RACING UP HILL

SELECTED PAPERS
OF AZERBAIJAN'S FIRST AMBASSADOR
TO THE UNITED STATES OF AMERICA

RACING UP HILL

Selected papers of Azerbaijan's first Ambassador
to the United States of America

Hafiz M. Pashayev

GLOBAL SCHOLARLY PUBLICATIONS
New York, New York
2006

Library of Congress Cataloging-in-Publication Data:

Pashaev, Kh. M.
Racing up Hill: Selected Papers of Azerbaijan's First Ambassador to the United States of America / Hafiz M. Pashayev.
p. cm.
Includes index.
ISBN-13: 978-1-59267-065-9 (pbk. : alk. paper)
ISBN-10: 1-59267-065-2 (pbk. : alk. paper)
1. United States--Foreign relations--Azerbaijan. 2. Azerbaijan--Foreign relations--United States. I. Title.
E183.8.A98P37 2006
327.4754073--dc22
2006022303

Director: Parviz Morewedge
Production Manager: Marina Zalesski
Layout design: Shalahudin Kafrawi
Cover Design: Anna Starr Townsend
Editors: Taleh Ziyadov; Marja Snyder

Published and distributed by
Global Scholarly Publications
220 Madison Avenue, Suite 11G
New York, NY 10016
www.gsp-online.org
books@gsp-online.org
Phone: (212) 679-6410

Table of Contents

To my wonderful wife, Rana Khanum

Acknowledgements

Throughout my years spent in Washington, I have met countless officials and private individuals who have enhanced my understanding of the United States and the American people. Although it is impossible to name everybody, I thank them all for their friendship and cooperation.

While working on a manuscript for this book, I continuously recalled those whose editing and typing efforts have helped me to construct speeches, articles, and letters over the years. I express my gratitude to the former and current staff members of the Azerbaijani Embassy in Washington, particularly Elmar Mammadyarov, Tahir Tagizadeh, Galib Mammad, and Aysel Yagubova for their ideas and contributions.

It gives me great pleasure to thank Edvin Graves for his cooperation during the early years of my tenure in Washington. Not only was he an indispensable source of information as he guided me through the political labyrinths at Capitol Hill, but he was also a good friend with a delightful Alabaman accent.

While in the process of planning and writing, I received valuable and enlightening advice from Dr. Frederick Starr. In addition to my strong admiration of his personality, I thank him for all his kindness.

I express deep appreciation for Dr. Rob Sobhani's encouragement and support throughout the course of my writings.

I thank Taleh Ziyadov and Marja Snyder's meticulous reading and editing of the entire manuscript that has effectively improved the text's readability ease. The author claims responsibility for any remaining shortcomings.

Preface

This story explains how the Republic of Azerbaijan, a small, distant, and new country, established a strong and highly regarded diplomatic presence in Washington between 1993 and 2006. It is also a record of the work of one man, Hafiz M. Pashayev, Azerbaijan's first ambassador to the United States and its representative throughout these years, who did much to achieve this. It is a tale of formidable obstacles and of decisive advantages, of lofty principles and low cunning, of steady learning and willful ignorance. It is, in short, a microcosm of diplomacy itself.

Pashayev's assignment could not have been clearer: to garner solid American support for Azerbaijan's independence and territorial integrity; help in the difficult transformation from a planned socialist economy to a market system, and from a Soviet-type government to a more open and democratic one; and to facilitate American active participation in the development of the country's hydrocarbon resources so as to strengthen rather than erode these other processes. Thirteen years on, it appears that Pashayev's efforts have borne fruit in all three areas.

None of this was inevitable. Azerbaijan's small size (a mere eight million people) and its location on the southern doorstep of Russia, with which Washington wanted to build a new and cordial relationship, threatened to relegate Azerbaijan to the a subordinate status. Worse, just six months before Pashayev presented his credentials to President Clinton in April 1993, the U.S. Senate passed the Freedom Support Act that included a little-noticed Section 907 that banned all U.S. aid, including humanitarian assistance, to Azerbaijan.

Several years earlier Azerbaijan's neighbor, Armenia, with strong Russian support, had laid claim to Azerbaijan's Karabakh district. In the course of a brief but fierce war, Armenia occupied a fifth of Azerbaijan's territory, displacing fully a million Azeris from their homes. The well-oiled Armenian lobby in America then brazenly charged that it was Azerbaijan that had applied "the offensive use of force" against Armenia, rather than visa versa. Senator John Kerry, responding to his Armenian constituents and unencumbered by any independent knowledge of the situation, slipped Section 907 into the foreign aid legislation, thus threatening to derail Pashayev's mission before it began.

From rented rooms on McPherson Square, Pashayev immediately launched what was in effect a massive educational campaign to inform Americans about his country. He pointed out its location between Russia and Iran and its critical links with NATO member Turkey. He talked about its aspiration to become a modern, Western-oriented and secular state, while affirming its traditional and moderate Muslim identity. Additionally, he did not fail to argue for the importance of his country's oil and gas reserves, which Soviet officials had denigrated for a decade before the collapse of the USSR.

This pedagogical role was easy for Pashayev, who had been teaching at Baku State University for twenty years. But his field was physics which, even after Einstein, allowed a far greater place for certainty than diplomacy, within which relativity has reigned supreme. Worse, Pashayev faced a Newtonian challenge, in which every action he took seemed to evoke an equal and opposite reaction from some quarter. The peculiar openness of the American system further complicated things. Pashayev had read that the Constitution had made the President responsible for foreign policy. Yet even though the White House wanted to abolish 907, it could not gain the Senate's approval to do so. Thus, the Armenian lobby could effectively dictate U.S. policy on this issue, thanks to the fact that few Azeris have ever immigrated to America and those who have done so were unorganized. It was all very perplexing and, to a scientist, thoroughly irrational.

Pashayev's qualifications as a physicist were formidable. After many years' work at Moscow's distinguished Kurchatov Institute of Atomic Energy, he had earned his doctorate in 1971, followed a few years later by research at the University of California, Irvine. He was soon solidly established as a leading international authority in the arcane but important field of high temperature superconductivity. Named director of the Metal Physics Laboratory at the Azerbaijan Academy of Science's Institute of Physics and having produced several important monographs, Pashayev was, by the 1980s, ideally situated to spend the next twenty years as an honored academician. This was not to be.

When the Red Army attacked the independence-minded Republic of Azerbaijan in 1990, Moscow cut off all funding for science there, effectively closing down Pashayev's institute. But the scientists labored on, now lending their strong support to the independence movement and undertaking such unlikely projects as a picture dictionary for young people. Amidst this confusion, the USSR collapsed at the end of 1991. Months later a new president of the independent Azerbaijan, former dissident Abulfaz Elchibey, was searching for skilled and untainted talent to fill key diplomatic posts. Professor Pashayev seemed a natural for the United Nations and might have been sent there had other considerations not intervened. Elchibey was eager to get a political rival, the former Soviet-era prime minister, out of Baku. He therefore named that minister, Hasanov, to the UN post and sent Pashayev instead to Washington. Elchibey was himself overthrown within months, but his successor, Heydar Aliyev, understood the wisdom of Pashayev's appointment and confirmed it, as did his son and successor, Ilham Aliyev, in 2003. In due course Pashayev's ambassadorial responsibilities were extended to Canada and Mexico.

Each year the rational and optimistic Pashayev hoped, and even predicted, that Section 907 would soon be abolished. Yet it continued on the books throughout the 1990s, as indeed it does today. Fortunately, over the years Pashayev mastered the art of the possible, collaborating with a diverse and bipartisan group of congressmen and senators to dilute the amendment they could not abolish. They accomplished this through two means: first, through adroit "carve-outs", by which the force of 907 was steadily eaten away, and, second, through "presidential waivers" which, under President Bush, have been issued on an annual basis.

Although clever from an American standpoint, this arrangement placed on Pashayev the responsibility for explaining to his own government why Azerbaijan continued to be singled out for punishment, even when the punishments were then suspended. Daily, Washington seemed to be posing Baku the old question "Are you still beating your wife?" The situation seemed to have been drawn directly from the pages of Franz Kafka's *The Trial*.

Fortunately, Section 907 was not the whole story of Pashayev's ambassadorship. Meanwhile, modern Western prospecting techniques had turned up impressive reserves of both oil and gas in Azerbaijan. When American, British, Norwegian and other western firms stepped up to develop these fields both Russia and Iran vehemently protested the appearance of outsiders in "their back yards." But by now, the Americans, Azeris, and Europeans understood their common interest and were prepared to shrug off Russian and Iranian objections. In September 1994, Pashayev beamingly stood by as President Heydar Aliyev and high ranking government officials from many countries witnessed the signing of the eight

billion dollar "Contract of the Century," opening all of Azerbaijan and its Caspian shoreline to intensive Western energy
development.

This in turn was followed by the commitment of Azerbaijan and a consortium of Western firms to develop an export
pipeline linking the Caspian and the Mediterranean Seas. With
enormous economic, social, political, and geopolitical significance, the three billion dollar Baku-Ceyhan Pipeline is argua-
bly the most significant project undertaken by the U.S. in the
area of the former USSR. In all the participating countries,
including the U.S., Baku-Ceyhan was a sustained and thoroughly bi-partisan undertaking. It has many fathers, notably
the U.S. Government, which assumed most of the risk. Yet
among those many actors the Azerbaijan embassy in Washington played a critical role, quietly nudging all parties to get
on with what was, after all, in their individual and common
interest.

The looming Caspian oil boom was not without its negative side, and this was felt particularly in Ambassador Pashayev's office. Suddenly, he was inundated with lobbying
and consulting firms of every description, eager to peddle
their services in exchange for what they assumed would be an
instant flood of petrodollars. Worse, sleazy operators appeared in many countries, some with the most baroque designs for milking the government that Pashayev represented.
One schemed to corner the market for Azerbaijan privatization vouchers, and thereby gain control of the country's most
valuable asset. Another proposed to bribe the Democratic
National Committee in order to gain access to the pipeline
deal. In every case it fell to Pashayev to help decipher these
intricate designs and to protect both Baku and Washington
from their potential damage. He did not do this alone, of
course, but his sound judgments were nonetheless essential in
every instance.

Addressing all these earnest issues, and the many others that have arisen over the years, Pashayev has the immense advantage of not taking them all that seriously. He had a life before becoming an ambassador, and he never forgot that he will have one afterwards. His wife, Rana, values her career as a scholar (of Arabic literature), and both Pashayevs consider their family (son, daughter and four grandsons) and circle of Baku friends to be far more important than any challenges that might rise up before them in Washington. Thanks to this, Pashayev has been able to maintain his wry sense of humor even in the worst of times.

This is partly a matter of genes. Hafiz Pashayev's father was a writer of droll and wise short stories and sketches that are beloved by all Azeri readers. Mir Jalal, as he was known, kept his distance from the pretenses and outright lies of Soviet life. Reading him, however, one senses that Mir Jalal might have been equally sardonic in his treatment of pre-Soviet life, or post-Soviet life. Far more than public life, he revered the private, the immediate, and the intimate. His son, Hafiz, is not a writer, but he is an obsessive caricaturist, whose sketches of friends and colleagues, like his father's literary gems, focus not on his subject's rank or role, but on his persona. Back in 1975, he sketched all his fellow members of the Academy of Sciences and presented them at an exhibition in Baku.

Mir Jalal's perspective on life gave him a solid basis for dealing calmly with all that befell him on the "outside." Hafiz Pashayev observed that "Mir Jalal provided a sense of serenity to those who associated with him." Members of the ambassador's staff would say the same of Hafiz. No wonder that Pashayev's embassy has been a training ground for many of Azerbaijan's most promising future leaders, among them the present Foreign Minister, Elmar Mammadyarov. Hafiz Pashayev remains a pedagogue, and a good one.

The opening of U.S.-Azerbaijan relations has occurred amidst a whirlwind of change and complexity on both sides. Azerbaijan is still struggling to put in place the institutions of a modern, Western society. Law courts, political parties, and the parliament itself are only slowly emerging from the chrysalis of post-Soviet change and will doubtless require many more years before they fully meet the needs and demands of modern citizenship. Weak institutions have afforded too much space for corruption, which will diminish only as the new institutions gain strength and public support. And the unresolved question of Karabakh still hangs over Baku, along with it its unresolved relations with its northern and southern neighbors.

For its part, the United States has had to reckon with energy crises, major challenges from rogue regimes, and then with 9/11 and its aftermaths in Afghanistan and Iraq. In its dealings with other countries it has placed renewed emphasis on the importance of democracy and civil society, yet at the same time, has shown perplexity in how best to advance them. Even now, it wrestles over the relations between democracy, security and economic development. At one moment it proposes to erect democracy as an absolute test that must be passed before the other issues are addressed, and then at another moment, it proposes to promote the three together.

Notwithstanding these complexities on both sides, U.S.-Azerbaijan relations have come a long way since 1993. The United States recognizes Azerbaijan as a potential model for the development of modern, open, and secular institutions in a traditionally Muslim society. It appreciates the centrality of Azerbaijan as the key axis of a future East-West transport corridor for goods and energy stretching from Europe to China and India. Azerbaijan, for its part, understands that while it is sometimes difficult to be a friend of the United

States, this is due more often than not to the very nature of democracy itself. It realizes that America, for all the cacophony that is audible behind every vote or action, is solidly supportive of Azerbaijan's independence and development as a modern and Western-oriented state and will remain so far into the future.

As Hafiz Pashayev completes his tour in Washington, he can fairly claim a worthy role in the complex process by which each side has come to these important understandings. To the extent this is so, it is not the result of Pashayev's hectoring or of his practice of power-politics in the usual sense. Rather, it is because he has consistently taken the time to ask obvious questions, patiently to explain matters as he sees them, and to put high-flown issues into a human perspective. Indeed, in some respects he remains to this day more of a scientist than a politician, more of a teacher than a diplomat. He once remarked that "Life is easier when you're simple and direct." Diplomacy is certainly so.

S. Frederick Starr
Chairman,
Central Asia-Caucasus Institute/Silk Road Studies Program,
Washington and Uppsala

Maps

Azerbaijan in the Caspian Region

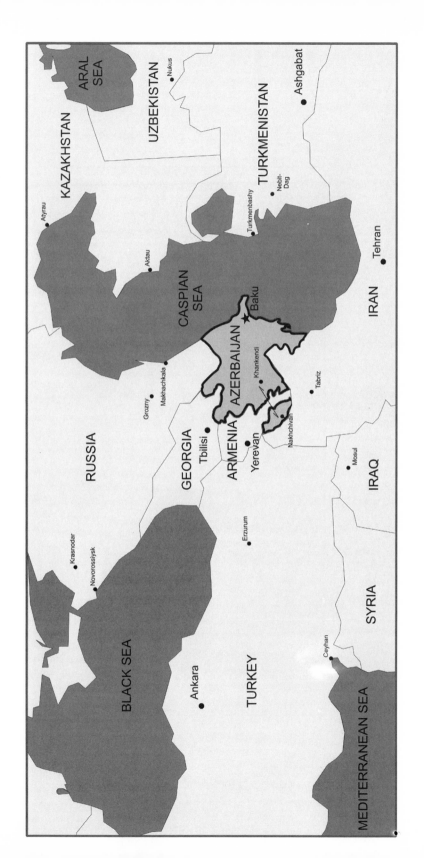

Map of Oil Pipelines

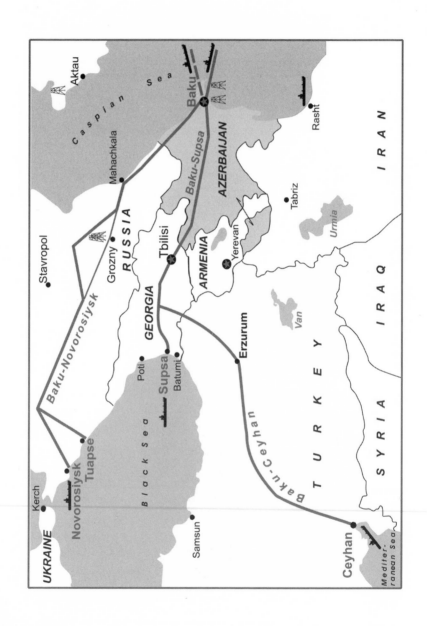

RESULTS OF ARMENIAN AGGRESSION

Occupied territories of Azerbaijan

Nagorny-Karabakh region

Territory	- 4 388 sq. km
Population (1989)	- 189 085
Armenians	- 145 450 (76,9%)
Azerbaijanis	- 40 688 (21,5%)
Russians	- 1922 (1%)
Others	- 1025 (0,6%)

Shusha district

Territory	- 289 sq. km
Population (1989)	- 20 579
Azerbaijanis	- 19 036 (92,5%)
Armenians	- 1 377 (6,7%)
Occupied	- May 8, 1992

Districts outside Nagorny-Karabakh region

	Occupation	Expulsion
Lachin	- May 18, 1992	- 71 000
Kelbajar	- April 2, 1993	- 74 000
Aghdam	- July 23, 1993	- 165 600
Fizuli	- August 23, 1993	- 146 000
Jabrayil	- August 26, 1993	- 66 000
Gubadly	- August 31, 1993	- 37 900
Zangilan	- October 28, 1993	- 39 500

Victims of aggression

Killed - 20 000   Disabled - 50 000   Missing - 4 866

Destructions and damage

Settlements	- 890
Houses	- 150 000
Public Buildings	- 7 000
Schools	- 693
Kindergartens	- 855
Health Care Facilities	- 695
Libraries	- 927
Temples	- 44
Mosques	- 9
Historical Places	- 9
Museum Exhibits	- 40 000
Industrial and Agricultural Enterprises	- 6 000
Motor Ways	- 800 km
Bridges	- 160
Water Pipelines	- 2 300 km
Gas Pipelines	- 2 000 km
Electricity Lines	- 15 000 km
Forests	- 280 000 ha
Sowing Area	- 1 000 000 ha
Irrigation Systems	- 1 200 km

Historical Monuments and Museum - 464

The total damage is estimated up to 60 billions US $

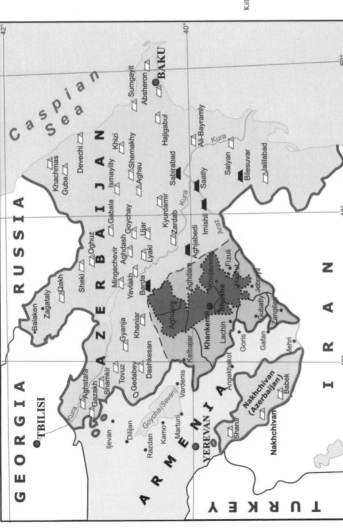

| Temporary Refugee/IDP settlements |
| IDP tent camps |
| Occupied territories |
| Line of occupation |
| Admin. line of the former NKAO of Az.SSR |

Armenian Armed Forces in the occupied territories

Tanks - 316	Artillery - 322		
ACV - 324	Personnel - 40 000		

Settlers illegally transferred to occupied territories

Nagorny-Karabakh	- 8 500
Lachin	- 13 000
Kelbajar	- 700
Zangilan	- 520
Jabrayil	- 280
Total	**- 23 000**

Refugees and IDP

Refugees from Armenia	- 250 000
Internally displaced persons from the occupied territories	- 660 000
Internally displaced persons from regions along the border with Armenia and line of occupation	- 100 000
Total	**-1 010 000**

Copyright 2004
Ministry of Foreign Affairs of Azerbaijan
All rights reserved

Introduction

Mohandas Gandhi once stated, "Satisfaction lies in the effort, not in the attainment; full effort is full victory." As I reflect on the last thirteen years of my life in the United States as Azerbaijan's Ambassador to Washington, DC, I can say that although we have achieved a lot in terms of U.S.-Azerbaijan relations, much is still yet to be done. However, along the way of my uphill race to establish a strong, mutually beneficial relationship between the United States and Azerbaijan, the single most important satisfaction has been the friends that I have made. This, in fact, has been true of my life in academics as well, for when I worked as a physicist, I came across many outstanding personalities in both the former Soviet Union and the United States. These friendships with the highest officials, titans of business, journalists, academics, and ordinary Americans from "sea to shining sea" have made me better appreciate and understand the United States for the great country that it is and for the challenges facing this great nation in the twenty-first century.

Therefore, this is not just the story of Hafiz Pashayev, the Ambassador of a once unknown country on the edge of the Caspian Sea. It is also a personal reflection of life in America and the history behind a new and enduring relationship between a superpower and a small country surrounded by larger powers. As my mission in Washington was extended from one year to the next, I also witnessed the evolution of my own country-from raising its head above the ashes of Soviet communism to becoming an independent, vibrant, and modern country.

During these thirteen years, my primary goal has consisted of becoming an "Ambassador" for Azerbaijan. In other words, not only did I want to simply represent my country, but I wanted to convey to Americans the hopes, aspirations, dreams, and fears of my people from all walks of life. I wanted to convey the culture, history and heritage of Azerbaijan, in addition to the daily routine of briefing congressmen and senators about the importance of my country and why it was critical for them to reconsider legislation such as Section 907 of the Freedom Support Act.

I will begin the journey of my life in Washington with Section 907 of the Freedom Support Act because this Act, in many ways, represents the ups and downs of U.S.-Azerbaijan relations.

When I arrived in America in February 1993 as Azerbaijan's first ambassador in Washington, U.S.-Azerbaijan relations were non-existent. Few American policymakers and even fewer American lawmakers had even heard of or had any interest in Azerbaijan. I always remember an episode when Etibar Mammadov, a member of Azerbaijan's Parliament, was meeting with Congressman Ben Gilman. A few minutes into the meeting the Congressman simply fell asleep. Little was known about my country other than it being a former republic of the Soviet Union, and yet, as soon as I arrived in Washington, I was thrust into the complex web of Section 907. It was like being asked to climb Mount Everest with little knowledge of the peculiarities of this giant peak.

During this period, a war was brewing between Azerbaijan and its neighbor Armenia over Azerbaijan's territory of Nagorno-Karabakh. While Armenian forces had occupied about 20 percent of the landmass of Azerbaijan and expelled one million people from their homes, Armenia's friends and allies on Capitol Hill were preoccupied with passing a piece of legislation called Section 907 of the Freedom Support Act. In short, this Act prevented Azerbaijan from receiving any direct aid, including humanitarian assistance, from the United States. For Azerbaijanis, this piece of legislation became to be known as the "Freedom Denial Act." My country had the distinction of being the only country in the world not eligible for even direct humanitarian assistance. How could a world statesman like former President Bush allow for such discrimination, we asked? Why would Congress impose such a draconian law on a country that was moving away from the Soviet sphere of influence and wanted to establish relations with the U.S? The answers, of course, rest in what I now understand and appreciate in the U.S. political system to be public advocacy, lobbying and internal politics. The U.S. political system is a transparent, yet complex process of influencing both the Legislative and Executive branches of government. This also creates a loophole in the representative democracy, whereby, special interest groups can hold the fundamental principles like humanitarianism and national interests of the country a hostage to their own agenda. To my dismay, ethnic groups, like Armenian-Americans, can import their hatred into the United States and turn it into the government policy and legal precedent of that country.

For example, on February 25, 1993, a mere few weeks after my arrival to Washington, Congressman Bonier of Michigan introduced a resolution that was later defeated when I made my introductory rounds on Capitol Hill. It was very apparent to me back then that the system was also a fair one in a sense that all sides do get to have their "day on the Hill." When these same members who supported Section 907 retired, and left their venerable positions on the Hill, they became advocates for the removal of Section 907. Another conclusion I have drawn from my years working on this issue is that the Armenian lobby (and similar lobbies) thrive on keeping the flames of hatred and misunderstanding alive on Capitol Hill because it justifies their existence. The lobbies' raison d'être is to be "holier than the Pope."

Today, although Section 907 is still on the books, it has been watered down considerably. Since 2002, President George Bush has been signing a waiver each year that allows for direct assistance to Azerbaijan. Yes, we have come a long way from congressmen and senators who used to fall asleep in a meeting with their Azerbaijani counterparts and who could not even locate Azerbaijan on a map or pronounce the country's name properly, to a deep-seated full strategic partnership.

The state of U.S.-Azerbaijan relations can be divided into different periods. The first phase coincides with Azerbaijan's independence in 1991 to 1994. Within Azerbaijan, chaos ruled supreme. Our independence from Moscow was being internally challenged by various groups vying for power in the vacuum left by the central authorities in Moscow. And externally, Armenian forces (often supported by extremist groupings in Moscow) threatened us with land grabs, and the expansionist tendencies of our former masters in Moscow lingered. During this period, Washington's policy towards Azerbaijan was being crafted around a central theme: maintain Azerbaijan's independence and territorial integrity.

My task during these formative years was to ensure that Washington had a full picture of what was happening on the ground in Azerbaijan and to educate Americans about our nation and vision of the future. By the end of the first period, it was very apparent that relations between our two countries were beginning to revolve around five major issues:

(1) Azerbaijan's significant geo-political location between a resurgent Russia and theocratic Iran.
(2) Azerbaijan's future role as both an exporter and provider of energy resources from the Caspian Sea, an oil-rich region.

(3) Shared values of independence, democracy, free markets and human rights.
(4) Integration of our young country into international institutions such as the World Bank and the International Monetary Fund.
(5) A peaceful resolution of the conflict with Armenia.

On this last point, I had my first encounter with an American President when I visited Emory University in Atlanta for a conference on conflict resolution. On February 18, 1993, (a mere ten days after my arrival) I spoke with President Jimmy Carter who was very gracious and told me that he would study the conflict in more detail before signing on as a mediator.

On a more personal level, the issue of Section 907 always curbed a more rapid strengthening of ties between Baku and Washington. I struggled to find friends and allies on Capitol Hill who would be sympathetic to our cause and who would share the frustration I felt over this "un-American" piece of legislation. At the same time, there was a positive side of it. Namely, we at the Embassy were obliged to be fast learners of the U.S. political system. It did not take too long to identify supporters, mainly from the oil-producing states of Texas, Oklahoma and Alaska. Indeed, it became apparent to me that I had a major card to play: Azerbaijan's vast energy resources and potential as a transport hub for the export of millions of barrels of oil from the Caspian Sea to international markets.

By the end of this first period, and as a result of spending 80 percent of my time lobbying on Capitol Hill, the Azerbaijan Embassy became a beacon for colleagues in other Embassies in understanding the intricacies of the U.S. political system. Fellow Diplomats would ask us for advice on how to deal with Washington.

The second phase of relations between the U.S. and Azerbaijan coincided with President Bill Clinton's engagement with the former republics of the Soviet Union at a much higher level, when departure from the "Russia First" policy became more efficacious to diplomacy. From 1994 until the tragedy of 9/11, energy concerns took center stage in terms of ties between Baku and Washington.

And it was during this period that I came to realize another truth about American politics: The stars and stripes do indeed follow the U.S. dollar. In my meetings with the CEOs of Amoco, Pennzoil, McDermott, Unocal and others, it became apparent that I could elevate relations to a much higher level by leveraging the development of Azerbaijan's most prolific oil fields: Azeri, Chirag and Guneshli.

Thus, in September 1994, a consortium of international oil companies led by Amoco and BP signed what came to be known as the Contract of the Century. This consortium, later called AIOC, would develop the six billion barrel Azeri, Chirag, Guneshli fields in the offshore waters of the Caspian Sea. In many respects, we had managed to not only get the commitment of these major oil companies to invest billions of dollars in Azerbaijan, but their presence would be an insurance policy for our new-found independence. The Consortium of Companies was deliberately designed as a mini-United Nations in terms of the number of participating countries.

Immediately following the signing ceremony in Baku, former President Heydar Aliyev, the father of modern Azerbaijan and architect of its revival, met with President Bill Clinton in New York on September 26, 1994. It was a proud moment for me but one filled with trepidation because the following day, the deputy Speaker of Azerbaijan's Parliament was assassinated along with a senior official from the Interior Ministry. Old thinking groups from our neighbors to the north and south, who viewed the Caspian Sea region as their sphere of influence, were not happy about our independently driven foreign policy. Nonetheless, the United States now had a clearer and more focused foreign policy goal as it concerned Azerbaijan: The uninterrupted exploration, development and transportation of Azerbaijan's oil and gas to international markets. In Washington, the office of the Vice-President and National Security Council took the lead on this and other policy issues. Thus, the seeds of an enduring relationship were being sowed. I was anxious to see these seeds blossom into an official visit for President Aliyev to Washington.

In the meantime, the landscape of Azerbaijan was changing rapidly. Oil companies and their employees soon made their way to Baku. The rush of "petrodollars" had an immediate impact on the local economy and Azerbaijan's international standing. A new sense of purpose and optimism filled the social, economic and political life of Azerbaijan's eight million citizens. Meanwhile in Washington, we were engaged in putting together a regional alliance of like-mined former republics with a view towards integration into the Western security system: GUAM (Georgia, Ukraine, Azerbaijan and Moldova) was formed. But like a bad toothache, Section 907 kept hovering over me, reminding me of my unfinished business. I decided to focus instead on what would become the highlight of my career in America; namely, the official visit of President Heydar Aliyev to Washington.

In 1997, America had also found a new sense of optimism. The dot-com era had begun and companies like eBay, Yahoo, and Amazon were fast becoming household names and making millionaires of those investing in the booming stock market. While his detractors focused on Whitewater, Travelgate and rumors of extra-marital affairs, President Clinton forged ahead. His slogan, "It's the economy, stupid" was

right on target for as the American economy expanded, so
did the ranks of legal and illegal immigrants. The "color of
America" was changing, albeit slowly, from black and white
to brown. While my personal observation was that many of
these new immigrants assimilated easily into the fabric of
American society, some stubbornly refused to cut the umbili-
cal cord with their motherland. As one who grew up behind
the Iron Curtain, I could sense a creeping Balkanization
within America.

The seeds that I had so diligently planted since my arrival
to America blossomed in July 1997 with President Aliyev's
official visit to the White House. I had wanted the President
to get a sense of history during his first visit to Washington.
The Blair House was the ideal venue because it has hosted
many heads-of-state. I also used this opportunity to bring
President Aliyev, a former member of the Politburo, face-to-
face with his former "rivals." Thus, a meeting was arranged
with the help of Dr. Zbigniew Brzezinski, whereby, Brent
Scowcroft, Dick Cheney, James Schlesinger, Richard Armitage and Colin Powel had a roundtable discussion on world affairs. This and the official meeting between President Clinton
and President Aliyev catapulted U.S.-Azerbaijan relations to a
new strategic level.

During the intervening three years, a major foreign policy
goal of both Baku and Washington was to construct the $3
billion Baku-Tbilisi-Ceyhan pipeline and to transport Azerbaijan's oil to international markets. President Clinton and Vice-
President Gore took the lead in keeping this issue on top of
their foreign policy agenda, and at the same time, President
Heydar Aliyev shrugged off Russian and Iranian objections to
this world-class project that would connect the landlocked
Caspian Sea to the Mediterranean. In 2000, the BTC host
country agreements were ratified and basic engineering work
was started. The process was indeed arduous because it in-

volved legal, financial, diplomatic, and security agreements that had to be reached at many levels in London, Washington, Houston, Istanbul, Tbilisi and Baku.

As I look back at this period between 1994 and 2001, there is no doubt in my mind that while relations between Baku and Washington were strengthened, we also witnessed the transformation of both American and Azerbaijani societies. While Monica Lewinsky became a household name in America, the people of Azerbaijan became even more interested in the world around them-including life in America. We were both puzzled and amused by the whole affair. In the end, not only did it offer a glimpse into the complex life of politics in America, but it also pointed out the strength of the American political system in which one can indeed question authority without resorting to violence and mayhem. The lesson learned was that the President of the most powerful country on earth could be held accountable. Not surprisingly, good governance, democracy and human rights started to creep into the lexicon of Azerbaijan's political culture. Another powerful phrase was also about to impinge on international affairs: the War on Terror.

But before the War on Terror would dominate the headlines, President George W. Bush asked his Secretary of State to hold a summit in Key West, Florida in order to address the conflict between Azerbaijan and Armenia. I recall my meeting before the summit with President Aliyev in which he expressed optimism and hope for a major breakthrough. Unfortunately, unlike the Dayton Peace Accord, this time the U.S. delegation had not prepared the groundwork. This historic moment was lost and the U.S. never showed any further interest in this conflict that has been frozen. In hindsight, it seems to me that some U.S. Special Envoys used their position to advance their own careers rather than making a genuine effort at resolving this festering regional conflict. Fur-

thermore, the various non-profit organizations interested in
conflict resolution seemed more eager to secure their internal
budgets and to maintain their existence rather than to channel
serious effort into bringing lasting peace between Azerbaijan
and Armenia.

September 11, 2001 marks the beginning of the third
phase of U.S.-Azerbaijan relations. I remember briefing late
President Aliyev immediately after the tragic events of that
day and soon afterwards, he invited the U.S. Ambassador in
Baku to his office to offer Azerbaijan's full and unconditional
support. When President Bush took the podium and declared
that "you are either with us or against us," Azerbaijan's answer, "We are with you," was unequivocal. Since then, relations between Baku and Washington have blossomed into a
mutual strategic partnership. Cooperation between the two
countries in the War on Terror consists of cutting off funding
for terrorists working in the region of the Caucasus, sending
Azerbaijani troops to Iraq and Afghanistan, and increasing
military training through the Pentagon. The U.S. Administration applauded Azerbaijan's "sacrifices" and "contribution"
to the coalition's activity in Iraq. President Bush emphasized
"Azerbaijan's unwavering support and determination in
bringing peace and democracy to Iraq," and the fact that
"Azerbaijan's forces have conducted themselves with skill
and bravery." In recognition of Azerbaijan's significant contribution to the War on Terror and as a means of increasing
bilateral military ties, President Bush signed a waiver lifting
Section 907 on an annual basis. The law, however, still remains on the books as a lingering irritant to U.S.-Azerbaijan
relations. While President Bush showed leadership in waiving
Section 907, his drive to promote democracy as an antidote
to authoritarianism created fissures between Baku and Washington. Indeed, this notion that democracy is "the one glove
that can fit all" reminded me of the Brezhnev Doctrine, when

we were told that communism is the answer to all the problems of mankind, whether they exist in Azerbaijan, Georgia, Ukraine, Vietnam or Hungary.

In 2003, Ilham Aliyev won the Presidency in an election process that although did not accordingly conform to Western standards, it confirmed what the people of my country wanted: progress through stability. Whatever its flaws, Azerbaijan's election showed real progress by any fair standard and led to a peaceful transfer of power. While some in Washington chose to see the glass of democracy as half empty, more astute observers recognized the imperative of stability in the increasingly significant Caspian Sea region. Indeed, Azerbaijan's transition from a satellite state of the Soviet Union a mere fifteen years ago to a democracy allied with the West took another major step forward on November 6, 2005, when the people of Azerbaijan went to the polls to elect their representatives to the *Milli Majlis* or Parliament. While the results seem to have disappointed some members of the international press who were hoping for another "color revolution" in the post-Soviet era, the true winners were the people of Azerbaijan. They did not vote for a revolution, instead, they voted for the stability inherent in gradual reform.

President Ilham Aliyev's insistence that these elections be free and fair was based on the premise that democratic pluralism in Azerbaijan would ensure a peaceful avenue for expressing dissent, thus, eliminating the need for violent alternatives. All Azerbaijani citizens were free to advocate their position peacefully, regardless of ethnicity or political persuasion. Washington must understand that the doctrine of democracy is not an absolute. Azerbaijan's complex geopolitical, economic, social and military challenges have to be taken into account when rushing to the scorecard of whether it passed or failed in carrying out free and fair elections. I believe that these parliamentary elections will become a watershed in the life of Azerbaijan because they proved that Azerbaijan has successfully transitioned from authoritarianism to democratic pluralism. The United States could easily employ it as a model for other Muslim countries.

In short, this book expounds on my thirteen years in Washington, DC as Azerbaijan's first Ambassador to the United States. It is not a memoir, but rather a record of my uphill race through published articles and statements. Fifteen years since the restoration of Azerbaijan's independence, this post-Soviet state has evolved into an active and reliable international actor with a niche of its own in the global arena. This period has been most productive in the framework of the bilateral relations with the United States. Azerbaijan's conscious political choices and growing U.S. interest in the region triggered the Republic's evolution from a "country of interest" to an "important nation" to a "strategic partner and ally" of Washington. And I can proudly say that my service in Washington was part of that process.

Chapter 1
Putting Azerbaijan on Washington's Map
(1993-1994)

In 1993, I began my first and most complex year of diplomatic service. Azerbaijan was then a little known country to the United States, and my primary goal was to increase awareness about it. My job, in essence, consisted of laying out a foundation for U.S.-Azerbaijani relations, which were practically non-existent at the time. What I found was that U.S.-Azerbaijani relations in 1993 were not even on the radar of most U.S. politicians. Ironically, it was the U.S. Congress that downgraded these relations to this status by placing the first obstacle in the path of U.S.-Azerbaijani bilateral relations.

In October of 1992, the U.S. Congress passed the U.S. Freedom Support Act aimed at aiding the newly independent former Soviet republics in their transitions from communist systems to democracies and market economies. Most congressmen and senators were unaware of a provision that would paralyze U.S.-Azerbaijani relations. What most U.S. lawmakers did not know was that the strong Armenian-American lobby groups in Washington, with the help of senators like John F. Kerry, had quietly inserted into the bill a provision named Section 907, which banned all U.S. Government assistance, including humanitarian aid, to the Republic of Azerbaijan.

In his speech before the U.S. Senate on October 1, 1992, Senator Kerry defined Section 907 to be "a modified version of a provision that I first offered in the Senate Foreign Relations Committee. As accepted by the Conference Committee, the provision prohibits assistance to the Government of Azerbaijan unless and until the President determines, and so reports to Congress, that Azerbaijan 'is taking demonstrable steps to cease all blockades and other offensive uses of force against Armenia and Nagorno-Karabakh'."

Senator Kerry's statement and the cryptic wording of Section 907 revealed that neither Senator Kerry nor the U.S. Congress had an accurate picture of the current events in Azerbaijan. Very few on the Hill knew that Azerbaijan never "used offensive force against Armenia" and that the Nagorno-Karabakh region was an internationally recognized territory of Azerbaijan. Even as Armenian forces were implementing their ethnic cleansing policies in the region and continuing the occupation of Azerbaijani lands, no one on the Hill stood up to highlight this ongoing tragedy. Instead, by supporting Section 907, the U.S. Congress unknowingly facilitated the growing humanitarian crisis in Azerbaijan and allowed the Armenian lobby to hold hostage U.S. strategic interest in the region for many subsequent years.

The two major issues that I had to cope with during the first two years of my Ambassadorship were Section 907 and the conflict between Armenia and Azerbaijan. My efforts focused on educating the makers of U.S. policy and law, as well as the American public, about the real situation in Azerbaijan, the unfair and immoral side of Section 907, Armenian aggression and the negative propaganda fueled by the Armenian lobby. Understanding the importance of public opinion in the United States, I did my best to respond to invitations to give public speeches and interviews, write articles and participate in many conferences on U.S.-Azerbaijan relations. I also wrote letters to and conducted countless meetings with U.S. congressmen, senators and U.S. Government officials.

Just one month after my arrival to Washington, I came to realize at the Congressional hearing on March 8, 1993 that Azerbaijan was not only facing aggression and terrorism at home, but that it was also a target of Armenian political manipulation and harassment abroad. I could not have imagined that my first public appearance on the Hill would be with Mr. Mourad Topalian, the Chairman of the Armenian National Committee of America (ANCA), who would soon be convicted for his ties to explosives used in terrorist acts against Turkish diplomats in the 1980s. According to a Cleveland paper, "The Plain Dealer," Mr. Topalian, also tried to disrupt the 1997 visit of President Heydar Aliyev to Washington, DC. As the Chairman of ANCA, Mr. Topalian was a key figure who helped raise funds to enact the unfair Section 907 and mislead the U.S. Congress about the conflict between Armenia and Azerbaijan. The very fact that I was presenting my case before the U.S. Congress with a person who represented one of the most powerful lobbies in Washington and who turned out to be a "terrorist in hiding" is a telling story. It is unfortunate that some members of the U.S. Congress still fall prey to the Armenian lobby groups, which have now lost a great deal of credibility by protecting such criminals and justifying Armenian attacks and territorial claims against Azerbaijan.

As I struggled to make my voice heard in Washington, Armenian forces continued their occupation of Azerbaijan's territory throughout 1993 and 1994. Armenia and the separatist forces in Karabakh came to control about 20 percent of Azerbaijan's internationally recognized territory. Ironically, Armenia tried to pretend that it had nothing to do with the war and that it was merely an interested bystander. But Armenians in Karabakh did not have the capacity to produce helicopters, tanks, armored personnel carriers or rocket launchers. Most of their military equipment, as well as military personnel, came from Armenia and the Russian military units stationed in Armenia and Nagorno-Karabakh.

The U.S. news media that covered the war used to routinely carry the Armenian denial of involvement, thanks to the information given to them by the Armenian-American lobbying groups. As the war progressed, however, more and more of these news agencies became reluctant to repeat this fiction, even when it was attributed to Armenian spokesmen. By 1994, the news agencies had learned the truth through the eyes and ears of their on-the-scene reporters. It was difficult for them to cover funerals in Yerevan for Armenian soldiers killed in the fighting around Karabakh, and to state that Armenia was not directly involved. During this time, I had many conversations with U.S. congressmen, many of whom were pro-Armenian, who told me privately that they too did not believe the Armenian officials' claims that Armenia was not involved.

When the fiction of non-involvement became insupportable, Armenia then claimed that all Armenian soldiers in Azerbaijan were volunteers. But as much as the Armenian government tried to come up with a new creative disguise and pretext for their involvement, it did not work. On April 16, 1994, the *New York Times* reported that "The Armenian Government has long considered that the only Armenian citizens fighting in Karabakh have been volunteers like Mr. Gevorkian and that no Government troops have fought there. But the Martyrs' Cemetery tells a different story." The article then quoted Mr. Yeghoian, an Armenian commanding officer, to have said that "six more of his soldiers were killed in the battle," and that all of them "were members of the Armenian Government's Internal Forces, a special military branch of the Ministry of Internal Affairs."

Indeed, regular Armenian army troops openly patrolled the occupied territories, and the then-defense ministers of the so-called Nagorno-Karabakh Republic and Armenia were one and the same. Just as Serbia incited and initiated the war through the Bosnian Serbs, Armenia incited and initiated the war in Karabakh through the Karabakh Armenians. The big-

gest difference between the two situations was that Armenia
played a far greater role in the actual conduct of the Karabakh
war than did Serbia in the Bosnian conflict.

As a result of the war, almost a million Azerbaijanis lost
their homes and became refugees and internally displaced
persons. My country had the highest number of internally
displaced persons per capita in the world, with about one in
every eight persons in Azerbaijan being either a refugee or
displaced. They had to live in boxcars, dugout shelters, tent
camps, and if they were lucky, in filthy public buildings in
Baku and other industrial cities of Azerbaijan. Torn apart by
internal political instability, occupation and a collapsed economy, Azerbaijan was facing the greatest humanitarian catas-
trophe since its independence. Here, I have to note that the
first ever U.S. humanitarian aid to my country via non-
governmental channels was provided to the Nakhchivan region of Azerbaijan thanks to efforts by Ambassador Richard
Armitage, the then coordinator of U.S. foreign assistance to
the new independent post-Soviet states.

Yet again, Section 907 remained the major impediment to
U.S. delivery of much needed aid to Azerbaijan. I continued
to write letters to the U.S. Congress asking them to revoke
Section 907 and urging the U.S. Government to help the
Azerbaijani government mitigate the country's humanitarian
crisis. Although the provision was not rescinded, it was eventually revised to allow some humanitarian aid to go through.
However an insufficient step, it was nonetheless a first step in
the right direction.

During this first period of my Ambassadorship, the issues
of Section 907 and the Nagorno-Karabakh conflict were the
two main topics that were reflected in my speeches, articles,
interviews and letters delivered and written at this time. These
two issues were also highlighted by President Bill Clinton in
his reply to my Letter of Credence.

President Bill Clinton's Reply to the Remarks of the Newly Appointed Ambassador of the Republic of Azerbaijan Hafiz Mir Jalal Pashayev Upon the Occasion of the Presentation of his Letter of Credence
April 14, 1993

Mr. Ambassador:

It is with pleasure that I accept your Letter of Credence and welcome the Republic of Azerbaijan's first Ambassador to the United States. The establishment of the Republic of Azerbaijan's embassy in Washington serves as a symbol of our growing bilateral relations and will enable a greater exchange of views between our governments.

I commend the Republic of Azerbaijan on the progress it has made towards democracy, and I encourage the Azerbaijani government to continue along this path. The measures taken by Azerbaijan to open up its economy to foreign investment are an important step towards the economic reform necessary for a prosperous future. I am also encouraged by Azerbaijan's commitment to reforming its political and economic system and fully support expanding business relations between our two countries.

Unfortunately, the Republic of Azerbaijan's development as a democratic, free-market economy is complicated by the Nagorno-Karabakh conflict. I am deeply concerned about the continued fighting in and around Nagorno-Karabakh and saddened by the many casualties suffered on both sides. The United States Government has made a major commitment to the efforts of the CSCE Minsk Group which is attempting to help resolve this conflict, and we fully support the work of the Minsk Group to obtain a cease-fire and deployment of observers.

The recent meetings in Rome, which led to the final agreement on the Terms of Reference for the Advance Monitor Group, are a significant step towards a peaceful settlement to the Nagorno-Karabakh conflict. However, further progress depends on the immediate cessation of the fighting. Military action has brought no victory for either side, only death, and demonstrates that a lasting solution to the conflict will not come through military means. The United States Government stands ready to continue to do what it can to reach a peaceful solution under the auspices of the CSCE. It is my home that all the parties can come to the negotiating table with the resolve to implement a successful cease-fire and the lifting of blockades. The U.S. Government expects Armenia and Azerbaijan to do everything in their power to halt the current fighting and prevent further bloodshed.

I realize that the Government of Azerbaijan is concerned by the FREEDOM Support Act provision passed by Congress prohibiting government-to-government assistance to Azerbaijan. I assure you that the United States Government wants to build good relations with the Government of Azerbaijan, and we sincerely hope that conditions will soon remove this irritant in our relations.

I am certain that through continued negotiations there will be a peaceful resolution to the Nagorno-Karabakh conflict, which will remove many of the obstacles hindering Azerbaijan's move towards democracy and a free market economy and will pave the way for the strong, cooperative partnership we want to have with Azerbaijan. Your country's diplomatic presence in Washington will enable us to further our discussions on issues of mutual importance. I look forward to increased contacts between our governments and our people.

Statement Before the U.S. Congress Commission on Security and Cooperation in Europe
March 8, 1993

Azerbaijan was the first of the independent republics of the former Soviet Union to enact legislation guaranteeing full civil rights, including religious, ethnic, linguistic, cultural, and political rights for all of its citizens. More than seventy ethnic groups live in Azerbaijan, including Russians, Armenians, Jews, Kurds and others. The rights of all are protected under the constitution of the Republic of Azerbaijan. Thus, the conflict over Nagorno-Karabakh is not about either religious or minority rights.

The true nature of the conflict over Nagorno-Karabakh is territorial. The roots of this conflict, both historical and im-

mediate, lie in ultra-nationalistic impulses of powerful extremist movements to expand Armenia's current borders at the
expense of its neighbors. Such an effort, carried out against
Azerbaijan by force of arms and by legislative acts of the Armenian parliament, is contrary to all international law respecting the territorial integrity of sovereign states and finds no basis in the history of the region.

At the end of World War I, the Versailles Peace Conference recognized the independent states of Azerbaijan, Armenia and Georgia. In 1918, as an independent state, Azerbaijan
set out to establish the first democratic and free market nation in the Near East and Middle East. At the same time,
newly independent Armenia promptly declared war on Georgia and Azerbaijan in order to expand its territories, and to
assert a territorial claim to Nagorno-Karabakh. But this same
Versailles Conference that recognized the independence of
Armenia and Azerbaijan, also recognized that Karabakh,
along with Nakhchivan and Zangezur, were integral parts of
Azerbaijan. The international community has always recognized Karabakh to be an integral part of Azerbaijan and has
never recognized it as either a part of Armenia or as an independent Armenian state.

Nagorno-Karabakh remained a part of Azerbaijan even
after the Democratic Republic of Azerbaijan lost its independence in 1920 upon its forced incorporation into the Soviet Union. Zangezur, on the other hand, was carved from
Azerbaijan by Joseph Stalin and ceded to Armenia. This left
the larger part of Azerbaijan completely separated from
Nakhchivan, another area of Azerbaijan, by this newly created
Armenian territory.

Both the old constitution of the former Soviet Union and
the new Treaty of the Commonwealth of Independent
States—of which Armenia voluntarily is a member—have
recognized Nagorno-Karabakh's legal status as an integral

part of Azerbaijan. Neither constitution has ever recognized Nagorno-Karabakh as a part of Armenia, or as an independent Armenian state.

On February 20, 1988, when the Armenian-dominated local parliament of Nagorno-Karabakh voted to secede from Azerbaijan and unite with Armenia, the Supreme Soviet of the USSR rejected this demand as illegal, based on the USSR Constitution of 1977 (then legally enforced). The declaration by ethnic Armenian citizens of Azerbaijan residing in Nagorno-Karabakh, the 1989 resolution adopted by the parliament of the Republic of Armenia on unification of Nagorno-Karabakh with Armenia, and Armenia's continued occupation and use of force against Azerbaijan, are in direct and open violation of the Commonwealth treaty into which Armenia freely entered. More importantly, these steps and Armenia's other hostile acts against neighboring Azerbaijan for the purpose of territorial aggrandizement are also in violation of the UN Charter, UN resolutions, and the internationally recognized principles set forth in the Helsinki Final Act, adopted by the CSCE. The Helsinki Final Act rejects the threat or use of force against the territorial integrity and political independence of any state. With the collapse of the Soviet Union, both NATO and the Helsinki signatories declared that the existing borders of the republics of the former Soviet Union should not be changed by the use of force.

Today, regular and irregular Armenian military forces occupy large portions of the internationally recognized territory of the Republic of Azerbaijan. These forces continue to seize Azerbaijani villages in addition to over two hundred towns and villages they already occupy. Of these, fifty-six had preponderantly Azerbaijani populations, all of which were expelled in ethnic cleansing operations. Indeed, all of the fighting has taken place on Azerbaijani territory, bringing death and destruction to all those men, women and children who have been caught in its horrors.

In contrast, Azerbaijani forces do not, nor have they ever, sought to occupy one inch of the territory of Armenia.

These actions by Armenian and Armenian-backed forces have created over half a million of Azerbaijani refugees. An additional 200,000 ethnic Azerbaijanis have been driven from homes and farms they and their forebears occupied for generations in Armenia and are now refugees in multi-ethnic Azerbaijan. While significant numbers of Armenians continue to reside in Azerbaijan as citizens of Azerbaijan (albeit at fewer numbers than before the conflict began), Armenia has been emptied of Azerbaijanis. Armenian militants are also continuing their blockade-first imposed in 1989-against the Azerbaijani territory of Nakhchivan, which is separated from Azerbaijan by Armenian territory.

In response to continued aggression against its citizens and territory, and to the Armenian blockade of Nakhchivan, Azerbaijan has been forced to suspend economic ties with Armenia. The term, "blockade," when used to describe Azerbaijan's action, completely obscures an obvious fact that an invader cannot expect that those who are invaded and are the victims of ongoing military assault should readily conduct trade and commercial activities with the invader on a "business-as-usual" basis. When the invader is using scarce economic resources to sustain a deadly military campaign of conquest that takes Azerbaijani lives and territory daily, Azerbaijanis ought not to be expected to collaborate in their own destruction. In any case, of all the means available to meet Armenian aggression, the suspension of economic ties is by far the most humane. Consider, for example, that Azerbaijan has not launched a counter offensive to seize Armenian territory to alter the military balance.

Over and over, we have witnessed on television tragic scenes of suffering in Armenia stemming from economic shortages. The suffering is genuine, and I do not mean to belittle it. I am deeply regretful of all the pain that this conflict is bringing to people of the entire region, but I am puzzled that there has been so little reporting of Azerbaijan's motivations in suspending economic ties, or of the initial Armenian blockade of Nakhchivan. Furthermore, Azerbaijan accounts for less than one-half of Armenia's borders. Armenia shares borders with Iran, Turkey, and Georgia, as well.

Azerbaijan has permitted humanitarian assistance to reach Armenia only to discover that such assistance, rather than going exclusively to the relief of civilians, is instead being used by Armenian forces occupying Azerbaijani territory and which are continuing attacks on the citizens of Azerbaijan. Even when the most recent round of talks in Rome were about to begin, Armenians attacked and seized eighteen additional villages and killed scores of Azerbaijanis. Among the Armenian forces were elements of the Russian Seventh Army. Indeed, the history of Russian involvement in this conflict has been, to say the least, troubling. As the Soviet Union was in its final stages of dissolution, Moscow stationed troops in Baku, our capital, imposed martial law, and prevented democratic elections from taking place.

Yet no such restrictions were placed on Armenia. While Azerbaijan remained sealed off from contact with the rest of the world under the weight of Soviet martial law, Armenia was purchasing weapons on the world market and obtaining weapons from Soviet troops still stationed there. Soviet troops were also involved in the worst atrocity to take place in this conflict: the massacre by Armenian militants of about one thousand Azerbaijani civilians from the town of Khojaly in 1992.

Today, as always, the people and Government of Azerbaijan remain convinced that neither side can win this war. The hostilities in Nagorno-Karabakh have already taken far too great a toll in human suffering and misery from both sides. The people of Azerbaijan welcome the progress made in Rome toward stopping the bloodshed. Indeed, they have contributed by far the greater portion of that progress, bearing in mind their expressed readiness to resume commercial, transportation and communication ties as part of the cease-fire arrangements and prior to resolution of the status of Nagorno-Karabakh. We look forward to the international conference in Minsk that will resolve the status of Nagorno-Karabakh in a way consistent with international law. Peace will come not through force of arms, but can be achieved through a negotiated settlement based on international law, guarantees of basic human rights, minority rights, and respect for the principle that the territorial integrity and international borders of sovereign countries cannot be changed by force of arms.

The United States, not only as a CSCE member, but also as the world's sole remaining superpower, has a particular responsibility to look soberly, unsparingly, and with impartiality at the facts and history of this issue. Passions inflamed by ethnic partisanship should not be allowed to obscure them, irrespective of their source. The preconceived and prejudicial notions reflected in the Freedom Support-Act and in pending House Resolution 86 are at odds with fulfillment of this responsibility. They reduce a complex situation to a one-sided caricature of the present conflict. For us, the penalty embodied in the conditions which the Act imposed solely on Azerbaijan was not economic, nor the denial of assistance. It was the rebuff of a people who have opted to build a multi-ethnic, diverse, and secular representative democracy. Our new republic is proof that the best values of the West can take root in countries with diverse religious and historical traditions.

During the long decades of Soviet rule, our people were forced to conceal the respect and admiration they held for the United States as a symbol of the strength and possibilities of the democratic ideal. This respect helped sustain their belief in democracy during the darkest periods. Now, as they finally begin to realize their own democratic aspirations, many see the Freedom Support Act amendment as a repudiation of the faith they have placed in the American model. But I do not believe that the resulting disillusionment is too far along to be irreversible.

A peaceful, prosperous future beckons to both Armenia and Azerbaijan. If it is to be realized, this conflict must be resolved peacefully. Impartial, vigorous encouragement by the United States will be a necessary condition for its resolution. But a skewed involvement will almost certainly fuel intransigence on the part of the "favored" side. In all likelihood, this would doom prospects for a settlement and for the promising future in which not only the parties and the region, but for all we know, the whole world, have crucial stakes.

What is the Solution to the Armenia-Azerbaijan Conflict? Peace Depends Upon Armenian Acceptance of a Modern Multi-Ethnic State
Washington Report on Middle East Affairs
June, 1994

In the long development of human history, mankind has struggled to maintain stability and to reduce conflict between and among ethnic groups, nations and groups of nations. Often, it has appeared that whenever progress was made, it was quickly overtaken by new conflicts and animosities. One of the most significant advances since World War II has been a gradual acceptance, with the notable exception of the Soviet

Empire, of the inviolability of international law with respect to state sovereignty and borders. This universal principle has been acknowledged repeatedly in the United Nations and other international agreements and conferences. Inherent in this principle is acceptance and recognition of multiethnic states, because almost no country is racially or ethnically pure, and any attempt to create such purity would bring nothing but chaos and endless conflict.

Under the Soviets, Russia dominated and ruled its neighbors in the "near abroad" by making them republics of the Soviet Union. In the process of doing so, Soviet rulers changed borders, played one republic and ethnic group against another and generally exercised a policy of divide and rule.

The collapse of the Soviet Empire led to the hope that this kind of division and ethnic fratricide could be replaced by democracy, respect for human rights and acceptance of internationally recognized law, sovereignty and borders. Since World War II, these international principles have pretty well held up throughout Western Europe.

As we know, the end of the Cold War has put these principles to new tests. Unfortunately, my country of Azerbaijan has literally become the battleground upon which adherence to these international norms is being tested. No sooner had the controls of the Soviet Union begun to loosen than Armenian ultra-nationalists began to act upon their decades-old vision of a "Greater Armenia." To achieve this dream required more land.

Since their territorial claims against Turkey and Georgia seemed unattainable, the ultra-nationalist Armenians turned to the territory of Nagorno-Karabakh within Azerbaijan. This option was attractive because Nagorno-Karabakh had an ethnic Armenian majority, Azerbaijan had an almost nonexistent military, and only a small strip of land separated Armenia from Nagorno-Karabakh. No doubt if Armenians are successful in Azerbaijan, they will then turn to other neighbors in their quest for more territory.

After a period of military stalemate, the Armenians launched a series of major offensives in 1993, which resulted in the capture and occupation of seven major regions of Azerbaijan. Scores and scores of villages and towns were looted, burned and destroyed. Thousands of civilians have been killed as a result of the fighting, exposure or malnutrition. Thousands of soldiers have lost their lives or suffered grievous wounds.

Repeatedly, the United Nations, the Conference on Security and Cooperation in Europe (CSCE), the United States, European nations and Russia have urged and even demanded that Armenia withdraw from the occupied territories and respect the internationally recognized sovereignty of Azerbaijan. Armenia, having viewed the inaction of the world community in the face of Serbian aggression and territorial conquest in Bosnia, ignored the appeal of the world community, and proclaimed to the world that it was the true victim.

The courage of the world community prevented Iraq from violating the principle of state sovereignty and securing borders when it invaded Kuwait. But, because oil was not involved, the world turned a blind eye to Serbian and Armenian aggression.

Finally, at long last, the West and NATO have begun to assert themselves in Bosnia to preserve a portion of the Bosnian state, but not before major portions of that state have been gobbled up by Serbia and its surrogates in Bosnia.

The world community has done very little, however, to halt or reverse the Armenian aggression in Azerbaijan beyond making statements and passing resolutions. Consequently, Armenia refuses to withdraw and demands independence (which would constitute de facto unification with Armenia) for Nagorno-Karabakh.

Armenians have ethnically cleansed both Armenia and Nagorno-Karabakh of Azerbaijanis. Armenian President Levon Ter-Petrossian was surprisingly candid about this ethnic cleansing in an April 12, 1992 interview with the Moscow News, in which he stated that "The worldwide process of creation of ethnic states is taking place now. It already has happened in Armenia. We have a mono-ethnic republic. History shows that the federative system of state is the weakest one."

Thus, Armenia is attempting to reverse the historic progress the world community has made toward peace. If successful, the Armenian example will tell the world that internationally recognized sovereignty and borders are mere conventions to be violated at the discretion of individual states. The prevailing principle of inviolability of sovereignty will be replaced by the principle of "might makes right." Likewise, the concept of multiethnic societies and states will be dealt a severe blow. It will further encourage ethnic cleansing and notions of racial and ethnic purity, as well as the corresponding notion of racial and ethnic inferiority. This concept was morally wrong when practiced by Adolf Hitler in Germany and the white supremacists of the pre-Civil War American South or of South Africa, and it is just as wrong when practiced today by the Armenians or Serbians.

The world community learned in World War II that aggression undeterred merely encourages more aggression. It learned the lesson all over again in Bosnia. Now, it is learning the lesson once again in Azerbaijan. Let us hope the world community acts before the principle of sovereignty and the sanctity of borders are dealt a severe setback.

Remarks on Ambassador Maresca's Proposal at the Briefing for the Helsinki Commission, CSCE
July 29, 1994

Ambassador John J. Maresca, then special U.S. mediator for the Nagorno-Karabakh conflict, had a proposal for the settlement of this conflict. His proposal was based on the following elements:

(1) Nagorno-Karabakh would be reconstituted as the Republic of Nagorno-Karabakh (RNK), a self-governing legal entity within and freely associated with the sovereign Republic of Azerbaijan.

(2) Armenia and Azerbaijan would sign a treaty on mutual transit rights across each other's territory.

(3) Refugees would be permitted to return to their homes, with certain villages designated for international monitoring.

(4) All of Armenia and Azerbaijan, including RNK, would be a free trade area.

(5) All agreed arrangements would be included in the two documents, which would be the basis for a diplomatic solution signed at the Minsk Conference.

(6) The provisions of these documents would be guaranteed by the CSCE and the UN Security Council.

(7) The United States should not be involved on the ground in the Caucasus, but should take the lead in building good road connections between the RNK and Armenia, and between Azerbaijan and Nakhchivan, an exclave of Azerbaijan.

(8) A donor's conference would be organized to raise funding for the economic reconstruction of the region.

It is a genuine pleasure to appear before the Helsinki Commission today to address the proposal of Ambassador

Jack Maresca for settlement of the conflict over Nagorno-Karabakh. Let me say initially that certain principles must be recognized in approaching this issue:

First, we must recognize that this conflict did not start in 1988, but goes back to history. Both sides can cite historical facts to justify their objectives- depending on how far back in history each side wishes to go. As a result, we must recognize the historical component of this matter-on both the Azerbaijani side and the Armenian side.

Second, there are at least four distinct sets of relationships that must be worked out:

(1) The armed conflict on a state level between the Republics of Azerbaijan and Armenia.

(2) The conflict between the Azerbaijani central government and the ethnic Armenians of Nagorno-Karabakh.

(3) The conflict between exiled Azerbaijani community of Nagorno-Karabakh and ethnic Armenians of Nagorno-Karabakh and the Republic of Armenia.

(4) The conflict between Azerbaijani refugees who were expelled from Armenia itself and the Republic of Armenia.

All of these conflicts must be taken into account and resolved before there can be any real solution to the problem.

Third, no settlement of this issue is possible without some degree of balance. Some observers believe that because Armenia currently has the upper hand militarily it can dictate the settlement. Remember, there are one hundred years of history to the conflict and relative positions can change with time. The Azerbaijani government could not, even if it wanted to, accept a dictated settlement that destroys its sovereignty. An unjust or unbalanced settlement would merely postpone the conflict to a later time, in much the same way that the dictated settlement of World War I set the stage for World War II. Both sides must compromise or the conflict will continue.

Fourth, despite the long history of this conflict, any permanent settlement requires that both parties look to the future rather than the past. If we remain obsessed by perceived or real grievances of the past, we will never be able to look to the future of cooperation and mutual progress for our people. We cannot forget the past, but we cannot remain mired in the past.

Before commenting on specific aspects of the proposal, let me first say I wholeheartedly agree with Ambassador Maresca on the need for active involvement by the United States and the West in efforts to settle this conflict. The fact is that the United States is the only remaining superpower in the world, and, as such, bears a special responsibility to provide leadership in matters such as this. No one is asking for American military involvement, but we do need the active, consistent and full-time diplomatic involvement of the United States.

Inherent in the proposition that the United States should assume a stronger role in these negotiations is the requirement that the U.S. be even-handed in its approach. In this connection, I was very pleased with Ambassador Maresca's earlier recommendation that Section 907 of the Freedom Support Act, which prohibits even humanitarian assistance to Azerbaijan, be repealed. Azerbaijan also appreciates the forthright opposition to Section 907 by the Clinton Administration. We understand and appreciate that there is a large Armenian Diaspora in the United States, but that is no excuse for a great power like the United States to prevent Azerbaijan from receiving the same kind of humanitarian relief that is being supplied to Rwanda, Bosnia and Somalia. Even the illegal government in Haiti receives humanitarian relief from the United States-but not Azerbaijan. The U.S., particularly Congress, should be ashamed of such a policy.

Now, I would like to briefly comment on several aspects of Ambassador Maresca's proposal. We are in total agreement with Ambassador Maresca, and the United States Government, that the solution and the monitoring and enforcement of that solution should be carried out under the auspices of the Conference on Security and Cooperation in Europe (CSCE). Azerbaijan, which is experiencing true independence for the second time within this century, is naturally concerned about its long-term independence. We have a long and complicated history of both cooperation and conflict with our neighbors, but we do not want to be dominated or dictated to by any other country—whether it be Russia, Turkey, Iran and anyone else. For that reason, we think it is in the best interest of Azerbaijan and everyone in the region that the solution to this conflict should be an international one – the CSCE proposal being the logical mechanism for achieving that solution-which Azerbaijan has already agreed to and signed. Azerbaijan has suffered too long and hard for independence to place it at risk in the settlement of this tragic, unfortunate conflict. So, we believe any peacekeepers or observers should be international in makeup and under international command and control.

While Ambassador Maresca did not address the issue of withdrawal of forces-since that matter is currently under negotiation-we believe this is an essential ingredient for any settlement. Armenian forces currently occupy more than 20 percent of Azerbaijan, including seven major regions outside of Nagorno-Karabakh. No settlement is possible unless it is agreed that those occupation forces will withdraw from those regions, with adequate safeguards that they will not resume their aggression in an effort to influence later negotiations on Nagorno-Karabakh. This position is consistent with United Nations resolutions, international law, and United States policy.

We agree with the Ambassador that in any settlement, Nagorno-Karabakh should remain "within and freely associated with the sovereign Republic of Azerbaijan." The exact status of Nagorno-Karabakh, in terms of local autonomy, is, of course, subject to discussion and negotiation. President Heydar Aliyev has indicated on many occasions that Azerbaijan is prepared to be flexible and forthcoming in providing a maximum amount of local autonomy, but we cannot grant total independence-which would amount to dismemberment of a sovereign nation that is recognized by the United Nations, the United States, CSCE and every other international body or institution. By the same token, I would have to take issue with Ambassador Maresca's suggestion that Nagorno-Karabakh maintain "permanent representatives" in certain foreign capitals. I do not believe such action could be taken without infringement on the sovereignty of Azerbaijan. Settlement of issues of sovereignty must be consistent with international law. But I would remind you that there was a great deal of local autonomy in Nagorno-Karabakh before the conflict began, and we are prepared to agree on further steps. And I ask you: Would the United States agree to give independence to a state like Texas that wanted to join up with Mexico? The answer would surely be of course not. In fact, the United States has already faced that issue during the Civil War and we know what the outcome was.

We agree with Ambassador Maresca that refugees and displaced persons should be allowed to return to their homes, villages and towns—and that most definitely includes Azerbaijanis who were forced to leave Armenia and Nagorno-Karabakh—as well as any Armenians who left Azerbaijani territory. Azerbaijan is a multi-ethnic, multi-religious society and we intend for that to remain so. In fact, one of the first laws enacted after our independence was one to guarantee the human rights of all ethnic minorities. Today, we have about one million refugees in Azerbaijan—one of every seven citizens in the country. We cannot accept a solution to this conflict that does not allow those people to return to their homes, if they haven't been burned down, and to their villages and towns. Right now the world's attention is rightly focused on the refugees of Rwanda and the Darfur region of Sudan, but we also have a major refugee crisis in Azerbaijan. Think for a moment what it would be like if one-seventh of all Americans were refugees—that would mean about 36 million Americans without adequate food, shelter or medical care, often living in "tent cities" along major highways and roads. Ethnic cleansing is not acceptable.

We also strongly agree with Ambassador Maresca that any agreement should be accompanied by international guarantees under the CSCE and the UN Security Council. We have lost count of the number of times that we have agreed to cease-fires that have been promptly broken. As a result, we cannot place our fate in the hands of mere promises; there must be international guarantees.

Azerbaijan could easily agree on a treaty of mutual rights and access, free trade agreements and similar measures once the fighting has stopped and all parties agree to peace. As I said before, we are a multi-ethnic society and will remain so. We also desire friendly relations with all our neighbors, including Armenia. We believe there are great opportunities for our mutual economic benefit such as development of our Caspian Sea oil reserves. We also need the cooperation of our neighbors in building democracy and free markets. None of these proposals for mutual cooperation are out of the question once the war has been concluded.

Finally, let me commend and congratulate Ambassador Maresca for his proposal and his contributions towards settlement of this conflict. The only hope for solutions to human conflicts is hard work by men and women of good will. Azerbaijan pledges its good faith efforts to go the extra mile to settle this truly senseless war. There are enough dead, enough grieving mothers and fathers, homeless and destitute refugees, and enough impoverished and hungry people on both sides. History will not be kind to any of us if we do not seize this opportunity to settle this conflict and begin building for the future.

Excerpts from Ambassador's Speeches Delivered at the University of Michigan on March 30, 1996 and the University of Florida, Tampa on November 9, 1994

It is difficult to understand the Nagorno-Karabakh conflict or devise a solution unless one considers the issue within the larger regional and geopolitical context.

Azerbaijan is unique in the fact that it is surrounded by three major regional powers, all with significant economic and military resources, but with differing cultures, political and diplomatic objectives. These regional powers are Russia, Turkey and Iran. Our history shows examples of Azerbaijan being used by big powers in a game of divide and conquer.

I am always somewhat amused when I hear Americans urge Azerbaijan to ignore its neighbors when they make unacceptable demands. That is easy to say when you are the world's only superpower, but it is totally unrealistic when you are a small country with a weak economy, a small population, and a small army, and only a few years of independence. Besides, we believe it is in our best interests to get along with our neighbors, who, after all, are our major trading partners and with whom we have long cultural ties.

But the fact remains that we do face challenges that impinge on our sovereignty and independence. We have done our best to deal with those challenges. For instance, we are the only former Soviet republic that has no foreign troops on its soil, although there are those who would wish otherwise. As you know, we have huge oil deposits that we are beginning to develop. We are willing to have our neighbors share in that production and distribution, but we are unwilling to have our sovereignty over those resources, or the economic benefits to be derived from them, taken away from us. This has been a constant struggle over the past two years. Thus far President Heydar Aliyev has skillfully managed to proceed on this front without major confrontations.

Azerbaijan has no desire to be in conflict with its neighbors and we will go to great lengths to avoid it. But, by the same token, we refuse to compromise our independence or sovereignty. As I have said, we have only known a few years of true independence throughout our history, and no Azerbaijani is willing to surrender that independence now.

We also want the active support and involvement of the United States. Although we are not asking for U.S. soldiers on the ground, we want America to strongly support our independence and sovereignty in the United Nations, the CSCE and other international forums. Azerbaijan is a small country, but it is also a test case of whether the international community will support the former Soviet republics as they struggle to maintain their independence and restore their economic well-being.

As far as the United States is concerned, Azerbaijan has been pleased both with the interest and action taken by America in recent months to help and support Azerbaijan. President Clinton, Vice-President Gore and United Nations Ambassador Madeline Albright have all admirably spoken up in defense of the recently-signed Azerbaijan oil contract, as

well as our independence and sovereignty. U.S support, and
help from American companies will be vital as Azerbaijan and
other oil-producing states in the region decide where to build
a new pipeline to deliver this oil to the Mediterranean.

Unfortunately, the strong support Azerbaijan has received
from the Clinton and Bush Administrations has not been
matched by Congress, which is unduly influenced by the Armenian-American lobby. When the Freedom Support Act
was passed in 1992, the Armenian American lobby prevailed
upon certain members of Congress to include a ban on all direct assistance to Azerbaijan, despite the opposition of the
Bush Administration. This year, the Clinton Administration
sought an exception to the ban for humanitarian assistance,
but this, too, was blocked by the Armenian-American lobby.

To its credit, the U.S. Government is providing humanitarian assistance to Azerbaijan through non-governmental organizations, but that is very inefficient since the government
is running all humanitarian relief efforts. It is our hope that in
1995, this ban will be lifted.

The Armenian-American lobby is very effective. They
have convinced many throughout the world and in this country that they are the "victims" in this war—despite the fact
that they occupy 20 percent of our territory, have killed more
than twenty thousand Azerbaijani soldiers and civilians, and
despite the fact that they have made one out of every seven
Azerbaijanis a refugee.

But I do not ask you to simply take my word for it. Consider a report published by the U.S. Army War College in December, 1993, written by three distinguished scholars on military history and U.S. foreign policy interests. In this article,
the authors urge the U.S. Government to apply pressure on
Armenia to halt its aggression against Azerbaijan. They stated
that "Although this means taking on the Armenian lobby
here, the stakes are worth it because this war is no longer in

defense of a threatened minority, but a war to destroy Azerbaijan."

Interview Published in *The Washington International* (by Patricia Keegan) August–September, 1993

Q: Mr. Ambassador, could you summarize the ethnic conflict between Armenia and Azerbaijan in the Nagorno-Karabakh region; when and how did it start?

A: The Armenian-Azerbaijani conflict, the so-called Nagorno-Karabakh conflict, was instigated five years ago when right-wing extremists in Armenia and Nagorno-Karabakh began to claim that the Nagorno-Karabakh Autonomous Region of Azerbaijan has historically been Armenian territory and must be returned to Armenia. Initially a local conflict, lately a large-scale war, it has been claimed necessary to protect the right of self-determination of the Armenian community of Nagorno-Karabakh. But Nagorno-Karabakh is not now, nor has it ever been a part of Armenia. It is completely contained within the borders of the Republic of Azerbaijan and has always been an integral part of Azerbaijan. Moreover, the Armenian population of Karabakh has always been free to express and promote its linguistic and cultural heritage.

The truth is that this war is over territory. It is fueled by powerful, ultra-nationalistic and extremist movements driven by a vision of a "Greater Armenia," and the desire to expand Armenia's borders at the expense of its neighbors.

The spark that ignited the war occurred on February 20, 1988 when the Nagorno-Karabakh regional council voted to secede from Azerbaijan and demanded unification with Armenia. Later the Parliament of Armenia adopted the measure. That was followed by the deportation of 200,000 Azerbaijanis from Armenia performed in the wildest manner one could ever imagine.

In 1988, 25 percent of Nagorno-Karabakh's population was ethnic Azerbaijani. Today, all of the Azerbaijani residents have been driven from their homes, and the entire enclave is under Armenian military control. Moreover, Armenian military forces occupy large Azerbaijani territories beyond Nagorno-Karabakh. Currently, 20 percent of Azerbaijani territory is under Armenian occupation. Armenian aggression has created more than 700,000 refugees and displaced people. In violation of all norms and principles of International law, a racial policy against a peaceful Azerbaijani population is being pursued. For justification, the Armenians use the idea of a mythical threat to the security of Nagorno-Karabakh.

After recent Armenian seizures of the large Azerbaijani regions of Kalbajar and Aghdam (population 300,000), and the looting and burning of cities and villages, UN Security Council resolutions (822 and 853) and statements by the U.S. State Department have condemned the aggression and demanded the unconditional and immediate withdrawal of the Armenian armed forces. However, condemnation of "local Armenian forces" has not contributed to settlement of the conflict. Moreover, new occupation of the Fizuli and Jabrail regions of Azerbaijan demonstrate the aggressor's disregard of these resolutions and its firm belief in absolute impunity.

Q: Although we can see reports of the war in Azerbaijan every evening on Moscow Evening News (C-SPAN), there seems to be a blackout on other news channels. What is your understanding of this apparent neglect?

A: You are absolutely right. Armenian aggression has no coverage here. Hundreds of thousands of refugees and displaced people in Azerbaijan is not adequate to attract the attention of the international community. The Armenian lobby in this country is very strong; they do everything possible to present a one-sided story. It used to be popular in the mass media to give religious and ethnic colors to this war, but the actual reason is obvious-an Armenian territorial claim on Azerbaijan.

Armenian aggression against Azerbaijan looks very much like Serb aggression in Bosnia. The latter has pretty good coverage in American press and television and so far there has been no time for our conflict. In my view, the United States has not fully determined and clarified its strategic approach towards our region, which constitutes another reason for the region's lack of coverage by the American press.

Q: How do you see this war in Azerbaijan being resolved?

A: Through peaceful and political means. Several CSCE peace plans have been under consideration and even signed by both parties, but the Armenian side repeatedly violated the results of the negotiations, and unfortunately, there is no real mechanism to solve this conflict in the CSCE framework.

Q: What is the relationship between Azerbaijan and the U.S. regarding the Freedom Support Act? Most Americans know very little about your country. What is being done to rectify that?

A: Taking advantage of the almost total absence of Azerbaijani representation in the U.S., citizens of Armenian origin have exerted a strong influence on congressmen and senators.

As a result, Congress has adopted a special amendment (Section 907) to the Freedom Support Act, which bans rendering economic and humanitarian aid to the Republic of Azerbaijan, and it is the only republic among the fifteen republics of the former USSR banned from assistance.

The paradox of this situation is that a country subjected to outside aggression is condemned and punished by the U.S. This amendment, adopted by Congress, has significantly reduced the country's progress toward pro-Western democratic development, and has created a political atmosphere that strongly encourages Armenian aggression.

At the same time, Western countries render to Armenia substantial financial and humanitarian assistance, used by the Armenians to strengthen military forces on Azerbaijan territory. Nevertheless, continuing Armenian aggression and occupation of vast Azerbaijani territory have brought on strong condemnation by authoritative international organizations and the State Department.

As for informing Americans about my country, the Azerbaijani Embassy just opened in Washington several months ago, and that should do a lot to rectify the lack of information.

Interview Published in the *U.S.-Iran Review* (Volume 1, No. 6) September 1993

Q: What is your assessment of Iran's role in the conflict between Armenia and Azerbaijan? Has Iran served as an "honest broker?"

A: Since the beginning of the Azerbaijani-Armenian conflict, Iran has repeatedly tried to contribute to the peaceful solution of the conflict, but every time, the Armenian side has impudently violated the achieved agreements, demonstrating its disregard with any peaceful initiatives by capturing new Azerbaijani territories. During the meeting of the acting Azerbaijani President Haidar Aliyev with Iranian Foreign Minister Ali Akbar Velayati on August 16, 1993, the latter expressed regret that the Armenian aggression against Azerbaijan was going on, and said that Iran always came out in defense of the territorial integrity of Azerbaijan and, at the same time, didn't interfere in the internal affairs of the sovereign state.

The continuing Armenian aggression and capturing of new Azerbaijani southern territories bordering with Iran brought a new element in the Iranian approach to the situation in the region. Now, the aggression is taking place just near the borders of the Islamic Republic and it is understandable that in its latest statements, Iran has expressed a serious concern about the developments in the region, and has sharply condemned the Armenian attacks.

Unfortunately, real understanding by the international community, including Iran, of the threat of Armenian aggression against Azerbaijan is currently occurring, however, only after huge hardships were suffered by the Azerbaijani people. In comments addressed to Armenian leaders, speaker of the Iranian parliament Nateq Nouri said the dispute in Azerbaijan "could not be solved through acts of violence." We can see the continuation of the Iranian efforts in seeking an efficient mechanism for halting the Armenian aggression. Having considerable economic and political potential, Iran evidently can effectively influence the solution of the conflict.

Q: How do you see the role of Turkey in the conflict?

A: The Azerbaijani leadership qualifies Turkey as a supporter of the economic and political development of Azerbaijan. Our historical and cultural ties create more opportunities for development and the deepening of present relations between Turkey and Azerbaijan. The Azerbaijani leadership highly esteems the role of Turkey in the tandem with Russia and the United States, in the development of a peaceful resolution for the Armenian-Azerbaijani conflict, as well as its participation in the CSCE frameworks.

Q: How does Russia enter into the picture?

A: Russia is a large world power having historically close ties with the republics of the former USSR. This evident geopolitical reality cannot be ignored. If some people think that the two hundred year link with Russia can be obliterated in the space of one or two years, they are simply very far removed from life, from reality, and from politics. Azerbaijani-Russian bilateral relations are to be developed and expanded, but not at the expense of their independence. Having strong potential and traditional links with both Armenia and Azerbaijan, Russia has a real chance to positively and efficiently affect the settlement of the Azerbaijani-Armenian conflict through authoritative international organizations.

Q: Given Iran's role in the conflict, what suggestions do you have for U.S. policymakers regarding U.S. policy towards Iran?

A: In the new geopolitical situation, the United States should not be very much concerned with the so-called "Iranian factor" in the region. This factor might be positive in its affect on the processes under way here. It can be noted that the fruitful and close economic cooperation between the countries of the region could be a very good guarantee for a future stable peace in this part of the world.

Q: How do you view the role of international actors, including the CSCE and the UN in mediating the conflict?

A: For five years, an unprecedented aggression of Armenia against Azerbaijan has been going on. In spite of the repeated efforts of international organizations, and in particular of CSCE, to settle the conflict by peaceful means, the achieved agreements have been continuously violated by the Armenian capture of new Azerbaijani territories.

Only after recent Armenian occupation of the large Azerbaijani regions of Kelbajar and Aghdarn, with a total population of 300,000 people, when the cities and nearby villages had been looted and then burned down, were UN Security Council resolutions adopted and the U.S. State Department made a number of statements condemning the aggression.

But unfortunately, UN Security Council Resolutions 822 and 853, the resolutions of the CSCE, and other resolutions condemning the Armenian aggression and demanding the immediate withdrawal of Armenian forces from the occupied Azerbaijani territories have not yet been fulfilled. Moreover, Armenian forces occupied new Azerbaijani regions, namely, Jabrail and Gubatli. The necessity is evident for real mechanisms, for the implementation of decisions and resolutions, and the adoption of such diplomatic tools by respected international organizations.

Remarks before the Federation of Turkish-American Societies
New York City
May 16, 1993

Thank you for the opportunity to address this seminar on Turkey and the Caucasus.

To begin my remarks, I know you are all familiar with the very close cultural and linguistic ties that exist between Turkey and Azerbaijan, and to a significant extent, the other independent Turkic republics that have emerged from the ruins of the former Soviet Union to take their rightful place among the community of nations.

Beyond these ties, Azerbaijan, of all the Turkic republics, has joined most closely with Turkey in embracing the model of a modern, secular, Western-style democracy. Like Turkey, we realize that this form of government, based as it is on the rule of law and guarantees of equal rights for all citizens, regardless of religion or ethnic origin, offers the best opportunity for realizing peace and economic prosperity for our people and for the people of the entire region.

Unfortunately, there is another model that many of the newly emerging nations, in the South Caucasus and elsewhere, are choosing to follow, a model that is in stark contrast to the one I just described.

This is a model based on irredentism and ultra-nationalism; a model in which those not of the proper ethnic origin forfeit their rights under the law and must be cleansed from the community (most often in campaigns of violence and bloodshed), while territories of neighboring countries in which ethnic kinfolk reside are fair game for military conquest. This model is based on a rejection of the very basis of international law that should govern the relations among civilized nations. Almost inevitably, the nation that makes this rejection plunges itself and its neighbors into war. That so many of the newly emerging nations have demonstrated a willingness to choose this model should be of concern to us all.

What is this fundamental element of international law, and why have so many nations dismissed it with scorn and contempt?

Central to any rule of international law is the principle that sovereign states are equal and therefore, their borders and their territorial integrity must remain inviolable. Any effort to change the borders of sovereign states through the use of force is impermissible and must be rejected if international law is to have any meaning. Indeed, this has been explicitly reaffirmed by all relevant international bodies, including, most prominently, the United Nations and the Helsinki signatories. Even those states of the former Soviet Union that chose to join the Commonwealth of Independent States did so by signing a treaty in which they explicitly committed themselves to respecting the existing borders.

Yet today, this very basic principle of international law is under attack and even, in some cases, rejected outright.

The justification for this rejection is found in the concept of self-determination. Consider these words of the Armenian minister of defense, quote, "The principle of the non-violability of borders may apply to Western countries whose borders were more or less solidly drawn up after two world wars. The principle of non-violability is not valid for Karabakh. The borders in the former Soviet Union were established in a capricious manner and must be changed."

Thus, in order to justify its war of territorial expansion against Azerbaijan for the purpose of creating a "Greater Armenia" that includes Azerbaijani territory, Armenia proclaims a distorted version of the principle of self-determination to override and cancel out the basic principle of territorial integrity and inviolability of borders of sovereign states. In so doing, Armenia stands in open violation of the United Nations, the CSCE, and of the Commonwealth of Independent States' treaty it freely chose to sign.

Now, it is indeed true that these two principles, the inviolability of borders and the right to self-determination, have their places, but the indiscriminate application of the principle of self determination, especially in the wake of the collapse of the former Soviet empire, can only lead to international anarchy, to continued war and bloodshed, and to a state of affairs where the force of arms replaces the rule of law.

The members of ethnic minorities each deserve full civil rights and individual liberties. But organizing and killing for sovereign statehood is another matter. Today, there is an Armenian state in the Caucasus, one that is bent on growing at the expense of its neighbors. Why not another in a part of California? Part of Massachusetts? Who is to say, under Armenian principles, whether full rights as citizens of California, Massachusetts and the United States are sufficient to satisfy Armenian ambitions for Armenian Americans, and whether the clamor for self-determination will be given voice here in America if Armenian logic is applied here as it is in the Caucasus?

Returning now to the conflict over Nagorno-Karabakh, we may ask the Armenian defense minister that if the principle of self-determination is absolute, if it provides sufficient justification for rejecting the entire body of international law respecting territorial integrity and the inviolability of borders, then where does it all end?

There are more than one half million citizens of Georgia who are ethnic Azerbaijanis. Many form majority communities in contiguous areas. Should we be justified in fomenting discontent among this community so that it can demand an Azerbaijani state of its own?

The Armenian defense minister also justifies his nation's bloody attempt to change borders in the former Soviet Union (which is really what the conflict in Nagorno-Karabakh is all about) by saying that these borders were established in a capricious fashion. But, I would point out that Nagorno-Karabakh has always been recognized by the international community as an integral part of Azerbaijan. Never has it been recognized as either a part of Armenia or as an independent state.

We understand that if every area that has a concentration of ethnic affinities were to assert and assume an absolute and unconditional right to self-determination, which, according to the logic of Armenian defense minister, that would necessitate the creation of a new state at the expense of the territorial integrity of another, then the result would only be international chaos and war.

This is why Azerbaijan makes no claims against the territory of Armenia. All of the fighting to date has taken place on Azerbaijan's territory. Azerbaijan is suffering from a war of aggression aimed at its dismemberment. This attempted redrawing of international boundaries by Armenian forces and this "cleansing" of lands of their inhabitants is all too likely to produce a crisis of global proportions if it proceeds unchecked and is not redressed.

Azerbaijan has been forthcoming in taking its case before the international community. We desire nothing more than peace for ourselves and the entire region, but we must insist on our territorial integrity and political independence. As a member of the United Nations, Azerbaijan's state territory is defined by international law. Its borders are internationally recognized. It cannot appease open aggression and brutal occupation.

At the beginning of my remarks, I said that Azerbaijan, more than any of the Turkic republics, has joined most closely with Turkey in embracing the model of secular democracy, based on equal rights, the rule of law, and open markets. The success of this model, not only in Azerbaijan but throughout Central Asia, is crucial if the newly emerging nations of the region are to avoid the threat of Iranian-fomented Islamic fundamentalism or the violent passions of irredentist ultra-nationalism.

We increasingly hear today that only the harsh, tyrannical communist systems of the former Soviet Union and Yugoslavia were capable of keeping the peace in the lands they once governed. In other words, the problems in the Balkans and the South Caucasus are intractable to democratic resolution. In reality, they can only be resolved by the brutal denial of freedom and human rights.

I do not believe this to be true. I believe that the pluralistic democratic path such as Azerbaijan has adopted for its multi-ethnic population offers the best chance to tame the irredentist passions of ultra-nationalism that threaten the peace, stability and future development of the entire region.

Letters to Members of the U.S. Congress and U.S. Administration

The following letter was one of my first official letters sent to the U.S. Congress since I assumed duties as Ambassador. This and similar letters were sent to Representatives Gary L. Ackerman (D-NY) and David Bonior (D-MI), co-sponsors of the House Resolution 86, also known as the

Bonior Resolution. The resolution was introduced in the House of Representatives on February 17, 1993 and called for the condemnation of the Republic of Azerbaijan for "violation of international law." It surprised me that at a time when Armenian forces were continuing to occupy more and more of Azerbaijan's territory and expelling thousands of Azerbaijanis in the process, this resolution was calling to condemn not the Armenian aggressors, but Azerbaijan. The text of this resolution was a testimony to how little the U.S. Congress knew about the Karabakh conflict and how grossly misinformed U.S. congressmen were about the war between Armenia and Azerbaijan. Similar letters were sent to all members of the U.S. Congress, and I personally met with and delivered letters to the co-sponsors of this resolution. As a result of our activities, we were able to stop this resolution from moving onto the House floor.

February 25, 1993

Dear Representative:

I urge you, as a co-sponsor of House Resolution 86, to carefully reconsider the impact that such a resolution would have on the prospects for peace in the ongoing conflict between Armenia and my country of Azerbaijan.

As you know, both sides have tentatively agreed to a cease-fire with international observers at the recent Rome peace talks under the auspices of the Conference on Security and Cooperation in Europe (CSCE). Azerbaijan agreed to such a cease-fire with no pre-conditions on the ultimate status of Nagorno-Karabakh, which would be negotiated as part of the Minsk peace process.

Both Turkey and Russia have taken an active role in promoting negotiations and both countries have urged the United States to join their efforts. The United States has played a very constructive role in the Rome negotiations, and Ambassador Maresca has continued those efforts in recent Geneva meetings.

Given the role of "honest broker" that the United States government plays and continues to do so, it is inconsistent and harmful to the peace process for Congress to take sides through the passage of legislation such as House Resolution 86.

I remind you that all the fighting has taken place on Azerbaijani soil, Azerbaijan has no territorial claims on Armenia and no soldiers in Armenia, and that Armenia wants to annex Azerbaijani territory and has both regular and irregular soldiers in Azerbaijan. Our country has 500,000 refugees as a result of the war, including 200,000 Azerbaijanis who were "ethnically cleansed" from Armenia, and despite the peace negotiations, Armenia has launched a major offensive in recent weeks that has resulted in many deaths and hundreds of additional refugees.

I would also call to your attention the attached article in The San Francisco Chronicle under the byline of Jill Hamburg concerning the situation in Armenia. The article points out that "ultra-nationalists" have limited Armenian President Ter-Petrossian's efforts to pursue a path of liberal reform. The article further states that "an extreme nationalistic opposition is surging, supported by a diaspora more concerned with the symbolic importance of the war than its price in misery."

Azerbaijan is a secular democracy seeking to implement a market economy. In many ways, we look to the United States as our model. Yet, when Congress passes resolutions, which take a one-sided view of the conflict, it makes it difficult for Azerbaijani citizens to view the United States as even-handed.

I commend to your reading the recent editorial in The Washington Post, The San Francisco Chronicle article, and my recent testimony before the Congressional Helsinki Commission.

Sincerely,
Hafiz Pashayev
Ambassador

Another issue was the fact that most statements and documents written by U.S. congressmen and senators highlighted the suffering of the Armenian people as a result of the so-called "blockade" of Armenia by Azerbaijan, while the misery of thousands of Azerbaijani refugees and internally displaced persons caused by Armenian aggression was not even on the agenda. A vivid example of that is a letter sent by Senator Bill Bradley (D-NJ), along with twenty-nine other U.S. senators, to the U.S. Secretary of State Warren Christopher on February 22, 1993. With my letter to Senator Bradley, I enclosed an editorial article from *The Washington Post*, a first one to present a balanced view about the situation in the region and the Karabakh conflict. That article was written after my meeting with Stephen Rosenfeld, the editor of *The Washington Post's* editorial page.

March 11, 1993

Dear Senator Bradley:

A copy of a letter to Secretary of State Christopher on February 22, signed by you and twenty-nine of your colleagues, has been brought to my attention. This letter addresses the suffering of the Armenian people as a result of the suspension of trading relations between Armenia and Azerbaijan.

The government of Azerbaijan shares your great concern over the suffering that has occurred on both sides and is as anxious as you are to end it. The people of my country have suffered as much and perhaps even more than the people of Armenia.

You should be advised that Azerbaijan stands ready to resume commercial, transportation, and communications ties immediately with Armenia as part of a CSCE-sponsored, cease-fire arrangement. This resumption of commerce and trade will occur upon the implementation of the cease-fire arrangement as discussed at the Rome talks and prior to the resolution of the status of Nagorno-Karabakh.

I have enclosed a copy of my statement to a hearing of the Commission on Security and Cooperation in Europe. This statement explains my position in greater detail than can be done in a letter. Moreover, I am

*taking the liberty of enclosing a copy of an editorial that appeared in to-
day's Washington Post.*
Sincerely,
Hafiz M. Pashayev
Ambassador

In March 1993, Armenian attacks against Azerbaijani villages and towns had intensified. Troops from the Republic of
Armenia and the separatist Armenian forces inside Azerbaijan, supported by heavy artillery and air assets, had moved
their offensive beyond the administrative borders of Nagorno-Karabakh. Lachin and Kelbajar regions of Azerbaijan,
both located outside of the Nagorno-Karabakh region, were
being continuously attacked by Armenian troops, which were
seizing ever larger portions of my country.

A lack of engagement on the part of the U.S. Government in trying to stop the continued Armenian offensives,
and the turning a blind eye towards the Armenian aggression,
was damaging the United States' image as an objective peace
broker. I wrote several letters to Secretary Christopher, urging
the U.S. Government to intervene. The following letter is one
of these, written on behalf of Tofik Gasymov, Foreign Minister of the Republic of Azerbaijan at the time.

April 5, 1993
Dear Secretary Christopher:
*I write on behalf of the Government of Azerbaijan to urge the
United States Government to re-examine its role as "honest broker" and
take full account of the terrible realities unfolding on the territory of
Azerbaijan. Surely, this role does not require the total omission of an
objective public assessment of what is happening on the ground. Surely, it
does not require turning a blind eye to rampaging aggression. To persist
in a posture of silence when the full dimension of Armenia's policy of ter-*

ritorial aggrandizement, executed with brute military force, is discernible to anyone with an eye for truth, only encourages such policy.

Past public exhortations by the United States, made to both sides with equal weight and equivalent content, have created the impression that the United States sees symmetrical grievances, provocations, hostilities, and aims between the parties (when the objective situation is decidedly otherwise).

This impression has fueled the aggressor's appetite as much as it has disheartened the victim. In the few days since our Ambassador in Washington, DC wrote to you on March 31, 1993, and in flagrant contempt for CSCE-sponsored peace efforts, the Armenians have greatly expanded their area of conquest, and systematic ethnic cleansing is proceeding even as I write. The city of Kelbajar was seized on April 3, thus sealing off from the rest of Azerbaijan a large territory between Kelbajar, Armenian-occupied Nagorno-Karabakh, Armenian-occupied Lachin, and Armenia. A new salient aimed at Fuzuli far to the south points to a campaign to envelop and isolate another large region of Azerbaijan. Savaged by an ultra-nationalist whose rapaciousness is equaled only by the Serbian equivalent in the Balkans, my country is suffering nothing less than a war to dismember it.

Armenia's contempt for "even-handed" appeals to stop hostilities has become exceedingly obvious. The Government of Azerbaijan expects that the Government of the United States, at long last and in keeping with the values and principles which form the stated foundation of American foreign policy, will disclose to the world what it knows to be true: that Armenia is attacking and seizing the territory of its neighbor in violation of all applicable international law; and that it has been negotiating in bad faith.

We call on the United States Government to insist publicly that these attacks immediately cease; that the Government of Armenia publicly repudiate the anschluss 1989 resolution of its parliament, which annexed the territory of Azerbaijan; that Armenian regular forces and mercenary gunmen withdraw immediately to restore the status quo at the outset of the Rome talks; that Armenia complete in good faith the talks to flesh out the cease-fire Terms of Reference developed in Rome; that Armenia implement a cease-fire in accordance with the arrangements envisioned in the terms of reference.

We ask further that you arrange for an immediate emergency meeting of the United Nations Security Council to condemn this aggression and to reverse its effects.

To date, Armenia has been reaping the rewards of aggression, while a too credulous international community has indulged itself in hand wringing or misplaced sympathy born either of ignorance or religious bias. Armenia's actions speak for themselves. Armenia is well advanced in a campaign to create an ethnically pure, Armenians-only, greatly enlarged Armenia. Neither our country, nor our region, nor the world can afford to allow this aggression, this redrawing of boundaries with blood and "cleansing" of lands of their inhabitants, to go on unnoticed and unchecked.

With best regards,
Sincerely,
Tofik Gasymov
Foreign Minister
(Signed by the Ambassador for the Foreign Minister)

On April 2, 1993, Armenian forces occupied the Kelbajar region of Azerbaijan. Some fifteen thousand families (roughly sixty thousand residents) lost their homes and became refugees in their own country. The international community, including the U.S. Government, condemned the Armenian aggression. On April 30, 1993, the United Nations Security Council (UNSC) adopted Resolution 822 expressing "grave concern," and declaring the "inadmissibility of the use of force for the acquisition of territory." The letter below was sent to U.S. senators informing them of the recent developments on the ground and urging them to be more active in the mediation of the Karabakh conflict.

April 14, 1993

Dear Senator:

Since I last corresponded with Congress, matters have taken a dramatic turn for the worse in Azerbaijan.

As you have probably heard, Armenia has launched two new offensives, totally outside of Nagorno-Karabakh, and Armenian forces now occupy an additional 10 percent of the territory of Azerbaijan. What is so disheartening is that these offensives occurred after both sides agreed in principle to a cease-fire with international observers, and just as talks commenced in Geneva on how and when the cease-fire would take place.

However, Azerbaijan is very grateful that the world community has condemned these new offensives. American Secretary of State Warren Christopher strongly denounced the offensive, as did the United Nations Security Council and other individual countries. The Security Council also reaffirmed the sovereignty and territorial integrity of all countries in the region.

Secretary Christopher said that "The U.S. Government condemns this offensive and has expressed its deep concern about the offensive to the highest level of the government of Armenia and to representatives of the Nagorno-Karabakh Armenians. We have called for the prompt and complete withdrawal of all ethnic Armenian forces from the Kelbajar district."

It is our hope that Congress, like the Clinton Administration and the Bush Administration, will play the role of "honest broker" and encourage Armenia to cease offensive actions, withdraw from conquered territories, and return to serious cease-fire negotiations under the auspices of the CSCE.

I have enclosed copies of Secretary Christopher's statement, the UN Security Council statement, and some clippings on the latest developments.

With best regards,

Sincerely,

Hafiz M. Pashayev
Ambassador

By June 1993, the internal political situation in Azerbaijan had deteriorated and Armenian forces continued to occupy additional Azerbaijani lands. This letter to Al Gore (D-TN), former Senate President and Vice-President of the United States (1993-2000), was written to draw the U.S. Senate's attention to the worsening situation in Azerbaijan and to urge it to do more to stop Armenia's occupation of Azerbaijan.

June 30, 1993
Dear Mr. Gore:

I write to urge you to encourage whatever steps may be necessary to stop the current and latest offensive by Armenian forces in Azerbaijan. With the ink not yet dry on a cease-fire agreement, the political crisis in Azerbaijan has been cynically exploited by Armenian forces as an opportunity to seize further Azerbaijani territory, in and outside of Nagorno-Karabakh. Armenian territorial appetites are apparently without limit and unfettered by any regard for international law, morality, or even simple decency.

The absence of effective action by the international community to stop Armenian aggression and ethnic cleansing is a primary factor in the erosion of public confidence in Azerbaijan's foreign policy and diplomacy-a policy that has been at once principled and forthcoming. This erosion has resulted in declining citizen confidence in the democratically-elected leadership of Azerbaijan. Democratic state-building is an arduous task under the best of circumstances, but in Azerbaijan, it has been burdened in time of crisis by the omission of substantial diplomatic and material support for the rule of law in international relations from democracy's most vocal proponents in the international community.

The hour is late. If Armenian aggression continues unabated and Western powers do not promptly move to reverse by all means necessary, the remnants of decency, self-restraint, and civility in the region may be swept aside by inchoate forces whose principal guideposts will be crude tribalism and vengeful grievances.

Conditions of more or less permanent warfare, accompanied by es-trangement from democracy and its moderating influences, as well as from the Western powers who did so little to foster it, will be the tragic prospect for years to come in the southern Caucasus-a bleak portent for all the countries of the former Soviet Union.

Sincerely,

Hafiz Pashayev

Ambassador

At the time, Section 907 restricted all types of U.S. assistance to the government of Azerbaijan, including humanitarian aid. With a rapidly growing number of internally displaced persons (IDPs) caused by new territorial gains by Armenian forces, Azerbaijan was facing the largest humanitarian crisis in its recent history. These two letters to Secretary Christopher highlighted the urgency of getting humanitarian assistance for Azerbaijani refugees and IDPs.

July 16, 1993

Dear Mr. Secretary:

As you know, Azerbaijan's refugee population continues to grow at an alarming rate and now totals approximately 600,000 in a total population of seven million. Acute shortages of the basic necessities of life-food, clothing, and rudimentary shelter-are growing not only for the refugees, but also for the general population.

In light of these desperate needs, and in keeping with a stated United States policy of impartiality in its relations with Armenia and Azerbaijan, I urge that the United States Government give favorable consideration to a formal request for greatly increased humanitarian assistance to Azerbaijan.

Assistance reaching Azerbaijan is deeply appreciated by the people of my country as evidence of the natural generosity for which the American people are so rightly known throughout the world. At the same time, however, the immense disparity between humanitarian assistance levels to

Armenia and Azerbaijan cannot be accounted for by reference to relative need or even to the existence of unfair restrictions contained in Section 907 of the Freedom Support Act. It is my understanding that United States Government-supported efforts have shipped foodstuffs to Armenia equivalent to 180 pounds for every man, woman, and child in that country, plus extensive medical supplies and fuel.

Mr. Secretary, Azerbaijan's need is great. Accordingly, I call it to your attention hoping that you can find means to help us to address it.
Sincerely,
Hafiz Pashayev
Ambassador

July 11, 1993

As I write, the Azerbaijani city of Agdam has been suffering for forty-eight hours from a renewed large scale offensive by Armenian forces attacking from three directions. Yesterday morning, after a massive artillery attack, armored elements advanced toward Agdam from Askeran, Agdera (formerly Mardakert) and Khojavend (formerly Martuni), and heavy fighting is underway in the Western suburbs. A total of forty have been killed, and over one hundred have been wounded; many which are civilians. Continuous heavy shelling of the Agdam-Baku highway and other arteries leading to Agdam make humanitarian relief very nearly impossible and successful military reinforcement unlikely.

Launched on the eve of renewed cease-fire talks in Rome, the Armenians have apparently concluded that Agdam's strategic value-the control of western Azerbaijan-transcends many aspirations for an end to the bloodletting, even if the Armenian seizure of Agdam dooms the southern Caucasus to endless warfare and the (possibly precipitous) erosion of self-restraint in an Azerbaijani population whose capacity to endure unredressed grievance approaches its limit.

Armenian aggression in the southern Caucasus is a growing phenomenon. Disclaimers by Yerevan authorities of involvement and responsibility ought to at least last to exceed the tolerance of the most credulous of third parties. They echo the denials by Belgrade of responsibility for the outrages committed in Bosnia.

Impartiality surely allows for the United States to acknowledge the fact of this aggression soberly, unsparingly, and publicly, and then to act to secure full compliance by Armenia with international law. This requires for Armenia to cease, and reverse the effects and violations of the territorial integrity of Azerbaijan.

Mr. Secretary, the hour is late; not only for efforts to end hostilities in the southern Caucasus, but also for democracy in the region. The suffering in Azerbaijan, caused by an unsought war, places a greater burden on our new democracy, and its ability to sustain and recover from setbacks everyday. The failure to secure a just peace and to secure democracy's foundation in the region is a bleak portent for all countries of the former Soviet Union.

Sincerely,

Hafiz Pashayev

Ambassador, Embassy of Azerbaijan

Washington, DC

By September 1993, Armenian troops had occupied Agdam and Fizuli districts of Azerbaijan, both of which are outside of Nagorno-Karabakh, and continued their rampage towards other southwestern regions of Azerbaijan such as Jabrail, Gubadli and Zengelan. On July 29, 1993, the UNSC adopted Resolution 853 condemning "the seizure of the district of Agdam and of all other recently occupied areas of the Azerbaijani Republic." Some 200,000 Azerbaijanis had been forcefully displaced by the advancing Armenian forces. Yet the U.S. Congress was still silent! Below are excerpts from my letter to the Speaker of the House, Thomas Foley.

September 1, 1993

Dear Speaker Foley:

Since I last corresponded with you about the ongoing conflict between Armenia and my country of Azerbaijan, several very tragic events have taken place. The latest attacks occurred in the Fizuli and southwestern region of Azerbaijan. The Armenian army captured the regions of Fizuli, Jabrail and Gubadli, which resulted in the creation of 200,000 refugees, many of whom are fleeing to the Iranian border.

Look at the results of this war of aggression:

(1) Some 20 percent of the landmass of Azerbaijan has been conquered and occupied by Armenian forces.

(2) By United Nations estimates, there are up to one million Azerbaijani refugees. In other words, one of every seven Azerbaijani is now a refugee.

(3) More than fifteen thousand-a very conservative estimate-have been killed in this war.

(4) Several hundred thousand Azerbaijanis are trapped in Armenian occupied Azerbaijani territory, cut off from the rest of the country to the east and vulnerable to continued Armenian ethnic cleansing.

(5) The Armenian forces have adopted a policy of looting and burning the villages and cities they conquer, trying to assure that no Azerbaijani will ever return to their homes. Most of this has occurred after Azerbaijan, Armenia and the Karabakh Armenians signed a CSCE cease-fire agreement. The Armenians signed the agreement and immediately began the Aghdam and Fizuli southwestern offensives.

The United Nations, the CSCE, the United States, Russia, Turkey, Iran and many others have condemned the Armenian offensives and demanded withdrawal from the occupied territories, but to no avail. These demands have been rhetorical, unaccompanied by even the threat of sanctions. As a result, the Armenians talk about cease-fire and continue to wage war.

The United States government has been outspoken in opposition to this aggression, and it has led efforts within the CSCE framework to negotiate a cease-fire and to secure withdrawal of occupying troops. But the United States Congress has been silent. It has refused to speak out against the atrocities being committed, the attempts to change borders through force, or even the creation of some one million refugees. Indeed, by acquiescing in the continuation of the ban on assistance to Azerbaijan, even for refugee needs, the United States Congress is in effect encouraging the Armenians to continue their policy of death, destruction and occupation.

I would urge the Congress of the United States to take an objective look at the situation and speak out forcefully in favor of territorial sovereignty and in opposition to this immoral Armenian war of aggression.
Sincerely Yours,
Hafiz Mir Jalal Pashayev
Ambassador

On October 10, 1993, Heydar Aliyev was elected President of Azerbaijan. On October 14, the UNSC adopted yet another Resolution (No. 874) supporting the CSCE Minsk Group's mediation effort and a timetable for the withdrawal of Armenian troops from the occupied Azerbaijani territories. Unfortunately, Armenia and Armenian forces never abided by the multiple cease-fire agreements signed during this time and shortly thereafter seized three more Azerbaijani districts-Jabrail, Gubadli and Zengelan-all of which are outside Nagorno-Karabakh. My letter to U.S. House Chairman Lee H. Hamilton highlighted these developments.

October 22, 1993
Dear Chairman Hamilton:
On Sunday, October 10, Heydar Aliyev was inaugurated as President of Azerbaijan after being overwhelmingly elected in a multi-candidate election on October 3.

The report of the Office of the Democratic Institutions and Human Rights of the Conference on Security and Cooperation in Europe (CSCE) affirms that the election "did allow the unimpeded expression of people's choice." In a congratulatory letter to President Aliyev, President Clinton expresses his hope to work with his Azerbaijani counterpart toward the implementation of the goals of democracy, political pluralism, market economic reform, and respect for human rights.

Upon his election, President Aliyev pledged to pursue a course of greater independence, sovereignty, democracy and free market reforms. Of course, the most immediate concern of President Aliyev is to seek resolution of the conflict with Armenia.

In that regard, the CSCE has proposed a timetable for the withdrawal of Armenian forces from the occupied territory of Azerbaijan. While my Government welcomes the CSCE initiative, and especially the United States' role in supporting the CSCE process, we continue to believe Armenian forces should first unconditionally withdraw from the 20 percent of Azerbaijani territory they currently occupy.

In a letter to the Chairman of the Minsk Conference of the CSCE, Foreign Minister Hassan Hassanov stated that "Azerbaijan is interested in the convocation of the Minsk Conference but it believes it can start work only after the full and unconditional withdrawal of Armenian troops occupying its territories," as provided for in two United Nations Security Council resolutions.

Our Government is also disappointed that the proposed withdrawal timetable does not include two key Azerbaijani towns, Lachin and Shusha, which are currently occupied by Armenian forces. The fact that Armenian forces unilaterally broke the current cease fire and captured four villages just days after the CSCE proposal was unveiled also causes us concerns about compliance and enforcement of any agreement we sign.

But we are continuing discussions with all interested parties in the hope and expectation that a reasonable solution can be found to these and other issues, so that a permanent ceasefire can be obtained and the Minsk Conference can proceed with negotiations on the ultimate status of Nagorno-Karabakh,

I also would remind you that the Armenian offensives have created about one million refugees within Azerbaijan, according to the United Nations, which means one out of every seven citizens in my country is a refugee. With winter coming on, you can imagine the hardships that will occur unless these people are able to return to the shelter of their homes—many of which have, unfortunately, been burnt and looted by the attacking Armenian forces. This brings me to my final point. Congressional prohibitions still prevent the United States government from providing any assistance to the government of Azerbaijan, despite the fact that it is Azerbaijan that is the victim of aggression, it is Azerbaijan that has one million refugees, and it is Azerbaijan that has 20 percent of its territory occupied by Armenian forces.

Simple decency and fairness, as well as the interests of the United States, dictate that this prohibition should be removed, and as advocated repeatedly by U.S. Ambassador Strobe Talbott, the U.S. Government could send no clearer signal on the need to halt the bloodshed than by removing this unjust prohibition.

It is my hope, and that of President Aliyev, that before the end of this year we will have achieved a clear course toward the resolution of this conflict, which has already resulted in more than fifteen thousand deaths and untold hardship and suffering.
With my very best wishes,
Sincerely yours,
Hafiz Mir Jalal Pashayev
Ambassador

In early March 1994, the Senate held a confirmation hearing for Ambassador Richard Kauzlarich, who was then Senior Deputy to the Secretary's and the President's Special Representative to the Newly Independent States. His nomination was confirmed, and he served as U.S. Ambassador to Azerbaijan from 1994 to 1997.

Due to the controversial Section 907, the U.S. Government still could not assist Azerbaijan in spite of the growing humanitarian crisis in the country. Although President Bill Clinton wanted Section 907 repealed, it was the Senate that had the final say. Below is my letter to Senator Biden urging him to support the Clinton Administration's initiative on re-pealing Section 907.

March 14, 1994
Dear Senator Biden:

I am aware that you questioned Ambassador designate Kauzlarich during his recent confirmation hearing about Section 907 of the Freedom Support Act. The Government of Azerbaijan is very appreciative of your interest in this issue.

You will know that as a result of recent Armenian offensives, there are now about one million refugees in Azerbaijan, according to estimates of the United Nations. This constitutes one in every seven citizens in the country.

At the same time, Armenian forces occupy about 20 percent of the landmass of my country. Some eighteen thousand Azerbaijanis have been killed, fifty thousand wounded, and scores of villages looted and burned.

These Armenian offensives have been condemned by the United Nations, the Conference on Security and Cooperation in Europe, the United States and European countries-but to no avail. That being the case, Azerbaijan finds it morally wrong that the United States Congress would punish the victim, Azerbaijan, and reward the aggressor in this conflict by continuation of Section 907.

The United States Congress should not let the Armenian American lobby determine American foreign policy.

For that reason, I urge you to support the Clinton Administration's recommendation that Section 907 be repealed during consideration of the foreign aid reform legislation.

I would be happy to meet with you at your convenience to discuss this matter.
Sincerely,
Hafiz Mir Jalal Pashayev
Ambassador

Thanks to the Armenian constituency in Massachusetts, Senator Edward M. Kennedy was one of the U.S. senators who occasionally wrote letters to the President urging the U.S. Government to help resolve the Karabakh conflict. I used this as an opportunity to communicate to him the Azerbaijani perspective on the problem and to update him about recent developments in the region.

April 13, 1994

Dear Senator Kennedy:

I have seen your letter of March 31 in which you urge President Clinton to take additional steps to seek a peaceful resolution of the "armed conflict in the Trans-Caucasus over Nagorno-Karabakh."

Your letter is very much on target. We would welcome a more active role by the United States in dealing with the two principals in the conflict, the Republic of Armenia and the Republic of Azerbaijan. Your recognition of the key role President Levon Ter-Petrosian continues to play in the war bodes well for its resolution. Without his active participation in efforts to end the fighting, there can be no peace, for his government is a combatant in the war.

The United Nations has repeatedly condemned Armenian aggression against Azerbaijan. Security Council Resolution 822 demanded "the immediate withdrawal of all occupying forces from... recently occupied areas of Azerbaijan." Resolution 853 reaffirmed "the sovereignty and territorial integrity of the Azerbaijani Republic," and "the inadmissibility of the use of force for the acquisition of territory." In November of 1993, Resolution 884 called upon the Government of Armenia "to use its influence... to ensure that the forces involved are not provided with the means to extend their military campaign further." Newsweek has characterized Armenia's actions as those of a "bully." Just this week, Armenian forces launched major new offensives in several regions of Azerbaijan.

P.L. 303-87 states that funds shall not "be made available to any government of the New Independent States of the former Soviet Union if

*that government directs any action in violation of the territorial integrity
or national sovereignty of any other New Independent State." Despite the
occupation of some 25 percent of Azerbaijan, Armenia continues to be
the largest per capita recipient of U.S. aid among the republics of the
former Soviet Union. Azerbaijan, on the other hand, is precluded from
any aid, including humanitarian assistance, under Section 907 of the
FREEDOM Support Act. As your letter correctly asserts, there are
more than one million refugees in Azerbaijan alone as a direct result of
this six-year war. Regarding this ban, Senator DeConcini has stated
that "in view of the humanitarian needs of the large number of Azerbaijani refugees, we should consider whether this course—which I initially
supported-is the wisest and fairest course of action" (11/22/93, Congressional Record S16917-8).*

*The United States has strong national interests in the region and it
could play a decisive role in ending the struggle. President Clinton's invitation could bring President Ter-Petrosian and President Heydar Aliyev
to Washington to negotiate its end and begin efforts to develop the economic potential of the area. There is much to be done to provide free and
safe transport of the natural resources of the region to the markets of the
west. The economic development that could be provided by a Trans-
Caucasus Enterprise Fund, as you have proposed, could be a stabilizing
force in the region.*

*I commend your continued leadership in seeking solutions to this
devastating war and support your plea for a stronger role for the United
States in seeking a lasting peace in our region. I look forward to working
with you in achieving these vitally important goals. Thank you.*
Sincerely,
Hafiz Pashayev
Ambassador

By 1994, the U.S. media had started to publish objective
and fair articles on the Armenia-Azerbaijan conflict. As I
came across such balanced news reports, I often wrote letters
to the U.S. Congress and to various departments in the U.S.

Government commenting on them and drawing further attention to the Karabakh conflict. Below is my letter to Secretary of Defense, William Perry, in which I compare the Karabakh conflict to the conflict in Bosnia.

April 21, 1994

Dear Mr. Perry:

I am sure you have already read the attached article from The Washington Post, but it so arrested my attention that I felt compelled to comment on it to you.

While I naturally do not agree with some of the author's rather gratuitous comments about the Administration, I do believe the article contains an essential truth: committed ultra-nationalists, when faced with uncertain opposition, can often achieve their goals despite the best efforts of a well meaning world community.

Ultra-nationalists-acting on perceived grievances often going back hundreds of years-are often willing to single-mindedly pursue a strategic objective, almost regardless of the cost to themselves or their opponents. Attempts to deal with such ultra-nationalists with rationality are often futile.

That is true with respect to the Serbs in Bosnia, and it is also true of the Armenians in my country of Azerbaijan.

The parallels between what the Serbs and Armenians are doing is so revealing that I devoted a major portion of a recent speech at George Mason University to the subject. Let me quote from that speech: "This conflict (over Nagorno-Karabakh) at its core represents an effort by a proud and extremely nationalistic ethnic group-the Armenians-to occupy, by force if necessary, lands they believe are theirs by historic right so as to create a Greater Armenia. It really is no different from what the Serbs and Bosnian Serbs are attempting in the Balkans." Because Americans understand what is going on in Bosnia, but not in Azerbaijan, let me describe the similarities between the two conflicts:

(1) The Armenians are seeking a "Greater Armenia", a
    dream they have held for decades if not centuries, just

as the Serbs want a *"Greater Serbia"*. *These dreams of territorial expansion, in both cases, are based on real or perceived injustices many decades ago.*

(2) *Both the Serbs and Armenians tell the Western world that this is a conflict between Christians and Muslims, when in fact it is a conflict over territorial expansion. Territory, not religion, is at the core of these conflicts.*

(3) *The Serbs claim they have no control over Bosnian Serbs; the Armenians make the same claim about the Karabakh Armenians. Yet the whole world knows who supplies the heavy artillery, the helicopters, the tanks and even the foot soldiers-it is the motherland of Serbia and Armenia. Armenia and the Karabakh Armenians even share the same defense minister. The New York Times recently detailed that regular Armenian soldiers fighting and dying in Azerbaijan.*

(4) *Armenia and the Serbs both claim they are the real victims, while at the same time Armenian forces occupy 20 percent of Azerbaijan and the Serbs occupy well over 50 percent of Bosnia. As Orwell would put it, the aggressors are victims and the victims are aggressors.*

(5) *Both the Serbs and Armenians think they can get away with their conquests because they believe the West and the United States do not care, and they believe Russia sides with them.*

(6) *Fighting in Bosnia has created two million refugees, while the Armenian offensives have created one million refugees-one of every seven citizens in Azerbaijan.*

(7) *The Armenian and Serbian offensives have been condemned by the United Nations, the Conference on Security and Cooperation in Europe (CSCE), the*

United States, and most of Europe and the rest of the world.

(8) *Likewise, the territorial ambitions of Serbs and Armenia have been rejected by all international organizations and by international law, which unanimously recognize Nagorno-Karabakh as part of the sovereign territory of Azerbaijan.*

(9) *Like Bosnia, Azerbaijan is a multi-ethnic society, which is being attacked by an ethnic group and a country seeking ethnic and racial purity. Just as the Serbs have ethnically cleansed major portions of Bosnia, the Armenians have ethnically cleansed Nagorno-Karabakh and Armenia itself. Armenian President Ter-Petrosian told the Moscow News on April 12, 1992 that "The worldwide process of creating ethnic states is taking place now. It has already happened in Armenia. We have a monotonic republic. History shows that the federative system of state is the weakest one." Azerbaijan, on the other hand, has more than fifty ethnic groups.*

We do not request military assistance from the United States-we will defend ourselves. However, that defense is made much more difficult when the world community and the West refuse to recognize and speak out forcefully against the ultra-nationalist ambitions of certain Armenians. And we ask that Congress redress the travesty of Section 907 of the Freedom Support Act, which denies direct assistance-even humanitarian aid-to Azerbaijan from the United States.

Like the Serbs, they will not be deterred by mere words. It will take deeds, such as outright condemnations in the United Nations, sanctions, and the threat of diplomatic isolation. What Mr. Williams says about the Serbs could just as easily be said about the Armenians: "From the day the war began two years ago, the Serbs have not wavered from their strategic goals: to conquer as much land in Bosnia as possible, expel the Muslims and at some point join their territory to next door Serbia. Dis-

ruptions in that drive, as in Srebrenica or Sarajevo, have been merely tactical."

The United States and the West took the lead in denying the territorial aggression of Germany in World War I, Hitler in World War II, the communists in Eastern Europe, and Saddam Hussein in Kuwait. It should do the same in Bosnia and Azerbaijan.
Sincerely,
Hafiz Mir Jalal Pashayev
Ambassador

Each year, the House Foreign Affairs Committee reviews the Foreign Aid Reform bill, which also raises the possibility of revising restrictions on Section 907. The U.S. Government clearly saw the worsening humanitarian situation in Azerbaijan and wanted to help, but for the U.S. Government to send humanitarian aid to Azerbaijan, Section 907 needed to be revised. Chairman of the Foreign Agriculture and Hunger Subcommittee of the House Agriculture Committee, Representative Timothy J. Penny acknowledged the humanitarian tragedy in Azerbaijan and urged the House to rescind Section 907 so that the U.S. Government could provide much needed humanitarian assistance to Azerbaijan. Representative Penny was the first member of Congress who officially presented a resolution to repeal Section 907. In the first of the letters below, I urged Chairman Hamilton to support Representative Penny's initiative. In the second letter, I thanked Representative Penny for his initiative and support.

May 18, 1994

Dear Chairman Hamilton:

As the House Foreign Affairs Committee prepares to deal with the Foreign Aid Reform Bill, I would like to draw your attention to a very courageous statement made on the House floor on May 16 by Congressman Timothy J. Penny.

In his statement, which I have attached, Congressman Penny makes clear that he is a very strong supporter of Armenia, but he is also aware of the humanitarian tragedy that is occurring in Azerbaijan, where one of every seven citizens (over one million by UN estimates) is a refugee.

My understanding is that Congressmen Penny, as Chairman of the Foreign Agriculture and Hunger Subcommittee of the House Agriculture Committee, held a recent hearing in which the refugee problem relating to the Armenian-Azerbaijani conflict was discussed.

Congressman Penny urges that Congress rescind Section 907 of the Freedom Support Act, which prohibits direct assistance to Azerbaijan from the United States. Let me quote Congressman Penny:

> *Section 907 also prohibits 'offensive uses of force.' During the past year, we have witnessed ethnic Armenians increasingly resort to offensive uses of force in Azerbaijan. The UN Security Council in 1993 condemned the continued aggression by ethnic Armenian forces outside Nagorno-Karabakh through resolutions 822, 853, 874 and 884. Azerbaijani forces have been in retreat during the past year, yet we continue to penalize them for using offensive uses of force.*

> *Mr. Speaker, both sides of this conflict must be held accountable for their actions. I am convinced that the prohibition of assistance to Azerbaijan as dictated under Section 907 runs counter to our strategic and humanitarian interests in the Caucasus. Our current strategy has not contributed to a peaceful solution to this conflict and has most certainly caused enormous suffering to innocent civilians. If we ever hope to play the role of an honest broker in the region, we must treat both parties in an even-handed manner and encourage them to move forward toward a lasting solution. Therefore, I propose that we rescind Section 907 of the Freedom Support Act.*

It is my hope that you and your committee share these sentiments.
Sincerely yours,
Hafiz Mir Jalal Pashayev
Ambassador

May 19, 1994

Dear Congressman Penny:

*On behalf of my government, let me express my heartfelt apprecia-
tion for the statement you made on Nagorno-Karabakh on May 16 on
the House floor.*

*Unfortunately, most Americans have little or no knowledge or un-
derstanding of Azerbaijan or the fact that one of every seven citizens is a
refugee in his or her own country. The human suffering is tremendous, yet
the world community seems to know little and care less.*

*Section 907 of the Freedom support Act is a source of great friction
between Azerbaijani people and the United States because it implies
that the United States is unwilling to help Azerbaijani refugees, in contrast to all other refugees in the world.*

*I have attached for your reading a special issue of Azerbaijan Inter-
national, which deals with the refugee problem.*

*Thank you again for your courageous statement, and I look forward
to meeting with you at your earliest convenience.*

Sincerely,

Hafiz Mir Jalal Pashayev

Ambassador

On May 25, 1994, Senator Paul Simon submitted Senate
Resolution 218 to the Senate's Committee on Foreign Relations and highlighted recent developments in the Karabakh
conflict. One of the provisions in Resolution 218 indicated
that "Section 907 of the Freedom Support Act (P.L. 102-511)
was not intended as an anti-Azeri initiative, is not so viewed
today, and it should be repealed as soon as Azerbaijani blockades are lifted." As much as I wanted to share Senator
Simon's account of Section 907's real intent, I disagreed.
Since its introduction in 1992, Section 907 had been viewed
as an anti-Azerbaijani initiative. The provision condemned
only Azerbaijan, while leaving Armenia blameless. Armenia
continued to occupy about 20 percent of Azerbaijan's terri-

tory and blockaded Nakhchivan, Azerbaijan's enclave. Yet, most senators and representatives unduly demanded that Azerbaijan open communications with Armenia, but never urged Armenia to pull its occupying troops out of Azerbaijan. The following letter was sent to Senator Simon.

May 31, 1994

Dear Senator Simon:

I read with a great deal of interest Senate Resolution 218-relating to the war in Nagorno-Karabakh-which you submitted along with Senator Reid. I am aware that you have closely followed this situation over the years and I know that your views will be taken very seriously by your colleagues and all interested parties.

First, let me state that your comments are most welcome. Your knowledge of the situation and your position as a senior member of the Foreign Relations Committee make you uniquely qualified to encourage the various parties to seek a quick resolution to this devastating struggle.

As has been widely reported, the only offensive actions now are those of the Armenian forces, whose seizure of Azerbaijan territory has been described as "a land grab exceeded only by what the Serbs have accomplished in Bosnia" (Newsweek, 11/29/93). Armenian forces now control one third of Azerbaijan's territory, Nagorno-Karabakh has been ethnically cleansed of Azerbaijanis, as has Armenia, and more than 1.1 million Azerbaijanis have become refugees as a result of these offensive actions.

I must regretfully report to you that Section 907 of the Freedom Support Act (P.L, 102-511) has been interpreted as an anti-Azeri initiative by the people of Azerbaijan, They remain puzzled that sanctions are imposed on Azerbaijan, while the Armenian blockade of Nakhichevan, and the offensive actions cited above, have largely been ignored by Congress and the media.

With these points in mind, I pledge the full cooperation of our government with you and your colleagues is pressing forward for peace. We welcome the CSCE's efforts through the Minsk Group and support your calls for UN *observers "to monitor the implementation of an effective cease-fire."*

Again, please accept my sincere gratitude for the bold leadership, which you have offered on this complex and emotional issue. I look forward to working with you toward the mutual goals of the cessation of hostilities and the establishment of political stability in our region.
With warmest personal regards,
Sincerely,
Hafiz Pashayev
Ambassador

The following letter to then Chairman of the Subcommittee on Economic Policy, Trade, Oceans and Environment, Senator Paul S. Sarbanes, and other senators, urges them to revoke Section 907. I had a hard time comprehending the logic behind the U.S. Congress's refusal to revoke Section 907 and failed to understand why the U.S. Congress would punish one million Azerbaijani refugees, since it was Azerbaijan that was being occupied.

June 8, 1994
Dear Senator Sarbanes:

As the Subcommittee begins consideration of the "Peace, Prosperity, and Democracy Act of 1994," I am writing to urge you and your colleagues to support President Clinton's proposed repeal of Section 907 of the Freedom Support Act (P.L. 102-511), which bans all aid to the government of Azerbaijan. Punishing Azerbaijan for "offensive actions" is not only misguided policy, it is contrary to the reality of current conditions.

Nagorno-Karabakh has been ethnically cleansed of Azerbaijanis, as has Armenia. The seizure by Armenian forces of more than 20 percent of the remainder of Azerbaijan has been described as "a land grab exceeded only by what the Serbs have accomplished in Bosnia" (Newsweek, 11/29/93). Yet, while the Serbs have been severely criticized in Con-

gress and the media, there is an eerie silence when it comes to the actions of the Armenians.

The fact that more than one million Azerbaijanis have become refugees as a result of the conflict with Armenia caused Senator DeConcini, Chairman of the Commission on Security and Cooperation in Europe, to ask whether Section 907, which he initially supported, "is the wisest and fairest course of action" (Congressional Record, 11/22/93).

Congressman Tim Penny, Chairman of the Subcommittee on Foreign Agriculture and Hunger, stated recently that: "Azerbaijani forces have been in retreat during the past year, yet we continue to penalize them for using offensive force. I am convinced that the prohibition of assistance to Azerbaijan [...] runs counter to our strategic and humanitarian interests in the Caucasus" (Congressional Record, 5/16/92).

Azerbaijan is engaged in no offensive actions against Armenians-not one inch of Armenian soil is occupied by Azerbaijani soldiers. The Government of Azerbaijan has publicly declared its support of the current efforts by the CSCE to forge a lasting cease-fire and begin resolving the other pressing problems of the region.

The Azerbaijani people remain puzzled by the tilting of U.S. policy toward Armenia. Our land is occupied, our province of Nakhchivan is blockaded by Armenia, and out cities overflow with refugees. In Sumgait, the Red Cross has found that "half the babies born in the squalid, disease-ridden housing die before the age of one" (New York Times, 6/2/94). I cannot believe that these conditions are what the proponents of 907 envisioned when they supported its passage.

Though America has turned its back on us, we make to no comments about seeking better treatment in other camps. This should be contrasted with the statement by an official of the Armenian Assembly who stated that if abandoned by Washington, "Armenia would have to look to Iran for security" (New York Times, 5/22/92). Such threats have no place in the business of relations between nations.

Azerbaijan will continue to extend its hand in friendship. By fairly reevaluating Section 907 on its merits, and by holding all parties to the same standards, the United States can rightfully claim its role as honest

broker, and more effectively assert its tremendous prestige and influence to
help all parties find a just and lasting peace.
With warmest personal regards,
Sincerely,
Hafiz Pashayev
Ambassador

Occasionally, I also sent letters to the European embassies in the United States. Below is a letter to the foreign missions of member countries of the European Union in Washington, in appreciation of the humanitarian assistance they were providing to Azerbaijan.

August 17, 1994

Your Excellency:

My government is extremely pleased with the decision of the European Union to provide up to 204 million euros worth of food supplies to the countries of Azerbaijan, Armenia, Georgia, Tajikistan and Kyrgyzstan.

I am writing to urge that your government give special consideration to the urgent plight of the 1.1 million refugees in Azerbaijan-which represents one-seventh of the entire population of the country. These refugees are a direct outcome of Armenian offensives, which have resulted in the occupation of more than 20 percent of Azerbaijan, accompanied by the looting and destruction of hundreds of towns and villages.

This refugee crisis has been made much worse by the U.S. Congress, which, at the instigation of the Armenian American lobby, passed an amendment which prohibits any assistance from the United States to Azerbaijan. We are thus essentially cut off from one of the main sources of humanitarian relief in the world.

Let me cite several other factors your government should consider when deciding how this EU assistance is allocated:

(1) Azerbaijan has the largest population, 7.4 million, of
any of the affected countries.

*(2) Azerbaijan has by far the greatest number of refugees,
      one million.*

*(3) Azerbaijan is the only country currently under occupa-
      tion by opposition forces. This occupation has been ac-
      companied by the destruction of much of the economy.*

*(4) Even during peacetime, Azerbaijan produces only 30
      percent of its food consumption needs.*

*Azerbaijan has converted many, many public facilities into refugee
centers, and we are struggling to feed, house and clothe all 1.1 million
refugees. But the task is beyond our current capacity, and therefore, we
must reach out to the world community for assistance. For that reason,
Azerbaijan commends your government and the European Union for
this great humanitarian effort, and you can be certain that the assistance
will be appreciated and put to urgent good use.*

Sincerely,

Hafiz Pashayev

Ambassador

The following was in response to a letter from Representative John E. Porter, Co-Chairman of the Congressional
Human Rights Caucus, who raised some questions regarding
the human rights situation in Azerbaijan. I welcomed his
comments but also asked the Caucus to provide a more balanced overview of the violations that had taken place as a result of the Karabakh conflict. Unfortunately, the Congressional Human Rights Caucus preferred to be silent on the
crimes committed by Armenian soldiers against Azerbaijani
prisoners of war and the civilian population.

August 25, 1994

Dear Representative Porter:

*I am in receipt of your letter of August 19 and, as you have re-
quested, I have forwarded your correspondence directly to President Ali-*

yev in Baku. I will, of course, provide all assistance to you that I can, in this and other efforts you may undertake in the future.

I would like to raise some concerns I have about the balance of treatment received by Azerbaijan from the Human Rights Caucus. While you have criticized our country for certain actions, the Caucus has, to the best of my knowledge, remained silent on any actions on the part of Armenia.

Just two weeks prior to your letter, Human Rights Watch/Helsinki called upon President Ter-Petrossian to "withdraw his forces from the conflict area," referring to Nagorno-Karabakh. The organization noted that "Ethnic Armenian forces presently occupy 25 percent of Azerbaijan" and called on Ter-Petrossian to, "Cease sending Armenian government military forces to the war in Nagorno-Karabakh. Such support merely widens the scope of the war, allowing the Karabakh Armenians to conduct offensive operations. We also repeat our call for an independent investigation into the deaths of eight Azerbaijani prisoners of war on January 29, 1994 and for the punishment of all guilty parties [...]"

The Washington Post recently asked, "Why the Armenian President has not responded to a request by international human rights monitors about the deaths earlier this year of eight Azeri prisoners of war in Armenia's capital, Yerevan." According to the Post, the representative of the Physicians for Human Rights who examined the bodies said that while he had been involved in similar forensic studies in areas of civil unrest elsewhere in the world, this was the first time he had examined "something in such clear violation of the Geneva Conventions."

Perhaps one CSCE staff member was correct when he stated in the Post that "making a fuss about dead Azeris is not right for the politics of this town."

Current U.S. policy bans direct aid, including humanitarian assistance, to the Government of Azerbaijan. The U.S. Committee for Refugees has called for the repeal of Section 907 for a number of compelling reasons: it has "undermined progress toward peace and respect for human rights in the region;" it is "a provocation, creating ill will on the part of

Azerbaijanis toward the United States; it "bolsters extremists among the Armenians who get away scot-free when they violate important international norms of behavior;" it does not address the "compelling humanitarian needs on the Azerbaijani side;" and it "precludes the United States from playing the role of honest broker."

Former U.S. Ambassador to the CSCE, John Maresca, recently stated that, "With almost a million internal refugees and one-fifth of its territory occupied, a unilateral prohibition of even humanitarian aid [to Azerbaijan] is deeply unfair" (Christian Science Monitor, 6/27/94).

CSCE Chairman Dennis DeConcini, an original supporter of 907, has questioned "[....] whether this course is the wisest and fairest course of action. Refugees are deserving of humanitarian assistance, whether they are Armenian or Azerbaijani" (Congressional Record, 11/22/93).

Representative Tim Penny has stated, "I am convinced that [...] Section 907 runs counter to our strategic and humanitarian interests in the Caucasus" (Congressional Record, 5/16/94).

I know that your concerns about Armenia are genuine, as are your questions about the treatment of prisoners of war. I pledge to assist you to the best of my ability to resolve any questions that you might have. In turn, I hope that the Human Rights Caucus will provide a balanced forum for discussion of issues vitally important to both of our nations.
With warmest regards.
Sincerely,
Hafiz Pashayev
Ambassador

A Doonesbury cartoon published in the Washington Post in 1993 illustrates well the realities of those early years when many Americans, including some U.S. officials, were not familiar with Azerbaijan.

One of my drawings: Panelists at the seminar on conflict resolution sponsored by the United States-Azerbaijan Chamber of Commerce, Vafa Quluzade (left), adviser to President of Azerbaijan, and Gerard Libaridian, adviser to President of Armenia. Both were principal negotiators in the peace process in 1990s.

Chapter 2
Developing Strong U.S.-Azerbaijan Relations (1995-2001)

A cease-fire between Armenia and Azerbaijan was signed in May of 1994, and it has remained intact since then. In my opinion, this was the time when the real state-building process began in Azerbaijan. During this period, President Heydar Aliyev stabilized the political situation in the country and invited foreign energy companies to take part in the exploration of Azerbaijan's oil and gas reserves. On September 20, 1994, the Azerbaijani government and a consortium of Western energy firms signed a production-sharing agreement, also known as the "Contract of the Century," at Gulistan Palace in Baku. This multibillion-dollar energy deal created new opportunities for expanding U.S.-Azerbaijani relations. Towards the end of 1994, U.S.-Azerbaijani energy relations had intensified and President Bill Clinton personally backed U.S. energy firms' involvement in projects in Azerbaijan. Also in September, for the first time, President Aliyev met with President Bill Clinton in New York on the sidelines of the UN General Assembly. This meeting marked the beginning of a new era in the U.S.-Azerbaijan cooperation and partnership.

From this time onward, U.S.-Azerbaijani relations developed in multiple directions; including the fields of energy and economic cooperation. At a reception in honor of President Heydar Aliyev in New York on September 29, 1994, I delivered the following speech, which highlighted this gradual change.

> During my nineteen months as Azerbaijan's Ambassador to the United States, we have witnessed many

"firsts" as a country, and in our relationship with America.

- I was honored to be the first Azerbaijani Ambassador to the United States.
- We opened the first Azerbaijani Embassy in the United States.
- We are now completing the first visit to the United States by a President of Azerbaijan.
- Today, the head of our state for the first time gave a speech at the UN General Assembly.
- Tonight we should mention another "first"-a major, $7 billion joint energy venture-which we hope will be the first of many joint economic projects between our two countries.
- And on Monday, we had the first meeting between a President of Azerbaijan and a President of the United States-a meeting which, I might add, was very warm and cordial and very productive.

In my view, the meeting between President Clinton and President Aliyev was the culmination of all these "firsts"-and it brings to a closure the first studying stage of the diplomatic and economic relations between the United States and Azerbaijan.

When the first stage of our relationship began, most Americans had never heard about Azerbaijan. The U.S. Government and the media paid little attention to our new, independent republic. On our side, we knew that the United States was a superpower and the world's leading democracy, but we had little knowledge or understanding of the American government, its economy, and even its people.

Today, as we enter the second stage of our relationship, all of that has changed. Many, many Americans-especially decision-makers in the U.S. Government-now know a great deal about Azerbaijan. The American media now recognize the crucial role that Azerbaijan can and does play in the geopolitics of our region. The American industry, and especially [the energy] industry,

knows the enormous potential of joint cooperation
with Azerbaijan. And most of all, Azerbaijanis and
Americans have developed a mutual trust, respect and
friendship that will hopefully last a lifetime.

In summary, the Americans and the Azerbaijanis
have become friends and partners.

So, I would like to propose a toast: To President
Clinton and President Aliyev, to the continued improvement in relations between our countries, to the
joint economic progress represented by the contract we
celebrate tonight, and especially to the friendship between individual Americans and Azerbaijanis.

Three years later, U.S.-Azerbaijan relations received another boost when President Aliyev came to Washington, DC
on his first official visit. It was a historical moment in the development of our bilateral ties with the United States.

The ten-day visit of President Heydar Aliyev, from July
27 to August 7, 1997, was one of the most exciting times in
my diplomatic career and I am proud to say that the visit was
a success. Previously, President Clinton and President Aliyev
had met twice in New York-in September, 1994 and October,
1995. President Clinton had recognized the importance of
Azerbaijan and was interested in strengthening U.S.-
Azerbaijan relations. "I am pleased with the development of
relations between the United States and Azerbaijan in recent
years [and] by the rapid growth of our commercial and investment ties," wrote President Clinton in his invitation letter
to President Aliyev on May 10, 1997.

The two Presidents met at the White House on August 1,
1997, and signed several documents aimed at further improving bilateral relations between the United States and Azerbaijan. "Presidents Clinton and Aliyev agreed on the importance
of expanding the partnership between the United States and
the Republic of Azerbaijan through strengthening bilateral
cooperation in the political, security, economic and commer-

cial spheres," read the joint declaration signed by both Presidents. President Clinton also reaffirmed U.S. support for Azerbaijan's territorial integrity, sovereignty and independence, noting that "close U.S.-Azerbaijan relations are important in promoting regional peace, stability and prosperity."

Additionally, President Aliyev attended some one hundred meetings and spent 150 hours at various receptions and in negotiations in Washington, Chicago, Houston, and New York, discussing topics ranging from bilateral economic and political cooperation to national security matters. With the help of Zbigniew Brzezinski, we organized a luncheon discussion with President Aliyev and several outstanding U.S. officials, scholars and representatives of the U.S. media at "the Blair House." Among the participants were Richard Cheney, Anthony Lake, Richard Armitage, Colin Powell, Brent Scowcroft and James Schlesinger. Nobody could have predicted that soon many of these participants would be in the U.S. Administration.

President Aliyev's political background as a former high-ranking Politburo member was of particular interest for many in the United States. He knew this and joked about it on many occasions. During the luncheon discussion one of the participants, referring to President Aliyev's lengthy experience in the Soviet Union, asked, "Mr. President, if you were the national security advisor to the future president of the United States, what would be your advice to the President on how to deal with Russia regarding the former Soviet countries?" President Aliyev laughed and replied, "I would provide him with good advice. I [would] ask you to appoint me to that post."

During the visit, the U.S.-Azerbaijan Chamber of Commerce sponsored several receptions in honor of President Aliyev. Below are excerpts from two of my remarks at these events:

You cannot imagine the sense of pride and pleasure that Azerbaijanis feel on the occasion of President Aliyev's visit to the United States and his official meeting with President Clinton on Friday.

Azerbaijan faced very difficult circumstances in 1993, when President Aliyev was elected. We were involved in a full-scale war, the economy was in bad shape, our independence was at risk, and the United States and the West knew very little about our new republic.

Now, under the guidance of President Aliyev, we have achieved great progress in terms of assuring our independence, economic development, democracy and improved relations with the United States and the West. In short, Azerbaijan has in the brief period of four years gone from an unstable, destitute former Soviet republic to a stable, independent democracy that has assumed its rightful place in the community of nations.

President Aliyev's meeting with President Clinton on Friday represents the culmination of all this, both symbolically and substantively.

The United States has been our partner in this progress. One of the first Americans to help us was Strobe Talbott, whom President Clinton appointed in 1993 to be Ambassador-at-Large with responsibility for Russia and the New Independent States of the former Soviet Union. Other Americans have been equally important, including Mr. Talbott's successor, James Collins, Ambassadors Dick Miles and Rich Kauzlarich, National Security Advisor Tony Lake, and Sandy Berger. Secretary of State Madeleine Albright was the highest-ranking American to visit Azerbaijan when she was UN Ambassador, and, of course, President Clinton and Vice-President Gore have had many meetings with President Aliyev and have been very attentive to our concerns.

Mr. Talbott, of course, is now Deputy Secretary of State, and we are very honored by his presence tonight. I will introduce Secretary Talbott by expressing to him the appreciation of all Azerbaijanis for the steadfast support of the United States during our transition to an independent, free, and democratic republic.

On this wonderful occasion, first let me welcome President Heydar Aliyev on his first official visit to Washington, DC, as President of the Republic of Azerbaijan.

This visit represents a new phase in the relationship between Azerbaijan and the United States. For those of you who have followed our progress over the years, you can feel the change that is taking place here in Washington.

More and more members of Congress are recognizing the importance of Azerbaijan and the role it can play in contributing to peace and prosperity in the world. The media is beginning to pay closer attention to the U.S.-Azerbaijan relationship. Outstanding Americans like Zbigniew Brzezinski, Henry Kissinger, Dick Cheney and Casper Weinberger have spoken out on our behalf.

The Clinton Administration is playing an increasingly active role in addressing Azerbaijan's problems and concerns, and in recognizing Azerbaijan's freedom and independence. President Clinton personally has sought out President Aliyev on matters of mutual concern, as has Vice-President Gore. Secretary of State Madeleine Albright knows Azerbaijan first-hand from her visit to Baku as United Nations Ambassador. National Security Advisor Sandy Berger and Deputy Secretary of State Strobe Talbott have also become strong friends and supporters of Azerbaijan. One of our newest friends in the Clinton Administration is Secretary of Energy Federico Pena, who is with us tonight.

Their attendance at this event tonight is further evidence of the change that is occurring in the U.S.-Azerbaijan relationship. We are becoming close allies in the true meaning of that term. So I would like to offer a toast: On behalf of everyone here, let us raise our glasses and salute both President Aliyev's visit to Washington and the new and improved American-Azerbaijani relationship that this visit represents. And finally let us drink a toast to the future in which Azer-

baijan and United States remain the closest of friends
and allies.

By 2000, Azerbaijan had become a critical player in the
U.S.-backed East-West Energy Transport Corridor. The first
pipeline that bypassed Russia and Iran, the Baku-Tbilisi-Supsa
oil pipeline, was completed in 1997 and had been successfully
operational for more than two years. Azerbaijan had signed
nineteen production sharing agreements with international
energy companies in excess of $60 billion in investments, but
the issue of how to deliver larger volumes of oil and gas to
the West remained unresolved. There were debates about different routes for the Main Export Pipeline (MEP) that would
carry the major portion of Azerbaijan's oil (fifty million tons
of oil per year) to Western markets. The political and legal
maneuvering surrounding the decision on the MEP was tremendous, in regards to questions as to who had ownership of
what sectors of the Caspian Sea and which countries would
host the pipeline. Moscow contended that most of the oil
should go through Russia, to its Black Sea port city of Novorossiysk. Tehran, on the other hand, proposed another route
through Iranian territory, which it argued was the most cost-
efficient option. The United States and Turkey supported a
route that would bypass both Russia and Iran.

Azerbaijan's position was that we should have multiple
pipelines, including one through Russia, but that the MEP
should bypass Russia and go to the Mediterranean Sea via
Turkey. Since Armenia continued to reject constructive solutions to the Nagorno-Karabakh conflict and still occupied
Azerbaijan's territories, it had no chance of becoming a transit country for this project. Thus, the Azerbaijani government
supported a route to Turkey that would go through Georgia.

This pipeline would also have geo-strategic significance
for Azerbaijan; tying into the question of guaranteeing Azerbaijan's independence and its pro-Western foreign policy and

of reducing the role of external players, particularly Russia, in the country's internal affairs. Fortunately, the United States and Azerbaijan positions coincided and soon the construction of the pipeline began. At that time, many doubted that this pipeline would ever be built. Some members of the U.S. Congress, who were upset about the fact that Armenia was left out, even tried to discredit the BTC project. But thanks to the continuous support of the United States, participating international energy companies, and a strong commitment by the Azerbaijani government to this pipeline, the Baku-Tbilisi-Ceyhan pipeline was successfully constructed and inaugurated on May 25, 2005.

The idea of a main pipeline had become an integral part of the plans aimed at restoring the ancient Silk Road Corridor stretching from China to Europe via Central Asia and the South Caucasus. The first large-scale summit of the Silk Road countries, under the auspices of the European Union, took place in Baku in 1998. Some thirty-two countries participated in the summit, including the U.S., and five documents were signed to facilitate trade along the Transport Corridor Europe Caucasus Asia (TRACECA) corridor.

Years of educating the U.S. Congress also started being fruitful. I was happy to see that as early as 1998, the House Appropriations Committee adopted language to eliminate Section 907. This effort in the House Appropriations Committee was led by Committee Chairman Bob Livingston of Louisiana, who was Azerbaijan's foremost champion in Congress at that time. In 1998, Chairman Livingston visited Azerbaijan and witnessed the great potential of my country. Overall, this was an exciting time to represent Azerbaijan in Washington because so many changes were taking place. As the first Azerbaijani Ambassador to the United States, I witnessed the process of establishing Azerbaijan on the American political map in its transition from "the great unknown" into a U.S. partner, and few years later into a "U.S. strategic partner."

Speech at the Central Asia-Caucasus Institute, Paul Nitze School of Advanced International Studies John Hopkins University October 23, 1996

In 1996, I was the first guest speaker at this newly established institute. My speech stressed the strategic role that Azerbaijan would play in the South Caucasus in the future and drew attention to the evolving relations between the United States and Azerbaijan, especially after the signing of the energy contract in 1994.

First, let me congratulate Johns Hopkins University and each of you on the opening of the new Central Asia Institute of the Paul Nitze School of Advanced International Studies. One thing amongst others that has most impressed me about the United States is the large number of private and university-affiliated foreign policy think-tanks, and the diversity and outstanding quality of scholarship produced there. Support of the international community is crucial for the independence of the Central Asian and Caucasus countries, and institutions like yours create awareness of these countries and bring attention to their problems. For that reason, I am especially honored to be the first speaker since your opening, which was celebrated only two days ago.

It is very appropriate that a representative of Azerbaijan would be your first speaker because Azerbaijan is the gateway to Central Asia-a twenty-first century gateway to a new political and economic "silk road." The beginning of this new "silk road" can be seen in the recent multilateral agreement to transport goods from the Central Asian countries through Azerbaijan and Georgia to the Black Sea.

Because of geography, abundant natural resources, and geopolitical circumstances, Azerbaijan will be at the very center of international politics and diplomacy over the next two decades. What happens in Azerbaijan, in my opinion, will have lasting consequences not only for the region, but for the entire world, including the United States.

Why do I make such sweeping statements, and what makes Azerbaijan unique? To understand my premise requires an examination of history and current developments in Azerbaijan, and an analysis of geo-political circumstances and trends.

Much of history concerns the discovery and development of new worlds, followed by struggles and wars among competing empires, seeking to dominate those new worlds. America was "discovered" a little over four hundred years ago. The first permanent settlements came about one hundred years later, which then the British, French and Spanish fought to control all or parts of America. Slowly but surely, the New World inhabitants decided to throw off the yoke of imperial domination, and in the relatively short period of two hundred years America emerged as the world's only superpower.

There are, of course, no new worlds to be discovered. There are, however, new regions and new republics emerging from imperial domination. The most important of these are the old Eastern European bloc and the former republics of the Soviet Union. In my view, the Eastern European nations are destined to become aligned politically and economically with the West. It is in the Caucasus and Central Asia where the next great geopolitical struggles will occur, hopefully in a nonviolent manner, and Azerbaijan will be crucial to those developments.

As mentioned earlier, Azerbaijan has only known seven years of true independence. The first two occurred right after World War I, and that brief taste of freedom was quickly replaced by seventy years of Soviet domination. The aspirations for freedom and independence always have been kept alive. The turning point in modern history of our struggle for independence was on January 20, 1990, when Soviet troops invaded Baku and killed hundreds of innocent people. Many in the West do not know about this event, but it had the same effect in Azerbaijan as the Soviet invasions of Budapest, Hungary in 1956, Prague, and Czechoslovakia in 1968.

The last five years of independence came with the collapse of the Soviet Union, and those years have not been without difficulty. There has been no shortage of those who would seek to dominate the new Republic of Azerbaijan; if not militarily, then economically or ideologically. The fact remains that today, Azerbaijan is the only former Soviet republic outside the Baltic States with no foreign troops on its soil. We have developed our own currency and our own military. We have refused to surrender our natural resources to others. We have maintained good relations with Russia, but we also have developed close ties with the United States, Western Europe, Iran, Turkey and Israel. We have joined many of the major international institutions.

We have in the short space of five years held two presidential elections and one for parliament. Some critics complain that democracy in Azerbaijan does not match that of the West. But let me remind you that America did not achieve direct election of senators until 1913 and women did not receive the right to vote until 1920. And while the American constitution was not adopted until eleven years after independence, Azerbaijan's constitution was approved four years after independence. Our constitution guarantees freedom of religion for everyone, including Christians, Jews and Muslims.

We are reforming our legal system to improve personal and intellectual property rights. Opposition political parties and opposition media are permitted and are flourishing. To be sure, we have not yet achieved perfection. Change does not and cannot occur overnight, but we are moving in the right direction.

Nothing is more important to our future independence and the development of democracy than the economic reforms currently underway. We have reduced the hyperinflation of recent years to 0.4 percent per month, instituted a progressive law on land privatization with the possibility of sales of private property, and enacted a new law on intellectual property. My personal participation in the last World Bank and International Monetary Fund annual meetings have convinced me that Azerbaijan is on the right track.

History teaches us that the key to survival of democracy is a broad middle class, in which all citizens have a stake in the system, both in terms of personal freedoms and economic security. Azerbaijan is blessed with abundant natural resources, especially energy. Some experts estimate that Azerbaijan's oil and gas reserves are equal to those of Kuwait. We have already signed an $8 billion oil development contract with a consortium of Western oil companies, including Amoco, Exxon, Pennzoil, Unocal and British Petroleum. Other oil contracts have been signed with participation of other Western oil companies, as well as the oil companies of Russia, Turkey and Iran.

We are talking with major international firms about infrastructure improvements necessary for a modern democracy, including communications, transportation, and various service industries. These developments are moving slower than some of us had hoped, but we are determined to do it, and to do it right. Western countries have no concept of the hardships involved in the transition from a centralized economy to one based on free markets. Going from a system that provided guaranteed jobs and pensions to one where markets and individual initiative rule is very unsettling, and it is being done without the benefit of a social safety net like that here in the United States. But we are on our way to a free market system, and there will be no turning back.

The reason [why] a small country like Azerbaijan is so important has [a] lot to do with geography. Russia is to our north, Iran to the south, the new Central Asian republics to the east across the Caspian Sea, and Turkey, Armenia and Georgia to our west. Throughout most of our history, we have been dominated by neighbors during their previous imperial regimes. Hopefully, that is now in the past. But all of our neighbors maintain a strong interest in what happens to Azerbaijan.

Speaking candidly, and without expressing opinions, let me briefly outline some of our neighbors' interests.

Russia has concerns about security on its southern border, the possible spread of Islamic fundamentalism, and the potential alliance of Turkey and other new Muslim republics. Russia also has economic interests and claims regarding energy resources of the Caspian. And needless to say, Russia would like to see new energy pipelines to go through Russia.

Turkey, in some ways, sees Azerbaijan and the new Central Asian republics as its natural allies in a loose confederation of secular Turkic republics. A friendly Azerbaijan lessens security concerns on its eastern flank. Turkey also wants new oil pipelines to travel via Turkey to the Mediterranean-both for economic reasons and to avoid environmental risks to Istanbul-if more oil tankers transit the Bosphorus Straits.

Armenia, of course, has territorial ambitions toward Azerbaijan, as is reflected in its aggression regarding Nagorno-Karabakh. And lately, some within Armenia have begun expressing an interest in seeing oil pipelines transit their country, both for economic and energy security reasons.

Georgia's interests are in the main economic at this point. It would like to host any new oil pipeline and increase trade and investment with Azerbaijan.

Thus, you have three major regional powers and two smaller countries, all with strong interests in what happens to Azerbaijan. Quite naturally, some of those interests are, or could be, in conflict with each other. But more importantly, from my point of view, they might conflict with Azerbaijan's own national objectives of independence and economic prosperity.

For those of you who think [that] the President of the United States has a tough job, try to imagine the difficulty of being President of Azerbaijan. President Aliyev must not only maintain good relations with all these neighbors with differing interests, but he also must govern a country whose economy has been wrecked by war and the transition from communism. On top of all this, one of every seven citizens is a refugee, again, because of the war with Armenia.

This brings us to the United States. Why should America care [about] what happens to a small country many thousands of miles away, a country with a very small diaspora in the United States, an independent republic that did not even exist five years ago?

I think you know the answer to my question. The United States cares deeply about the spread of democracy in the former republics of the Soviet Union, and what happens in Azerbaijan could have an impact on all the Central Asian Republics. The United States, as the world's only superpower, knows that the Caucasus can be just as volatile as the Balkans, and we know what happened in Bosnia. As the world's largest economy, Americans also know the importance of reliable, reasonably-priced energy. Last, but certainly not least, the

United States has a very strong interest in what happens in Turkey, Russia and Iran.

For those reasons, the relationship between the United States and Azerbaijan has grown tremendously in the past three years. President Aliyev has had two meetings with President Clinton and one with Vice-President Gore. I visit the State Department and National Security Council almost on a weekly basis, and we have been generally pleased with the growth of our relationship with the Administration.

The only criticisms I would make is that we would like to see the Administration take a more forceful and prominent role in solving the conflict over Nagorno-Karabakh, and there needs to be greater consistency in pursuing its stated policies.

Azerbaijan's relationship with Congress has been much less positive. My meetings and interaction with individual members of Congress have been good; however, many members seem incapable of opposing anything the Armenian-American lobby groups propose. Some members even admit privately that they know these proposals are against American interests, but say they cannot oppose these powerful lobby groups.

A senior staff delegation from the House Committee on International Relations recently made a trip to the region, and reported that one high-ranking Armenian official confidentially told them [that the] "anti-Turkish and anti-Azerbaijani" positions espoused by Armenian-American lobbying organizations do not help Armenia's efforts to obtain better relations with Turkey, or to resolve the conflict in Nagorno-Karabakh. Again, in confidence, that official said [that] both the Humanitarian Corridor Relief Act and Section 907 of the Freedom Support Act of 1992 were counter-productive.

In my opinion, the actions of these lobby groups are definitely un-American because their efforts are clearly against the national interests of the United States, and almost every knowledgeable person knows it.

I recognize that the actions of Congress do not represent the official position of the U.S. Government, but an average person in Azerbaijan does know these differences. They know from history how much money the U.S. has spent in faraway locations to make friends. So they ask why Azerbaijan makes such great efforts to improve relations with America when Congress continually insults our national pride and rewards the aggressor. Although the Administration opposes Section 907, it is still the law of the land in the United States.

Section 907, of course, results from the conflict over Nagorno-Karabakh. While this war has its origins in Armenian desires for territorial expansion, it has also been used as a "proxy" for other forces within the region with other objectives.

The Caucasus Region has long been subjugated-economically and politically-through the use of "divide and conquer" tactics, and there are elements within the region that would use the conflict to further economic objectives or to secure strategic strongholds within Azerbaijan. I do not believe this is necessarily the policy of any government, but there is no doubt that such elements exist.

And, as the Foreign Minister of Azerbaijan recently stated, the fact that Russia recently conducted joint military exercises with Armenia-with separatist leaders of Nagorno-Karabakh in attendance-does not lend credibility to its efforts to act as a mediator of the conflict.

The merits of the issue are not in doubt. All international organizations, and international law, support Azerbaijan's sovereignty over Nagorno-Karabakh. No country recognizes Nagorno-Karabakh as an independent region or country. What is in doubt is whether the United States and the world community will act upon its beliefs and policies.

Azerbaijan remains strongly in favor of a negotiated settlement, and we are working with the Organization for Security and Cooperation in Europe toward that objective. But, I must report that the current situation is not encouraging because of Armenian intransigence and the dubious Armenian election-which is likely to make the Armenian government even more hardliner [sic]. We will continue working for a peaceful resolution, but it should be clear that Azerbaijan will never compromise its territorial integrity.

In conclusion, it is inescapable that what happens in Azerbaijan will be important to the world community, and especially to the United States. It will influence the fate of the new Central Asian Republics. It will help determine whether secular republics with predominantly Muslim populations can survive. It will impact both the availability and price of world energy supplies. It will certainly influence the stability of the Caucasus. And finally, what happens to Azerbaijan will help determine the future of democracy and free markets in the entire region.

As *The Wall Street Journal* reported Monday in a front-page article (quote), "For the West, Azerbaijan's prize is another wellspring of oil beyond the stormy Persian Gulf. For Western oil companies, it potentially means an $8 billion investment, 30 years of production and $100 billion in revenues. But for Azerbaijan itself, which gets to keep 80 percent of the profits, the prize is a thing no country skewered between Russian and Iran can easily hope to hang onto: independence."

The United States has both a unique role and opportunity to play, not only because it is the world's only remaining superpower, and because American interests are at stake, but also because geography and geopolitical circumstances make Azerbaijan's fate of real consequence to the entire world community.

While Congress has done great harm to U.S.-Azerbaijan relations, we have no problem with official American policy toward Azerbaijan. In most cases, that policy has been carried out with diligence and care. What we do have a problem with is the lack of consistency and political will on issues like Nagorno-Karabakh. We saw in Bosnia what happens when American leadership is exerted, and we would like to see that leadership exercised in Azerbaijan. I am hopeful that once American elections are concluded, these matters will receive the consistent attention they need and deserve.

Speech at the Conference on Azerbaijan
U.S.-Azerbaijan Chamber of Commerce
February 18, 1997

It is a distinct pleasure to participate in this conference on Azerbaijan sponsored by the U.S.-Azerbaijan Chamber of Commerce. Just twelve days ago, I celebrated the fourth anniversary of my arrival at Dulles Airport as Azerbaijan's first Ambassador to the United States. The first official in State Department whom I met was Rich Kauzlarich, now Ambassador to my country. And I am very pleased to be with him at this conference.

But I also remember that I found almost no one in official Washington who had any knowledge or understanding about Azerbaijan. Most on Capitol Hill had never heard of Azerbaijan. Even those in foreign policy think tanks, with a few notable exceptions, knew little more than the fact that Azerbaijan was a former Soviet republic.

We have worked very, very hard over the past four years to better acquaint Americans with Azerbaijan. But, I must admit that [during] the first year or so, it was very difficult to get decision-makers to focus on Azerbaijan, and it was almost impossible to get the attention of members of Congress. Slowly but surely, however, we have made great strides.

It was an easier task to work with the U.S. Administration. The Clinton Administration very quickly understood the importance of Azerbaijan's independence and its role as a gateway to the new Central Asian republics. The administration was supportive from the very beginning although we were probably not very high on its priority list, probably because we had no nuclear weapons on our territory.

Congress was a different story. Members of Congress were too busy with other things and they only paid attention to Azerbaijan when ethnic lobby groups sought to impose one sanction or another on Azerbaijan, the worst of which was Section 907 of the Freedom Support Act.

But truth is coming and improvements have occurred, and I attribute the change to several basic factors:

(1) The first is what I called the basic American instinct to support freedom, democracy and independence. While most Americans do not know a lot about my country, they do understand our desire to be free and independent.

The American people, I believe, do not like the idea of one nation controlling or dominating another one. For this reason, I have found great receptivity among Americans on the matter of continued independence for Azerbaijan. My personal meetings with more than 150 members of Congress have proven that.

(2) A second milestone in the relationship between the United States and Azerbaijan occurred in September 1994, when Azerbaijan signed an $8 billion oil contract with Western oil companies. While this agreement was long in the making, and while many began to doubt that it would happen, President Heydar Aliyev

had the political courage to make it happen—
and many American oil companies have told
me of their appreciation for this forthright action in the face of considerable internal and
external opposition.

Azerbaijan, under the leadership of President
Aliyev, has now concluded five oil contracts
worth more than $15 billion. There is no
longer any question but that huge amounts of
oil will soon be flowing from Azerbaijan to
the rest of the world.

The significance of the agreements in terms of
U.S.-Azerbaijani relations cannot be overestimated. For this first time, Americans had a direct economic as well as political interest in
the future of Azerbaijan, both because of the
companies involved but also because of the
potential for providing a reliable, reasonably
priced supply of oil for the entire industrialized world.

A side benefit of these energy development
projects has been that literally thousands of
American and European businessmen and
women have visited Baku and Azerbaijan. We
have factual evidence of that through the consular section of our Embassy. I am a great be-
liever that no one can visit Azerbaijan and not
come away with not only a greater understanding of our problems and potential, but
also with a love for our people.

(3) A third reason I am so optimistic about the
future of U.S.-Azerbaijan relations is that our
geography and location dictate that Azerbaijan
cannot be ignored. We are surrounded by

three great regional powers, Russia, Turkey
and Iran. We are at the crossroads of East and
West, and I believe what happens to Azerbaijan will greatly influence what happens in
Central Asia and the former Soviet republics.

As you might know, we are the only former Soviet republic other than the Baltics that has no foreign troops on its soil.
We want to keep it that way. And we want to develop our
natural resources in a manner whereby our neighbors can
share in our good fortune but not dominate or dictate our internal decisions.

American policymakers have always understood this intel-
lectually, but now that the energy development projects are
beginning to occur, the attention paid to Azerbaijan has taken
on new and greater importance. It is no longer theoretical; it
is fast becoming reality.

These energy projects are not only about money. They
represent much more than that. It is the revenue from these
energy projects that will be used to build the infrastructure of
Azerbaijan: modern communications, better highways, larger
and safer airports; things that Americans often take for
granted.

It means the ability to improve our education system, the
ability to privatize our industries, providing new and better
jobs for our people. It means restoring those parts of the
health care system that have fallen into disrepair, and it also
means properly caring for the more than one million refugees
created by the various Armenian offensives against Azerbaijan.

In short, these oil projects are about providing Azerbaijan
the means necessary to maintain its long sought and finally
achieved independence.

I am pleased to say that our cooperation with the World Bank and the IMF helps to achieve these goals. Projects funded by these Institutions brought macroeconomic stability and we already have the first signs of economic growth. Now, more and more businesses outside of energy sector find their way to Azerbaijan. I witness great positive developments each time I visit Baku.

President Aliyev has already met twice with President Clinton. He has also had several meetings with Vice- President Gore, most recently at the Lisbon summit of the Organization on Security and Cooperation in Europe. Secretary of State Albright visited Azerbaijan when she was UN Ambassador.

When I stop and think about it, the changes that have occurred in the past four years have been amazing. Outstanding Americans like Zbigniew Brzezinski, Jim Baker, Henry Kissinger, Lloyd Bentsen, Senators Byrd, Stevens, Lugar and Murkowski, among others, have taken a personal interest in the freedom and independence of Azerbaijan. Whenever I meet President Clinton at various functions, he is always up-to-date on our issues; the same is true of Vice-President Gore.

But let me conclude with a word of caution. While most of us here firmly believe that relations between the U.S. and Azerbaijan are important, and while they have improved tremendously, there is still one major obstacle that we have not overcome-the Congressional ban on Azerbaijan-Section 907.

As *The Washington Post* pointed out in an editorial last week, foreign aid is a major tool of American foreign policy and should be used to promote free markets, democracy and human rights. Yet, in the case of Azerbaijan, the U.S. Government is forbidden by Congress from promoting free markets, human rights and democracy.

This restriction also badly damages relations between our countries, because in Azerbaijan, Section 907 is seen as a deliberate affront to our independence, our national pride and our dignity as a sovereign nation.

This is especially so when Azerbaijanis learn that Armenia, which militarily occupies 20 percent of Azerbaijan and which is responsible for Section 907, receives the second largest per capita assistance from the United States (after Israel).

At the same time [that] we are inviting American businesses into Azerbaijan to make billions of dollars that will benefit American workers and investors, the U.S. Congress is insisting that the American Government cannot have normal relations with Azerbaijan. This is a total distortion of American foreign policy, and, as many people believe, contrary to the best interests of all Americans.

So I would urge each of you, in your own way, to work for the repeal of this terrible law, because only when this law is repealed will we be able to have the kind of complete relationship common among allies.

This conference, sponsored by the U.S.-Azerbaijan Chamber of Commerce and others like it, will make a great contribution to the future of U.S. and Azerbaijan relations. On behalf of my government, let me express our appreciation for your participation in this important meeting, and I hope you leave here with renewed energy and dedication to improving the friendship between the United States and Azerbaijan.

Speech at the Conference Titled
"An Economy in Transition"
U.S.-Azerbaijan Chamber of Commerce
May 21, 1997

Since 1995, Azerbaijan began its economic recovery. Economic sustainability and political stability were essential for attracting direct foreign investments to Azerbaijan and for moving forward with regional energy projects such as the Baku-Supsa and the Baku-Tbilisi-Ceyhan oil pipelines. The following speech illuminates how dramatically the economic and political situation in the country had changed since 1994.

In considering the economic status and future growth of Azerbaijan, one cannot ignore geopolitical realities and governmental stability-a fact that international businessmen and women, including those in our audience today, know very well. Let me start first with governmental stability, and then I will touch on geopolitical factors.

I remember very well talking with American oil company officials in 1993-1994. They were very concerned about the stability of the government, and, needless to say, were somewhat reluctant to invest in a country whose future was in doubt. Many businessmen took an understandable "wait and see" attitude.

However, Azerbaijan has surprised even its most severe skeptics. Out of the chaos of 1993, Heydar Aliyev was elevated to the office of President-first by appointment under the constitution and then through direct election. We negotiated a ceasefire in the war with Armenia. Parliament began serious consideration of laws designed to make the transition to a market economy. Final negotiations on the first big oil contract were begun. Under the leadership of President Aliyev, Azerbaijan began formulation of a foreign policy based on independence, good relations with our neighbors, cooperation with the West, and close ties with the United States.

Some $17 billion in oil contracts have been signed with oil companies from the United States, Western Europe, Russia, Turkey, and Iran. Despite protests from time to time, none of these oil deals have come unraveled and all are progressing more or less on schedule. We have signed economic cooperation agreements with most of our neighbors, and we are full participants in the United Nations, [the] World Bank, [the] Ex-Im Bank and other international institutions. We have introduced our own currency-the manat-and it is very stable; with very low inflation. We have largely minimized, although not totally, attempts by outside groups to influence the internal politics of Azerbaijan.

As a result of all this, international business concerns now have faith in Azerbaijan and they are flocking to Baku to participate in the coming economic growth. These businesses would not be coming to Azerbaijan if they thought the government was unstable.

At the risk of sounding immodest, I believe Azerbaijan has achieved a great deal in a relatively short period of time-it seems especially so for those of us who lived with the problems on a daily basis for a decade, or more. But the reality is that we have gone from chaos to stability in only four years. That, I think, is a remarkable achievement-but it only the beginning.

Now, let me turn to the geopolitical realities, which have as much to do with the investment climate as internal stability. Many problems remain. Foremost among them is settling the war with Armenia so [that] our refugees can return to their homes, normal commerce can resume between Armenia and Azerbaijan, and we can live in peace with our Armenian neighbors. This is a key to maintaining economic stability and growth. Unfortunately, recent actions of the Republic of Armenia do not indicate the same desire for peace that we have. I cite three disturbing developments:

(1) We have recently learned that Armenia received about $1 billion in arms shipments from Russia, starting during the period of Armenian offensives that resulted in the current military occupation of parts of Azerbaijan. Many of these arms were transshipped from Armenia to the occupied territories of Azerbaijan. This has created a military imbalance in the region, but it has also created a backlash by governments and the international community. President Yeltsin has launched an investigation, as has the United States Senate. Prompted in part by these huge arms shipments, the United States and Azerbaijan have issued a joint declaration concerning foreign troops on Azerbaijan soil and the territorial integrity of our republic.

(2) Last January, in Lisbon, the fifty-four-member Organization for Security and Cooperation in Europe (OSCE) considered a statement of principles upon which to base negotiations for settlement of the Armenia-Azerbaijan conflict. Armenia was the only country out of fifty-four that refused to support these principles because Armenia was unwilling to affirm the territorial integrity of Azerbaijan. The net result of this stance has not been to enhance Armenia's position in the world community; rather, it has only served to isolate Armenia in the world community. In April, Armenia made the same mistake at the

Parliamentary Assembly of the Council of
Europe.

(3) And finally, Armenia recently appointed as
Prime Minister Robert Kocharian, the hard-
line leader of separatist elements in Nagorno-
Karabakh. Rather than appoint someone who
could foster the peace process, Armenia gave
in to the ultra-nationalists who increasingly
seem to control events in Yerevan. These
people would rather fight a war than make
peace, initiate aggression rather than negotiation and foolishly try to turn back the tides of
history rather than make history.

Despite these facts, I am more optimistic than ever, both
about the future of Azerbaijan, its economic growth potential, and even settlement of the conflict. You may ask why I
am optimistic about settlement of the conflict. For one simple reason-history and the facts are not on the side of the extremists in Armenia.

History in the twenty-first century will not be on the side
of aggression; history will not favor those who create a million refugees and then claim they are victims, and history will
not be kind to those who live in the past but do not learn
from it.

Like internal stability, geopolitical realities have improved
dramatically. I believe Azerbaijan's independence has
achieved permanence. Our strategic role in the region is universally recognized. Our neighbors-with the exception of
Armenia-are beginning to treat us as peers and partners,
rather than as enemies or bitter rivals. Moreover, U.S.-
Azerbaijan bilateral relations are improving as well. As I have
said many times, whether the Americans like it or not, they

are the world's only superpower. And with that role come grand responsibilities and opportunities.

Just in the last month, we have seen signs of just how far we have come and how much things are changing. Just Monday, the United States and Azerbaijan issued a joint declaration affirming the independence of Azerbaijan and its right to prevent the stationing of foreign troops on its soil. On Thursday, Prime Minister Rasizade will meet with Vice-President Gore. Two weeks ago, the House International Relations Committee rejected an amendment designed to infringe on Azerbaijan's sovereignty and another to cut humanitarian assistance. One week ago, the Senate adopted language requiring a study of the illegal arms shipments to Armenia. And finally, President Clinton has issued an invitation to President Aliyev to meet with him in the White House in late summer.

Problems remain, of course. Section 907 of the Freedom Support Act remains a discriminatory piece of legislation that is a constant source of disharmony. The Armenian lobby will no doubt continue its efforts to destroy good relations between the United States and Azerbaijan.

But more and more Americans want to focus on the future, not the past. They want to seize new opportunities-not throw them away. They believe in making new friends-not new enemies. They believe the future lies with commerce-not conflict. Naturally, I share those views.

I have found that most Americans are optimists, and perhaps I have acquired some of that optimism, but I see a bright and growing future between the United States and Azerbaijan. That future is bright for American business and consumers, and it is bright for all the people of Azerbaijan.

Remarks at the Meeting of Business Council for International Understanding (BCIU)
February 29, 2000

It is a pleasure to appear here today, though looking at all you people gathered here, I seriously doubt my ability to share with you anything new, as far as Azerbaijan's economic development is concerned. I realize that all of you are perfectly aware of my country's economic genesis, so let me suggest that after very brief remarks indeed, we put together an extensive Q&A session.

As you know, the Republic of Azerbaijan has consistently followed the path of economic and political reforms, and in the last five years, we have managed to back up our progress towards strengthening my country's independence and sovereignty with some considerable achievements in the economic field. Let me name only most striking of the results of Azerbaijan's economy. Inflation, which had reached 1600 percent in 1994, has been gradually curbed to the level of 3.7 in 1997, and now equals zero (according to the IMF, 2-5 percent yearly inflation would be normal for Azerbaijan).

Exchange rate for Azerbaijan's currency, the manat, has been stable since 1995, and currency reserves reached $715 million, while the gross domestic product in 1999 grew by 7.4 percent percent, reaching almost $4 billion. It is most appropriate to mention that over 32 percent of the GDP was provided by industry and construction; nearly 22 percent by the agriculture, 14.5 percent by transportation, communications and infrastructure, and 5.1 percent by trade and services sector.

Allow me also to mention two areas of my country's economic transformation that are of special interest.

First, privatization, which has been successfully developing since 1996, has already led to the denationalization of over 22,000 small and about 1,100 medium and large businesses [and] continues to be a top priority for my government.

Second, based on the Law on Land Reform, over 95 percent of 1.3 million hectares designated to become private property have already been distributed resulting in almost 770,000 households becoming land owners.

As far as Azerbaijan's place in the world economy is concerned, I would like to emphasize that it now has commercial relations with almost one hundred states compared to fifty-four in 1994. For the first time since 1994, my nation's foreign trade balance has become passive, which can be explained by the purchases of equipment and machinery for the oil projects. Besides traditional trade partners, among them Russia, other CIS countries, and also Iran, we pursue active commercial contacts with the West, where Turkey (over $190 million in eleven months of 1999), the U.S. (almost $88 million), and the UK (over $70 million) are our biggest partners.

It would be also appropriate to underline that investments in Azerbaijan's economy, including the oil and gas sector, have continued, totaling well over $800 million in the first nine months of 1999 despite allegations that the initial period of interest in the Caspian, including in my country, is over.

All of you know pretty much about the importance of oil and gas development, and also about how its production and transportation is doing in my country. That is why I am intentionally trying to concentrate on the economic performance in general, as well as on the non-energy sector. Nevertheless, I cannot help but mention a few of the recent figures describing progress in that area. In January 2000, over 119,000 tons of Azerbaijani oil were transported via the Baku-Novorossiysk pipeline, and the general drilling plan was completed at 111.2 percent, with well ever three thousand feet drilled in addition to what was initially scheduled for that period.

I would like to conclude my brief statement by mentioning that Azerbaijan is implementing its reforms not only successfully, but also in full compliance with the recommendations of the International Monetary Fund. The latter has recently been paying keen attention to the development of agriculture in my country, including privatization, management, training etc., as well as to the monetary policy pursued by the Azerbaijani Government. A number of IMF missions visiting Azerbaijan in the recent months have indicated that my country's progress is considerable and achievements significant.

"Challenge to the Global Oil & Gas Industry: Competition, Commercialization, Privatization" Remarks at the George Washington University October 13, 1998

It is a pleasure to be invited to discuss the challenges facing Azerbaijan's oil and gas industry. I am grateful to The George Washington University for sponsoring this important conference. We too hope to learn a great deal from the experiences and recommendations shared among the participants.

As many of you may know, prior to becoming Azerbaijan's first Ambassador to the United States, I was a physics professor. On occasion, that training has been helpful to me as a diplomat. Recent articles about Azerbaijan in last weekend's *Washington Post* and *New York Times* reminded me of an often-misunderstood idea in physics called the Uncertainty Principle. The Uncertainty Principle states that the closer one gets to observing the velocity of a particle, the further one gets from measuring its position-and vice-versa.

In other words, to casual observers, "uncertainty" may seem to be an apt description of Azerbaijan's nation-building process in the early years of its independence.

Some degree of uncertainty and upheaval are to be expected in any major reform movement. For this reason, the Uncertainty Principle may be the perfect metaphor for what is happening in Azerbaijan today. Political and economic transformations are difficult to measure, especially when they are happening quickly. The faster the changes, the more difficult it is to pinpoint their places in time. The impact of the changes that are underway in Azerbaijan today may difficult to measure, but in fact, new democratic rules and recognizable patterns of economic reform are emerging.

Following the break-up of the Soviet Union, Azerbaijan asserted its independence and emerged as a democratic republic in 1991. Situated on the borders of Russia, Iran and Turkey, our nation faced serious challenges from the start.

The dismantling of the Soviet Union and the war with Armenia caused Azerbaijan's economy to decline dramatically. Between 1991 and 1995, real GDP dropped by 60 percent, high inflation eroded incomes, and international reserves were nearly depleted.

Despite these obstacles, the Azerbaijan Government embarked on a privatization initiative soon after independence. In 1992, the State Property Committee was established and in 1993, the Law on Privatization of State Property was approved.

By 1995, Azerbaijan, in cooperation with the World Bank and the International Monetary Fund (IMF), began a comprehensive stabilization program. Fiscal and credit policies were tightened, structural reforms were introduced [and] foreign investment rules were changed to attract capital.

As a result of these and other economic reforms, by 1996, the country was poised to make a more predictable transition to a market economy, including the privatization of major industries.

Azerbaijan's oil and gas reserves are at the heart of this transition. Total proven oil reserves are estimated at nine to eleven billion barrels, with potential reserves of several times that amount. Foreign investment has helped revitalize this industry and produced strong growth throughout the first six months of this year. Total capital investment in the Azerbaijani economy has increased by 58 percent over the past year.

Such high levels of foreign direct investment are a sign that the private sector supports and has confidence in the reform program and its continuing implementation.

In July, President Aliyev signed three new production-sharing agreements for offshore oil fields. These agreements involve: BP and Statoil, which are partners in Azerbaijan; Monument of the United Kingdom; Amoco of the United States; Central Fuel Company (of Russia); and other oil companies from France, Italy, Norway, Japan, and other countries.

This brings [up] to fifteen the number of Production Sharing Agreements that have been signed thus far, with a total estimated value of more than $40 billion.

The outlook for 1999 remains positive. The oil sector will continue to expand as the main Western consortium, the Azerbaijan International Operating Consortium (AIOC), brings more wells into operation and smaller joint ventures invest in exploration. When the world oil price begins to recover in 1999, as expected, oil production is likely to grow beyond present levels.

In addition, a final decision on the route of the main export pipeline that will carry most of the oil and gas out of the Caspian Basin to Western markets will be announced within the next several weeks. This will allow construction work to begin and create a greater influx of capital.

We expect that there will be multiple pipelines, including one through Russia; however, the Azerbaijan Government believes the main export pipeline should run through Georgia and Turkey to the Mediterranean Coast. Azerbaijan and the United States favor this route from Baku to Ceyhan on the Mediterranean coast of Turkey. In our view, this route will protect Azerbaijan's economic future as well as the West's energy interests. All other alternatives would transport oil through neighboring Russia, Ukraine, or Iran.

In addition, the main pipeline is integral to restoration and modernization of the ancient Silk Road trade corridor. Last month, Azerbaijan hosted a summit meeting to promote cooperation in establishing a modern Silk Road. Eight heads of state attended the Summit. In total, thirty-two nations, including the United States, and thirteen international organizations participated in the event (at which five major agreements were signed).

The recent drop in oil prices and the concomitant decline in exports and tax revenue demonstrate the dangers of building an economy on a single sector. The Azerbaijani Government is aware that it cannot become overly dependent on oil and gas, for its sustained economic development. The goal is to create balanced growth over time, and to use revenues earned from energy exports to reinvest in modernizing manufacturing, transportation, telecommunications, and communications capabilities.

Investments in Azerbaijan's oil and gas industry have created a positive social and psychological climate that has made privatization possible in many other sectors. These privatization efforts are well underway. For example:

(1) More than 70 percent of small and medium-size businesses in the country have been privatized, and the remainder will be privatized by the end of the year.

(2) All residential real estate has been privatized, and several Western hotels have been completed, or are under construction.
(3) New laws have been enacted to protect intellectual property and limit taxes on businesses.
(4) Bank privatization will continue to streamline the financial sector, making investment easier and more attractive. The European Bank for Reconstruction and Development is lending $20 million to help build up Azerbaijan's banking.
(5) A progressive land privatization program is in the process of being implemented.

The Azerbaijani Government is also in the process of developing plans to privatize the oil and gas industry. Like other industries, this sector will go through an orderly transition to private sector management in the future. Obviously, the oil and gas industry is of great strategic importance to Azerbaijan's economic development, and thus, the Government has played an active role in its management to date.

The results of this management, as well as of macroeconomic policies, have been impressive. Today, annual inflation has been reduced to 4 percent while the growth rate for the first half of 1998 was more than 9 percent.

And, it is important to note that we have accomplished this despite the hardship created by a Congressional ban on direct U.S. assistance to Azerbaijan.

Just as Azerbaijan has sought a diversified economic base, so too has the Aliyev Government sought out a variety of Western investors and business partners. No one wants to return to the days when we were reliant on traditional trade links only to the Soviet Union. Today, Baku is truly an international city, much as it was centuries ago when commerce traveled between East and West via the "Silk Route."

Business executives from Israel, Turkey, northern Africa, Europe, North America, Latin America, Japan and Russia are all supporting Azerbaijan's goal to become a modern, open market economy with privately-owned and operated companies and consortia.

This is Azerbaijan's future. It is from this diversity of interests and investments that Azerbaijan will prosper. To the casual observer, such diversity may appear divisive, conflicting or chaotic at times. But to those who have studied Azerbaijan's history, it is road to a more prosperous and stable economic and political future. Given America's own history, Americans may be uniquely qualified to understand the challenges and opportunities associated with building a nation and a modern free-market economy.

This is why Sunday's presidential election was critical. Azerbaijan has adopted strong pro-democracy reforms. We have held four nationwide elections, three for President and one for the Parliament.

The October 11 Presidential election demonstrated how our new election law, a free media, and a cooperative relationship with monitoring groups and opposition parties, can work successfully. The high voter turnout and massive participation is also evidence that the Azerbaijani people place a high degree of confidence in the electoral system and in President Aliyev's leadership.

It has been said that a good leader inspires men to have confidence in him, but a great leader inspires them to have confidence in themselves. The goal of the Government is to inspire confidence in Azerbaijanis; that they can compete, succeed and prosper in an open market, a private sector economy. If we can accomplish this, Azerbaijan will have earned its true independence and ensured its future.

Thanks to gatherings like this one, we remain hopeful we will succeed at home as well as in building stronger relationships with the United States.

Remarks at the Second Annual Cambridge Energy Research Associates (CERA) Conference
"Caspian Pipelines: Building Solutions"
December 8-9, 1998

It is a great honor and pleasure to appear here and represent Azerbaijan on this distinguished panel. Despite being the only one on it with no direct relation to oil industry, I must confess that I do feel at ease.

As I begin my comments, I would like to start by briefly answering a question that I receive rather often. The question is the following: is oil good or bad?

Let me answer by saying, that in essence oil is definitely not bad, but of key importance is how the country deals with the difficulties that oil brings along. We, in Azerbaijan, view oil as definitely good, if it can be used as an instrument in solidifying our independence, pursuing political and economic reforms, and bringing prosperity to people. Everyone who analyzes energy-related development in my country has to look at it in the bigger geopolitical context.

Azerbaijan's geography dictates that it is a key in geo-strategic consideration of the Caucasus and Central Asia. At the crossroads-both commercially and politically-for all major issues facing the region, Azerbaijan resists efforts by those who wish to dominate it, regardless of where the efforts come from.

Most world energy experts rank Caspian oil reserves as second only to those of the Persian Gulf, and Azerbaijan's share is more than visible here. Azerbaijan was the country that opened up the Caspian for foreign partners, created reliable conditions for foreign businesses, and we remain committed to the accommodation we have reached with companies. We have entered into fifteen oil contracts with the participation of major Western oil companies. The contracts will bring total investments in my country's energy sector to almost $50 billion.

We know how much debate is going on now on the issue of the Main Export Pipeline, and this well-organized conference-already second in a row-is a good proof of that. My government remains committed to the Baku-Ceyhan route and we have confirmed this more than once. We believe that now it is time for the regional governments to act with the purpose of making this route commercially viable. The Ankara Declaration created a solid basis for that, reiterating the governments' commitment to Baku-Ceyhan line.

The universal rule applies-wherever there is oil, finding a way to get it to the world markets should follow. In the Caspian, that means pipelines. We do believe indeed, that a saying, "happiness is in multiple pipelines," is true. In Azerbaijan we view pipelines not only as means of transportation, but also as a backbone of the re-emerging "Silk Road," which would include transportation, infrastructure and other links.

Sometimes the question is raised of whether there will be enough oil for several pipelines. In answer to it, I would like to use figures, provided yesterday by Mr. Terry Koonce in his excellent presentation at the Central Asia-Caucasus Institute. Oil production from the Caspian basin can reach three to six billion barrels per year in a decade or two. And that will mean that we will need not one, but several pipelines the capacity of Baku-Ceyhan. Thus, the pessimistic estimates that have recently surfaced about the Caspian hydrocarbon volume seem unfounded to me.

Well, let the pessimists be. I am an optimist. In my six years in Washington, DC, I have followed closely, and in some cases participated in, the various stages of oil-related developments in my country, and let me tell you, all of them, including the signing of the first contract, defining the legal status of the Caspian, and the issue of an alternative early oil pipelines, have been accompanied by considerable difficulties. The latter have been aggravated by the continuing military aggression of neighboring Armenia.

United States was a great supporter to us in overcoming the difficulties. In this regard, I want to raise the question of whether there is now enough support from the U.S. Government to the Baku-Ceyhan route. Indeed, many of those involved would expect financial support to follow verbal support. But there is one issue on which America could achieve much in terms of implementing its own stated agenda by just showing some political will. I am, of course, talking about the infamous Section 907 of the Freedom Support Act. Its repeal or lifting could send a strong message to all parties about keen U.S. interest in Baku-Ceyhan. I would like to remind you that this will has already been shown once, when the U.S. established the office of the Special Advisor to the President and Secretary of State on Caspian Basin Energy Diplomacy.

Finally, let me say a few words about the overall economic climate in my country. Strictly, following the path of reforms, we have privatized most real estate and small businesses, as well as major business enterprises. Because of financial reforms, our inflation has been brought down to less than 4 percent over the past year. Growth of the GDP was 5.8 percent over the same period, and the share of the private economy will increase from 30 percent in 1997 to about 70 percent by the end of 1999.

In summary, I want to stress that we are determined to uphold our independence, and if this also means having multiple pipelines, as a tool, so be it. We will be even happier to combine these two objectives into one.

**Presentation at the Center for Strategic
and International Studies
July 19, 1999**

It is a pleasure for me to appear before the distinguished
CSIS audience today. On the agenda of your institution, there
are many topics related to our region. Developments in the
countries of former Soviet Union always get significant attention here. Three months ago, when President Aliyev visited
Washington to celebrate [the] fiftieth anniversary of NATO,
he made a presentation at the Statesmen's Forum. We are
thankful to the CSIS for the interest to Azerbaijan. Today, I
would like to express my special gratitude to the Turkish
Studies and Caspian Sea Study Group for inviting me here to
speak.

I have been asked to discuss future economic and political developments in Azerbaijan, especially in the light of energy projects, which have significant importance in shaping
the geopolitical image of the region. It is obvious that Azerbaijan's oil and gas development is not merely an issue of energy production and delivery. It is a matter of major geo-
strategic implications involving not only Azerbaijan, but also
Russia, Iran, Turkey, stability of the whole Caucasus region,
as well the economic interests of industrialized nations of the
West.

That is why Azerbaijan, under the leadership of President
Aliyev, has developed and persistently implemented its own
oil-development strategy with a major goal of strengthening
its independence and integrating with the international community.

I would remind you that in contrast with the image of
Azerbaijan as an energy-producing country, in 1993-1994, we
actually imported energy. By that time, it had been well understood in Azerbaijan that without Western technology and

investments, it would be impossible to develop new oil-fields in the Caspian Sea.

Overcoming internal and external obstacles, Azerbaijan managed to sign its first contract in 1994 and to create a consortium of twelve companies representing eight countries. Today, [the] Azerbaijan International Operating Company (AIOC) is producing more than expected-120,000 barrels per day. This is early oil. When in 1995, at the CERA conference, representatives of SOCAR made the statement that by 1997 we will have oil from the first project, few people took this seriously. But, we achieved our goal and that was the first success.

The second one came with early oil pipelines. In a relatively short period of time, we were able to put in operation two pipelines (Novorossiysk and Supsa). Again, the decision and implementation were not easy. Unfortunately, operation of the northern route in the recent period has not been as reliable as we would like it to be. This fact by itself shows that Azerbaijan's determination to construct the second pipeline to Supsa without delay reflected correct strategy.

Last week, we witnessed another success when BP-Amoco announced that the Shah Deniz field contains huge amounts of natural gas and significant volumes of condensate. In any event, this field alone has enough gas to cover all of Turkey's needs for decades to come.

The BP-Amoco announcement was a good answer to those skeptics in the media who have been predicting in recent months that Azerbaijan's projected energy resources have been overestimated.

Now, Azerbaijan will be a big gas, as well as oil, producer. In terms of gas, we are both exporters and a transit country. By the year 2003, production rate will be four billion cubic meters per year for export, and this amount will grow another five to six billion a year, until the volume reaches twenty billion cubic meters. And I would remind you that we have signed nineteen oil contracts worth over $50 billion with oil companies and governments representing many foreign nations.

To deliver huge oil and gas volumes produced in Azerbaijan and other Caspian states, we need to construct new pipelines. Issue of the main export pipeline (MEP) is under intensive discussion. And right now, we believe that negotiations around Baku-Ceyhan project are in a practical stage to guarantee financial terms of the project. Even as we speak, representatives of companies and the Government are preparing recommendations to finalize the decision.

Special working group on MEP, created in Azerbaijan by a decree of President Aliyev two years ago, already announced that it would not be necessary to evaluate other options like Supsa and Novorossiysk. In regard to gas pipeline, my understanding is that a similar working group committee will be created, comprised of government and company representatives to study this issue and prepare recommendations. And it should happen very soon.

Energy and energy-related industries are not the only components of our economy. My country's geographical location makes it regional and international hub. We are working closely with the EU, EBRD and other institutions over projects like TRACECA, restoration of the ancient Silk Road, etc.

Agriculture is of crucial importance to our country. We have totally privatized our agriculture system. Major structural reforms [and] macroeconomic transformations have been made to create a modern economic structure, and we are quite confident that in the nearest future, we will make a successful breakthrough as a result of these reforms.

There are many factors that could affect our economic developments, like a drop of world oil prices, energy resources' delivery difficulties, and so on. But for Azerbaijan, the ongoing conflict with neighboring Armenia over the Mountainous Karabakh region of Azerbaijan presents the major obstacle.

As many of you may know, Presidents of Azerbaijan and Armenia met in Geneva last Friday, as a continuation of two earlier meetings at NATO's fiftieth anniversary celebration and several subsequent telephone conversations. While much of these talks remain undisclosed, I consider it as a good sign of possible progress toward eventual settlement.

We must admit that efforts of the Co-Chairs of Minsk Group brought disappointment. After some initial progress at the Budapest and Lisbon Summits in 1994 and 1996, the Armenian *coup d'état* against former President Levon Ter-Petrossian in 1997 really threw the Co-Chairs into disarray. Late last year, the Co-Chairs agreed to a Russian-Primakov proposal for a "common state," which has no real meaning in diplomatic terms, and which is totally unacceptable for Azerbaijan because it effectively recognizes Mountainous Karabakh as a separate entity from Azerbaijan. Obviously, this proposal was another attempt to perpetuate the conflict.

Now, the "common state" proposal is out of question and the U.S. Secretary of State Madeleine Albright has reconfirmed to President Aliyev the United States' support for the territorial integrity of Azerbaijan.

For the Minsk Group to be successful, it must have active support and participation of top officials of the governments involved. At this moment, practically all the Co-Chairs of the Minsk Group have either resigned, or otherwise left their positions for another jobs.

I call upon the President of the United States to appoint a top-level diplomat, one with a personal relationship with both the President and the Secretary of State, as a special negotiator for the Armenia-Azerbaijan conflict. (We have the precedents: Richard Holbrooke's activity in Bosnia, Senator Mitchell's and Representative King's in Northern Ireland, the efforts of President Jimmy Carter and General Colin Powell in Haiti, personal involvement of President Clinton and Secretary Albright in the case of Kosovo). This conflict has been going on for eleven years now. It is time that the conflict were settled, rather than managed. We don't want "freezing instability" to be imposed on the region.

I would like to briefly address our security concerns in a situation where Russia has provided lots of arms to Armenia. Because Azerbaijan sees NATO's expansion as a stabilizing factor, we support the concept of NATO's enlargement. We are also actively involved in the PFP program. At the same time, we are concerned about Russia's reaction to NATO expansion and, in turn, to the U.S.' reaction to Russian concerns.

It is of utmost importance that the strategic concept of NATO also envisages and deals with the security needs of nations like Azerbaijan. That is why we are so sensitive about a possibility of the U.S. and Russia reaching expansion-related accommodations that overlook the independence and security needs of other countries.

Another aspect of our growing security-related interaction with the West is the U.S.-Azerbaijan security dialogue, which has been developing on steady, regular basis, and addresses both increasing bilateral cooperation in this area and Azerbaijan's security concerns.

Common security and economic interests have brought the five countries of GUUAM together. The last meeting of the GUUAM Presidents took place here, in Washington, DC, in April, and top officials of these countries got together regularly to discuss issues of mutual interest.

[The] Relationship between our two countries is based on shared values, foremost of which are independence of nations, democracy and commitment to free market economy principles. We have rapidly growing economic ties between the two countries, but Section 907 remains the major impediment to our relations. This law has been in force since 1992, despite the fact that there is no justification for these sanctions and despite the U.S.' other domestic political considerations. From the very beginning, the U.S. Administration has opposed this law, but as it turns out, policy-makers in this country have become hostages of politics.

The government and people of Azerbaijan do not understand how it is possible for the U.S. leadership to exercise the so-called "territorial integrity" waiver to let Armenia continue being one of the biggest per-capita recipients of American assistance in the world, and at the same time, uphold unfair sanctions against my country.

Just listen carefully to the language of 907, "U.S. assistance under this or any other Act (other than assistance under Title V of this Act) may not be provided to the Government of Azerbaijan until the President determines, and so reports to the Congress, that the Government of Azerbaijan is taking demonstrable steps to cease all blockades and other offensive uses of force against Armenia and Nagorno-Karabakh."

It is quite obvious what was, and, perhaps still is, the main reason why this law came into existence. But nowadays, even Armenian lobbyists rarely use the original set of "arguments" to justify keeping 907. Instead, they and their vocal supporters in Congress invent new "reasons" as to why the sanctions should be upheld. As an example, in a recent letter, pro-Armenian members of Congress argued that the oil factor is weakening and that Azerbaijan is becoming more flexible and receptive to the idea of an independent Mountainous Karabakh. In addition, to achieve that, Congress is supposed to keep Section 907.

I want to be frank with you. The provisions of 907 have nothing to do either with oil, or with the situation in Azerbaijan, and repealing these unjust sanctions would mean, on one hand, upholding [the] U.S.' image as a strong and unbiased advocate of democracy and democracy-related values throughout the world. On the other hand, it would be in the national interest of the United States to do so, to re-assert America's determination to show certain states in the region that South Caucasus is a region of consequence in the U.S. foreign policy.

"Azerbaijan: 10 Years After 'Black January'"
Briefing for Congressional Staff
Rayburn House Office Building
January 20, 2000

It was on Saturday, January 20, 1990 that 26,000 Soviet troops, under orders from Mikhail Gorbachev, invaded Baku, killing 140 innocent civilians, and set in motion the events which led to Azerbaijan's independence-a year and a half later. The significance of the KGB-inspired invasion cannot be overestimated, just as it cannot be overestimated in case of similar events, which have taken place in Vilnius, Lithuania, and Tbilisi, Georgia. Peaceful demonstrations had been taking place for several weeks in Baku, protesting Soviet control of Azerbaijan and the arbitrary decisions dictated by Moscow to the local communist officials.

In fact, Azerbaijan was one of the first of the former Soviet republics to mount a serious move toward independence, and it was the prospect of a breakup of the Soviet empire that prompted Gorbachev to send both armored troops and KGB officials into Baku. He succeeded temporarily in preventing independence, but he was unable to stop the quest for freedom, and, contradictory as it may sound, accelerated the process by enhancing nationalistic feelings among all Azerbaijani people. Before the January massacre, pro-Soviet sentiments were still alive in my country. After the slaughter started, there was little doubt that there was no future for Azerbaijan within the USSR. That is how it came [to be] that Azerbaijan became the first among the Soviet states to adopt a constitutional act on independence on October 18, 1991. In April 1993, it also ultimately succeeded in driving the Soviet troops, the embodiment of the oppression and brutality, from its soil.

It is interesting now, ten years later, to look back at those events and the world's reaction at the time. Gorbachev, of course, was something of a hero in the West because of his policies of glasnost and perestroika. But, in fact, Gorbachev had no intention of breaking up the Soviet Union, [for] he merely wanted to "reform" communism to extend its life.

The Washington Post stated on January 21, 1990 that the situation in Azerbaijan had "presented Gorbachev with his 'gravest crisis' since taking power in March 1985." On January 23, The Washington Times reported that some Soviet experts warned "that Azerbaijan could become Moscow's next Afghanistan, but some U.S. experts believe that it might become the Kremlin's Northern Ireland."

Throughout the seventy years of Soviet reign, Moscow used ethnic differences and tensions to maintain internal control. [As] Masters of the divide and conquer game, the Kremlin leaders transplanted thousands of people of various ethnic backgrounds to either dilute their strength or to counter other ethnic groups. In Azerbaijan's case, several hundred thousands Azerbaijanis have been expelled from Armenia and the latter has been given a strip of land separating Azerbaijan from its region of Nakhchivan; both to internally divide Azerbaijanis and to prevent a direct link between Azerbaijan proper and Turkey.

In 1988, the ethnic conflict between Armenia and Azerbaijan began when ethnic Armenians in the Azerbaijani region of Nagorno-Karabakh unilaterally declared their independence. While neither the Soviet Union nor any other nation gave recognition to this unilateral declaration of independence, reactionary forces used the conflict to keep Armenians and Azerbaijanis divided and, therefore, under tight Soviet control.

Soviet army and Spetsnaz [Soviet Special Forces] troops fired indiscriminately at civilians, some of whom were merely watching events from their windows or the sidewalks. Ambulances carrying the wounded were fired upon. *The Washington Post* reported [on] January 22 that a Russian photographer told Western reporters in Moscow, who were banned from traveling to Baku, that "Soviet soldiers fired at almost anything that moved in the early hours of their occupation." Again, in classic Soviet fashion, Soviet military authorities announced on January 23 that no one had been killed in Baku since the Saturday invasion, while at the same time more than one million Azerbaijanis gathered to mourn the dead who were buried in a park overlooking Baku, now known as the Martyr's Cemetery.

Under conditions of [the] informational blockade imposed by the Soviets, the West, misinformed and fearful of undermining Gorbachev, was very circumspect in its reaction. The press reported [on] January 26 that President Bush said Gorbachev had done a "remarkable job" in handling the situation in Azerbaijan and that British Prime Minister Margaret Thatcher told the House of Commons she had "great sympathy" for Gorbachev as "he tries to keep his nation from unraveling." *The Washington Post* reported on January 21 that the White House "expressed regret at the 'already heavy loss of life' in Azerbaijan, and called 'upon all involved to act with restraint in the use of force and to show respect for the rule of law and the rights of individuals concerned."

A more candid assessment of the West's reaction came in a *Washington Post* dispatch [on] January 21: "As ethnic strife and secessionist pressures buffet the Soviet Union, U.S. officials have been forced to acknowledge that the United States has a stake in President Mikhail Gorbachev's survival that now outweighs the old Cold War hope that the USSR. might fragment or fall apart." What the West failed to comprehend was that the events in Baku that January ten years ago were for Azerbaijan no different from what happened in Budapest, Hungary in 1956, Prague, and Czechoslovakia in 1968.

While some in the West may have been fooled by Gorbachev's justifications, the Azerbaijani people were not fooled. They instinctively knew-as did the people of Hungary and Czechoslovakia-that what was happening was the destruction of their freedom. That is why thousands of Azerbaijanis surrounded Communist Party headquarters demanding the resignation of the republic's leadership. That is why thousands of Azerbaijanis in Turkey rallied near Turkey's border with Azerbaijan. That is why the Baku City Council demanded that Soviet troops be withdrawn. That is why even the Soviet legislature in Azerbaijan condemned the occupation as "unconstitutional" and threatened to call a referendum on secession unless Soviet troops were withdrawn within forty-eight hours. That is why there were reports of mutiny by Soviet Azerbaijani military cadets, and why Azerbaijani oil tankers blocked Soviet naval vessels from reaching the Baku harbor.

Despite a news blackout, hundreds of Azerbaijanis in Moscow used short-wave radios to listen to Voice of America and to BBC to learn what was happening in Baku. Many of these Azerbaijanis gathered in Moscow seeking information and demanding explanations. At that point, on the day after the invasion, Azerbaijan's current President Heydar Aliyev-who was living in retirement in Moscow-made his first public appearance since his resignation from the Soviet Politburo and Government in 1987. He broke the information blockade in Moscow concerning the Soviet attack, and strongly urged international condemnation of the invasion.

Soviet troops were eventually withdrawn from Baku, but political control was maintained for almost another two years until Azerbaijan's parliament declared independence in October of 1991. Azerbaijan has maintained its independence since then, despite lingering economic and social problems from the Soviet era, and despite the military occupation of 20 percent of Azerbaijan by Armenia. The Republic of Azerbaijan has a freely elected president and parliament, the beginnings of free market reforms led by the energy sector, and, most importantly, no foreign troops on its soil. Indeed, January 20, 1990, in Baku, Azerbaijan, the fate of the Soviet empire was sealed, because it quickly became apparent that even the might of the Soviet military could not extinguish the hopes and dreams of a people seeking freedom and independence.

Human Rights Watch report, published in early 1991 and entitled "Black January in Azerbaijan," states, "Indeed, the violence used by the Soviet Army on the night of January 19-20 was so out of proportion to the resistance offered by Azerbaijanis as to constitute an exercise in collective punishment. Since Soviet officials have stated publicly that the purpose of the intervention of Soviet troops was to prevent the ouster of the Communist-dominated government of the Republic of Azerbaijan by the nationalist-minded, non-Communist opposition, the punishment inflicted on Baku by Soviet soldiers may have been intended as a warning to nationalists, not only in Azerbaijan, but in the other Republics of the Soviet Union." In their January 26, 1990 op-ed "Gorbachev's procrastination," published in *The Washington Post*,

Rowland Ewans and Robert Novak subscribe to the same point of view, stating similarities between both the Kremlin intervention in the Baltics and the Baku massacre and the importance of Black January for the then impending collapse of the USSR: "The Baltic independence has now been irretrievably affected by civil war in Azerbaijan though official opinions differ in what way. One school believes that the overwhelming military force killing Azeris is sending an unmistakable signal to the Baltics: Watch it-or you will get the same. More probable is the opposite: Gorbachev's preoccupation with the Trans-Caucasus crisis he failed to stop on time gives Baltic leaders more latitude to move faster on independence."

With the progress of time, lies used by the Soviet regime to cover what had been perpetrated in Baku have become transparent. As *The Wall Street Journal* editorial of January 4, 1995 stated, "It was Mr. Gorbachev, recall, who in January 1990 chose to defend his use of violence against the independence-seeking Azerbaijan on the grounds that the people of this then-Soviet republic were heavily armed gangs of hooligans and drug-traffickers who were destabilizing the country and quite possibly receiving support from foreign governments." By the way, it is ironic, that while Mikhail Gorbachev dismissed hundreds of thousands of protesters gathered in the capital of Azerbaijan as "heavily armed gangs of hooligans and drug-traffickers," it is exactly their leaders, who are being hailed as legitimate and pro-democratic opposition by the U.S. now.

For many in the U.S., it probably was just another case of violence in a faraway country. For somebody who has witnessed the gunfire, the bloodshed, [and] the suffering like I did, it is so much more. I know that the Black January started the process strengthening my people's determination to achieve independence and eventually leading to the restoration of Azerbaijan's sovereignty. I believe this determination will help us to prevail, despite any problems, on our path toward becoming rightful member of the twenty-first century international community, where governments will never even consider using troops against their own peoples.

Statement at the National War College
Washington, DC
January 31, 2000

First, let me say what a privilege it is to appear here today, especially with my good friend, Ambassador Japaridze. Together, we represent two of the three countries of the Southern Caucasus; the third, of course, is Armenia.

Let me begin by saying how much the rest of the world admires, and would like to emulate, the American military. We not only admire your efficiency and your modern weapon systems, but we also greatly appreciate your strict adherence to civilian control of the military. We also often look with envy on the professionalism and lack of politics within the American military establishment. Coming from an area of the world where in the past that has often not been the case, you have much to be proud of and thankful for.

In his invitation to me for today's event, Admiral Bowler asked that I address the topic, "Azerbaijan in 'The Geo-Strategic Context.'" This is an excellent topic, since all of Azerbaijan's problems and opportunities today are the result of the geo-strategic context in which it finds itself. To understand Azerbaijan geo-strategically, one must only look at a map and do some basic research on the mineral resources of my country.

The most important fact of life for Azerbaijan is, quite simply, the neighborhood in which it exists. With Russia as our northern neighbor, Iran to the south, and Georgia, Armenia and Turkey to the west, we are guaranteed an interesting existence, to say the least. And when you add the valuable and vast oil and gas deposits, both onshore and offshore, on our eastern boundary in the Caspian Sea, what was before an interesting existence quickly becomes a volatile and dangerous one. To make life even more precarious, consider the following: Azerbaijan is a secular Muslim country bordered by an Orthodox Russian and a fundamentalist Muslim Iranian state. Further complicating matters is the fact that twenty million people in northern Iran are ethnic Azerbaijanis (as opposed to the population of Azerbaijan of only eight million).

One must also keep in mind that throughout its history, Azerbaijan has—with the exception of a brief two-year period from 1918 to 1920-been part of someone else's empire, whether it be the Russian Empire of the czars, or the Soviets, or the Persian Empire, or the Ottoman Empire. As a result of this history, many longstanding friendships and animosities exist that cannot be ignored.

Our geography has been highlighted in recent weeks by the war in Chechnya. Both Georgia and Azerbaijan have been falsely accused by Russia of allowing our territory to be used to transport arms and fighters for the Chechnyan guerillas. There is no question that Russia is using the war in Chechnya to put pressure on both Georgia and Azerbaijan in an effort to extract concessions from us. So, what happens in the Northern Caucasus regions of the Russian Federation also vitally affects those of us in the Southern Caucasus.

You can see that by geography alone, Azerbaijan is a geostrategically important state. It is at the cross-roads of Central Asia with its five new republics; it is where East meets the West in this region of the world; it is Russia's important southern neighbor and Iran's important northern neighbor. As a result of this geography, it should come as no surprise that Azerbaijan's neighbors are constantly jockeying for position and influence over Azerbaijan.

When you add Azerbaijan's vast deposits of oil and gas both onshore and within the Caspian Sea to its geography, you gain an even greater appreciation for Azerbaijan's geo-strategic importance. Since October, 1994, Azerbaijan has signed some twenty production sharing agreements with oil companies from throughout the world, in excess of $50 billion. Oil industry experts predict that Azerbaijan and its neighbors will eventually have as much oil as Kuwait, and we have just recently made a natural gas discovery that could theoretically supply Turkey's energy needs for the next forty years.

Such mineral wealth merely adds to Azerbaijan's geo-strategic significance, and raises the stakes for those regional and world powers competing for influence in the country.

This competition for influence over Azerbaijan's energy resources has taken many forms since our independence was achieved in 1991. First, there was the question of true owner-ship of this mineral wealth buried beneath the waters of the Caspian Sea. First Russia and then Iran challenged Azerbai-jan's ownership of these resources, contending that the Cas-pian was a lake and not a sea, and that all the littoral states of the Caspian should share equally in the wealth of the Caspian. While this argument has pretty much been overcome, it is still not totally settled.

Secondly, there is the question of how this oil and gas wealth will be transported to Western markets. Russia con-tends that most of that transportation should be through Russia, to the Russian port city of Novorossiysk on the Black Sea. Iran contends that the cheapest route is through Iran. The United States, Georgia, Turkey and Azerbaijan support a route called Baku-Ceyhan, which would run from Baku in Azerbaijan through Georgia and Turkey, to the Turkish Mediterranean port city of Ceyhan. As alluded to earlier, this transportation issue not only encompasses the geo-strategic interest of all the interested governments, but also involves the question of cost to the oil companies, environmental questions relating to use of any Black Sea route, and the role of Iran in major energy development in the region. Thus, the major question now before us is the location of the Main Export Pipeline to transport the oil and gas of Azerbaijan and its neighbors to waiting markets.

This discussion of Azerbaijan's geography and mineral wealth alone should be enough to convince you of the geostrategic importance of the country. But if anyone needs further convincing, let me briefly discuss Azerbaijan's foreign policy priorities and why they are important to the United States.

After centuries of being dominated by its neighbors, Azerbaijan finally achieved true and lasting independence in 1991. Maintaining and strengthening that independence is and will remain the top foreign policy objective of Azerbaijan. For far too long, our very existence has been in the service of others. We are finally free of the yoke of seventy years of Soviet communism, and we are now enjoying the freedom to develop our own democracy and free market economy. We do not intend to relinquish that freedom ever again. So, our first priority is the elimination of threats and risks to the security, political independence, sovereignty, and territorial integrity of Azerbaijan.

A second major foreign policy objective is to settle the eleven-year-old conflict with our neighbor Armenia. This conflict began in 1988 when ethnic Armenians living within the Azerbaijani territory of Nagorno-Karabakh unilaterally declared their independence. This action, backed by Armenia, quickly developed into an all-out war. With the assistance of the Armenian army and more than $1 billion in illegal arms shipments from Russia, the Armenians, during 1993, captured Nagorno-Karabakh and seven surrounding regions. With more than thirty thousand dead, and in excess of 800,000 Azerbaijani refugees and displaced persons, and with Armenians controlling 20 percent of the territory of Azerbaijan, a cease fire was adopted in 1994. That cease fire has held for the succeeding six years, but all efforts to negotiate an end to the conflict have been to no avail.

We are now in the midst of the most promising set of negotiations since the ceasefire was put in place. Azerbaijan's president, Heydar Aliyev, and Armenian President Robert Kocharian met just last week in Moscow, which is a continuation of a series of bilateral meetings that started here in Washington during the fiftieth anniversary celebration of NATO, under the prompting of Secretary of State Albright. The overall negotiations are being conducted by the Organization for Security and Cooperation in Europe's Minsk Group, which is co-chaired by the United States, France and Russia. But our objective is clear: return of the captured territories and respect for our territorial integrity.

A third foreign policy objective of Azerbaijan is the establishment of security and stability within the Southern Caucasus region. President Aliyev and others in the region have advocated the establishment of a regional security pact to include Azerbaijan, Georgia, Turkey, Iran and Armenia. To the extent that such a pack could enhance stability in the region, Azerbaijan is supportive of the idea. We would go much further and advocate a total demilitarization of the Caspian Sea Basin and the establishment of a nuclear-free zone in the Southern Caucasus, as well as adherence to all existing global non-proliferation treaties and arms control agreements.

A fourth foreign policy objective for Azerbaijan is to enhance its strategic cooperation with the United States and the West. We share many values with the West, such as independence, democracy and free markets, and we need the support of the United States and other Western governments as we seek to implement these values. We are active participants in the Partnership for Peace program, and we hope to expand that cooperation with NATO in the near future. We seek further integration with European and Euro-Atlantic security structures. As has already been mentioned, we are under pressure constantly from some of our neighbors who either do not share our values, or who wish to control us. We cannot resist those pressures on our own; we must have Western support.

A fifth objective of Azerbaijan's foreign policy is the creation of a climate that will foster the economic development of Azerbaijan and the entire region, as well as integration with the Western economies. We have already discussed the oil Azerbaijan can provide for Western markets, but there are many other items of commerce that we can trade. We need to fully re-establish the old Silk Road by development of the Eurasian Transport Corridor, which will enhance regional cooperation through shared prosperity.

I have now discussed Azerbaijan's geo-strategic importance by looking at its geography and its mineral wealth, and I have outlined Azerbaijan's five basic foreign policy objectives. Now, let us turn to the United States' interests and how its foreign policy and geo-strategic interests are affected by Azerbaijan. My argument will be that the geo-strategic interests of the United States and Azerbaijan are largely consistent and compatible, which should give rise to more strategic co-operation between our two countries.

First, we share many of the same values as a nation and as a people. Independence is now taken for granted in the United States, but it is really only nine years old in Azerbaijan. Our feeling on independence is much like that of Patrick Henry and other great American patriots: "Give me liberty or give me death." We are in the process of implementing democracy in Azerbaijan and we have had three Presidential, one parliamentary and one local government elections. These elections have not been perfect, but we are improving. We are also in the process of implementing a free market economy. Almost all small businesses have been privatized. Most of the major sectors of the economy are in the process of being privatized. We are carrying out land reform. We believe in [the] separation of church and state. Although a largely Muslim country, we have a very secular government and protect the religious freedoms of all.

Second, I believe America does not want to see Russia reestablish the old czarist or Soviet empire. As such, the United States has an interest in the future independence of the former Soviet Republics such as Azerbaijan and Georgia. In fact, Azerbaijan is the only former Soviet republic other than the Baltics that has no Russian troops on its soil, and Georgia is in the process of removing Russian troops from its soil. We wish to have friendly relations with Russia, but we know old habits die hard with some Russians. If Russia were to re-exert control over Georgia and Azerbaijan, you would have the beginnings of a new Russian empire, and that would probably bring about a new Cold War with the West. It is for this reason that the United States has a strong interest in the continued independence of Azerbaijan and Georgia, and it is also why the United States must take those actions necessary to help us preserve our independence.

Third, the United States has a strong interest in development of energy supplies outside the Middle East. Taken together, the Caspian Sea Basin countries represent the best hope for new non-Middle Eastern energy supplies. The United States and Azerbaijan also share similar views on the best route for the Main Export Pipeline, specifically a route that is not under the control of the Russians, or the Iranians.

Fourth, the United States realizes that Azerbaijan is one key to the future development of the five new Central Asian republics. Whether a secular government committed to democracy and free markets can survive in Azerbaijan will have an influence on the new governments of Central Asia, as well as other Muslim countries throughout the world. The question before all of these countries is whether the Turkish or Iranian model will prevail. Those of us in Azerbaijan have decided in favor of the Turkish model, which is consistent with American geo-strategic interests.

Fifth, I believe the United States supports the arms control policies of Azerbaijan in the region. We are for [the] non-proliferation of weapons of mass destruction, we are for [the] de-militarization of the Caspian Sea Basin, and we support a nuclear-free zone in the Southern Caucasus. We support a mutual regional security pact for stability in the Southern Caucasus. We support all existing arms control treaties. In other words, we support de-militarization of the region, which I believe is also consistent with American foreign policy.

Sixth, the United States has a friend in Azerbaijan in its other foreign policy objectives. Azerbaijan supported American policy in Bosnia and Kosovo, and has sent a military unit to Kosovo under the auspices of Turkey. Azerbaijan supported NATO enlargement and its objective of maintaining a stable Europe. Azerbaijan is a strong friend of Israel. Azerbaijan has withstood Iranian pressure to impose a radical Islamic regime.

Seventh, the United States has strong relations with both Armenia and Azerbaijan, and it does not relish being constantly placed in the middle of this conflict. The United States does, however, support the concept of territorial integrity, which is at issue in the war. For this reason, the United States' interest is in seeing the conflict settled on internationally recognized principles.

But with all these areas of strategic cooperation, there is one item I must mention before closing. In 1992, when Congress was enacting the Freedom Support Act to provide assistance to the former Soviet republics, pro-Armenian members of Congress successfully supported an amendment-known as Section 907-which prohibits any direct American assistance to the government of Azerbaijan. This discriminatory piece of legislation was enacted at a time when Azerbaijan had no embassy, ambassador or other representation in Washington, and while we have successfully modified this provision over the years, Congress insists on retaining it.

Both the Clinton Administration and the Bush Administrations strongly oppose Section 907, but because of the politically active Armenian Diaspora, we have been unable to repeal this provision of law. Azerbaijan finds it inconsistent in the extreme for the United States to maintain Section 907 at a time when Azerbaijan has literally and figuratively cast its lot with the West. This, to my way of thinking, is a classic example of the negative impact of ethnic politics on American foreign policy, and it does not reflect well on the world's sole remaining superpower.

In conclusion, let me reiterate my original premise. The geo-strategic interests of the United States and Azerbaijan are largely consistent and compatible, and those interests argue for increased strategic cooperation between the two countries. Such increased cooperation will not only benefit both Azerbaijan and the United States, but I also believe it would be in the best interest of peace and stability in the world.

"Current Issues in International Relations and The U.S.-Azerbaijan Ties: An Ambassador's Perspective" Speech Before the Future World Leaders' Summit. Presidential Classroom Washington, DC July 9, 2000

It is a pleasure for me to be addressing so many outstanding student leaders today. This appearance takes me back a few years when I was a professor of physics in my own country of Azerbaijan. Since that time, I have done my best not to miss a single opportunity of meeting university-based audiences. It is always a thrill for me to meet with young people who one day will fill roles of leadership and influence the future. One of you may some day be your country's Ambassador to Azerbaijan; and who knows, there may be a future President or two in our midst today.

First, let me acquaint you with my country. Azerbaijan is a relatively small country of eight million people. We have a Muslim majority in our country, but we have a secular government. We are one of the fifteen former Soviet republics and re-established our independence in 1991. Azerbaijan is very important geo-politically, located at the crossroads between East and West, North and South, and neighboring Russia to our north, Iran to the south, and Turkey to the west. The Caspian Sea is on our eastern border. Azerbaijan is also becoming an important country economically, as we have signed about twenty production-sharing agreements worth $60 billion with oil companies from throughout the world since 1994. We are also strong allies of the United States and share a common viewpoint on independence, democracy, and free markets.

Though having only recently reacquired its independence, my country has a long and rich history. Throughout millennia, it has produced many outstanding poets and writers, scholars and scientists, being known as one of the cradles of civilization.

I thought I could make best use of my time this evening by describing for you what an ambassador does, how he [or she] does it, and what the consequences are of his or her actions.

Put in simplest terms, an ambassador's job is to represent the interests of his country in the country where he [or she] serves. It is my job to educate the American people about Azerbaijan, as I am doing tonight with you, and to work for improved relations between Azerbaijan and the United States. That means primarily working with the U.S. Government, both the executive and legislative branches, but also reaching out to other groups and individuals.

To that end, one of my highest priorities as Ambassador of Azerbaijan has been to encourage more student exchanges, with American students studying in Azerbaijan, and Azerbaijani students studying in the United States. We have faced some difficulties, which I will go into later, but we are making good progress. English is becoming the world's first language, so it is not hard to get Azerbaijani students interested in learning English, but we do not have enough American students who wish to learn the Azerbaijani language. However, Russian is a good second language in Azerbaijan, and since Azerbaijani belongs to a Turkic language group, we have no problem whatsoever communicating with other Turkic peoples.

I would like to encourage each of you to visit Azerbaijan sometime in the future. You will find our people to be extremely nice and friendly. We are a very family-oriented society and our culture teaches us to treat our visitors as if they were members of our family. In my seven years as Ambassador, I have never seen a foreigner who was disappointed by his or her visit to Azerbaijan.

A second education-related priority has been the establishment of learning centers about Azerbaijan in the United States. Last year, the U.S.-Azerbaijan Chamber of Commerce opened a Caspian Studies Program at Harvard University, and similar programs are in the process of being established at other universities. These programs will lead to greater knowledge of Azerbaijan in academic and political circles, and eventually this knowledge will spread among average citizens.

At the same time, more and more Americans are visiting Azerbaijan, in large part due to the great oil and gas exploration that is going on there. We have scores of American families living in Baku, whereas there were none during the Soviet era. The American media is beginning to pay attention to Azerbaijan and the last James Bond movie was filmed in part in Azerbaijan.

Having said all this, Azerbaijan is still relatively unknown to most Americans, in part because it is a small country that has only been independent for nine years, and in part because there are so many other things that occupy the time of Americans such as school, work, family, and entertainment. That does not leave much time for other things, but that is why you are so important, because you make the time for considering other things in life.

Perhaps you can best understand the role of an ambassador by looking at what happens when a country does not have an ambassador or an embassy. That was our situation here in the U.S. in 1992, right after Azerbaijan achieved independence from the former Soviet Union. Unfortunately, at that time-and still today-Azerbaijan was involved in a conflict with Armenia, resulting from the latter's territorial claims. The large Armenian Diaspora in the United States also has two rather large lobbying organizations that are very effective within Congress.

So, in 1992, when a legislation called Freedom Support Act came before Congress, the Armenian lobby groups approached their friends in Congress and persuaded them to enact an amendment denying any U.S. assistance to the government of Azerbaijan. This provision, known as Section 907, was placed in bills in the House and Senate and enacted into law because the Bush Administration, which opposed Section 907, did not believe it could veto the entire bill over one relatively small provision.

This was achieved primarily because Azerbaijan did not have an ambassador or an embassy at the time, and there was no appreciable Azerbaijani Diaspora in the United States. In other words, there was no one available to lobby against Section 907. What was the result of this provision of law? Only the unjust punishment of victims of aggression instead of the aggressor. It meant that for four years, hundreds of thousands of Azerbaijani refugees and internally displaced persons were ineligible even for American humanitarian aid. It also meant that the Government of Azerbaijan could receive no assistance from the U.S. in setting up democratic procedures or market reforms. It meant that no U.S. assistance could be made available for education, health or environmental programs.

So naturally, one of my first and major tasks upon my arrival to Washington in 1993 was to seek [the] elimination of Section 907.

In 1997, we were able to secure exceptions-sometimes called "carve-outs"-to Section 907 for democracy building, humanitarian assistance, and activities of the Foreign Commercial Service, the Trade Development Agency, OPIC and the Export Import Bank. We are working for additional exceptions this year, and our eventual goal remains outright repeal.

So you can see that as an ambassador, I had to learn American politics in a hurry. Some of you who have studied American government know how difficult it can be to secure real change in the American system. Unlike most governments, the American executive and legislative branches are not necessarily controlled by the same party, and even if they are, it does not guarantee coordinated policy direction. The Administration may favor one policy and the Congress another.

All the while these matters were going on, as Ambassador, I had many other challenging assignments. Between 1994 and now, we have had five Presidential visits here, with President Aliyev meeting President Clinton and other top-level U.S. officials. This has meant that the Embassy has had to coordinate meetings with the White House and other cabinet-level departments, participate in negotiations regarding joint statements to be issued, and follow up on comments and suggestions made by both sides. We have also had numerous ministerial visits etc. Just recently, our Foreign Minister-the equivalent of your Secretary of State -was in town for a host of meetings that we set up and attended; but that is only part of what we do. We must explore issues beforehand, brief our Foreign Minister, and make recommendations for the meetings he attends. We also arranged a very successful official visit for our Defense Minister last week.

Any time a foreign policy issue in the U.S. affects, or potentially affects, Azerbaijan, I must get involved. When American policy is potentially detrimental to Azerbaijan, I seek to change that policy. By the same token, I am constantly seeking cooperation of the U.S. on policies mutually beneficial to both countries. We also work closely with other like-minded embassies. Our Embassy is often the point of first contact for American firms wishing to do business in

Azerbaijan. The Embassy is also where Americans wishing to visit Azerbaijan can get the necessary travel visas.

In conclusion, let me encourage each of you to consider diplomacy as a career. For the most part, diplomacy is carried out by your State Department, but like me, you do not have to be a career diplomat to become an ambassador. But, you must be successful in some career field to become an effective ambassador. You must have an interest in international relations and the cross-currents that exist between nations. To do that, you must also have some familiarity with the history of the region you work in.

There is certainly no more challenging or rewarding a field of endeavor than diplomacy. It is in essence the art of making sure countries get along with each other-in other words, avoiding war as a method of settling disputes. It is an opportunity to pursue idealistic objectives, while operating in the most real parts of the "real world." It is the perfect job for someone who is patriotic and nationalistic. It gives you the opportunity to serve your nation in a most unselfish way.

And last, but not least, it is exciting and rewarding work. You never have a dull day. You never know when you wake up what you will be dealing with that day. You meet the most interesting and challenging people in the world. At the same time, I must warn you about the only thing on the tough side, which is to survive all diplomatic receptions, a little bit too diplomatic to the taste of someone who has made a transfer to diplomacy from an academic background.

Something on a personal note: I consider my whole career to be a success, and let me tell you why. I am very grateful to my previous scientific career for the opportunities to meet numerous outstanding people, including many Nobel Prize winners, and now, in the diplomatic community for almost seven years, I have had chances to meet and even make friends with so many personalities, for whom I have utmost respect, including Dr. Brzezinski, Secretary Kissinger, and many others. In that sense, I am a happy man.

I hope that I have been able to give you some insight into what being an ambassador is like, and I hope that I have been able to encourage some of you to pursue diplomacy as a career. And I hope to see many of you in Azerbaijan one day.

Remarks at American Culture Studies Program
Washington University
St. Louis, Missouri
November 2, 2000

It is a distinct pleasure for me to appear here for the second time already, to discuss habits of democracy in the context of Azerbaijan.

Today, I will try to concentrate, as our distinguished hosts have asked me to, on the interrelation between public debates and other forms of discourse on one hand, and historic and cultural traditions on the other.

To begin with, I would like to emphasize that the tradition of public debate in the Azerbaijani culture dates to the pre-Islamic period, as far back as [the] seventh century AD. It is exactly at that time that the ancient Turkic epic, "Kitab-i-Dede-Korkud," depicted [the] struggles between early feudal rulers of Azerbaijani principalities, dealt with both [the] political and moral responsibilities of individuals in emerging societies, [and] became the first documentation of how the problem had been tackled in the times of our ancestors. One of the most fascinating ideas of the whole book is attributed to one of the main protagonists, Bayandur-khan, who calls on his vassals and other rulers to "abandon grudge, and envy, and bitterness" to "pursue what is best for the people," [and] "not to resort to arms" when a problem can be solved "through wits." Would you consider, please, that this had been written almost one thousand years prior to Francois

Rablais' "Gargantua and Pantagruel," and Machiavelli's "The Prince."

This trend's foundations were laid by numerous outstanding thinkers, both philosophic and religious, who advocated human beings' right for independence of expression, be it through thought or action, and its peak was between the years of 1100 and 1200 AD.

It was not until the canonization of Islam that the ideas of public discourse started receding slowly. Even then, though, theories of liberal thinking have been very strong in Azerbaijan.

During the Soviet rule, the entity of a public debate became a considerably less-known notion to my people, since any kind of discourse had become largely formal in these times. Nevertheless, despite the lack of real hot-blooded discussions, the basic set of rules that applied has remained the same all through this period of seventy years; personal politeness bordering courtesy; non-aggressive argumentation; inadmissibility of personal attacks, etc.

Of course, it was much easier to follow this "game plan" under the Soviets when all sides basically advocated the same thing. After the restoration of Azerbaijan's independence following the collapse of the Soviet Union, discourse became much more heated and, sometimes, sides tended to turn ideological disagreements into personal quarrels and animosities. And this is where I wanted to say a couple of words on the interrelation between cultural traditions and political process in the United States.

I have been following, in my almost eight years as an Ambassador, both Presidential and Congressional races with great attention, and one thing is very unusual, not to say shocking, to me. What I have in mind is how the candidates treat or, should I say, mistreat each other using strong words and epithets, not shying away from sometimes vicious personal attacks. But it is okay, I guess, since the U.S. political culture allows people to remain on socially amicable terms after the unpleasantness of some of their exchanges of opinions.

In Azerbaijan, it is nothing like that. Once you humiliate your opponent (and any personal attack is considered humiliating in my country), you can never be on good terms again personally. This is a mistake many have made in Azerbaijan after the restoration of independence, by trying to impose Western traditions of public debate on our society without considering traditional specifics of our society.

Let me bring one more example to your attention: the Senate race in Missouri. After the tragic death of Governor Carnahan, it is certain now that his widow Jean will take his place if the Democratic candidate wins, but this involves extensive campaigning using the late Mel Carnahan's name. That type of a campaign is unthinkable in Azerbaijan, where we try to avoid bringing up the name of the deceased in any kind of debate before forty days have passed since the day of his death to "let his spirit rest in peace."

So, what I am trying to say is that we differ greatly as far as means of pursuing public discourse are concerned, but that does not necessarily change our commonality on the substance.

Presentation at GUUAM Workshop
Stanford University
San Francisco
November 18, 2000

I am very happy to be here today to speak on a topic, which is so thrilling for me, and not only for me, I guess. This workshop under the auspices of the distinguished Stanford University lives up to our expectations. These expectations are that the interest to our countries, shown by the U.S. on the level of political leadership, will be seconded by the academic community, creating the atmosphere of public discourse which has to be a part of any foreign policy discussion if it is to reach any level of prominence.

Since 1991, we all, the whole world, have lived in a period of transition. The definition of the "post-cold-war period" is not something lasting. The great powers and small countries alike have to be ready to address a new, broad set of multidimensional security issues.

The group of countries then called GUUAM came into existence during the most intensive discussions on CFE Flank Agreement in the mid-1990s, at the time when [the] "Russia First" approach was still dominating U.S. foreign policy, when any sort of political issue was looked at through the prism of development of U.S.-Russia relations. I do not think we have overcome this completely even now, and we still witness the same kind of an approach here in America on many instances: we keep being called "Newly Independent States," or the "Independent States of the Former Soviet Union," and some analysts still refer to us, on occasion, as Russia's "backyard." How long does a sovereign nation have to exist to become just a plain State, without adjectives, to disassociate itself from the former regime? I would like to urge decision-makers not to play into the hands of those who never accepted our country's independence.

But, back to the Conventional Forces in Europe Treaty. At that time, Azerbaijan, and three other states- Georgia, Moldova, and Ukraine-moved to address their mutual needs and concerns, seeking Western understanding and assistance. Despite occasional suspicions, the GUUAM had no aims against any other state. The four of us, indeed, sought U.S. support in either keeping foreign troops out of the region, or getting them withdrawn. By the time the CFE Flank Agreement discussions started to unveil, there were no foreign forces on Azerbaijani soil, with the exception of the so-called "gray area" under Armenian occupation, which currently is not under my Government's control, and, thus, can host unaccounted TLE (Treaty Limited Equipment). This very "gray zone" has become a factor in the transfers of WMD and sensitive technologies, as well as in drug-trafficking and the spread of terrorism. In this context, the struggle for power between the "leaders" of the puppet regime of NK also shows to the whole world that in this area of instability, which presents a real security challenge for all of us, the proclaimed ideas of separatism have been used to serve ulterior motives of personal enrichment.

So, as regards the Flank Agreement of 1997, it was not until Vice-President Gore's last minute phone call to President Aliyev that Azerbaijan agreed to compromise on some of its vital interests, in order not to undermine the CFE Treaty.

Since that time, the GUUAM group has passed through a number of important stages in its development, marked by the Joint Communiqué of the four Presidents, signed in Strasbourg in 1997 [which included] the accession of Uzbekistan, the adoption of a Declaration during the Washington Summit in 1999, and the signing of a memorandum during the New York Summit of 2000. Besides summits, new dimensions of GUUAM interaction have started to emerge to include cooperation on the level of foreign and defense ministers. The process has also gone far beyond cooperation on issues of arms control, expansion to include such areas as national security in general, as well as broad economic initiatives, including those within the framework of the TRACECA project. Regular meetings of national coordinators of the GUUAM countries have become a crucial element of the cooperation, turning into one of the pillars of the group.

CFE-related matters, which were at the cradle of GUUAM, still remain one of the pillars of participating states' interaction. Currently, as we approach the May 2001 CFE review conference, a number of new issues have arisen. After the OSCE Istanbul summit of 1999, we could already foresee that Russia, despite being cornered into agreeing to withdraw its troops from Georgia and Moldova, would try to avoid full compliance. By [the] redeployment of forces from Georgia to Armenia, Moscow continues to build up its military presence in Armenia, and by doing so, further complicate the uneasy situation in the region. Russia's policy in the region is aimed, as top military representatives in Moscow have more than once indicated, at staying in the region of South Caucasus. The bilateral military cooperation agreement between Moscow and Yerevan compromises Moscow's position as a mediator in its capacity as a Minsk Group co-chair. In this regard, I would remind you that the U.S., another co-chair, being barred from fully cooperating with Azerbaijan militarily as a result of an infamous congressional restriction (Section 907 of FSA), restrains from military cooperation with Armenia likewise.

Let me tell you, that it is not only about Kremlin's aspirations to retain a status of a military power, or even about the security of a couple of small states, like Azerbaijan, Georgia, and Moldova. We talk here about integrity of the whole CFE flank zone, about the backbone of the Treaty itself, and I can not but praise the resolute and principled approach of both Tbilisi and Chisinau here, which enables the international community to exercise tighter control over Russia so that it lives up to its Istanbul obligations.

It is also about the beginning of a qualitatively new dialogue between NATO and GUUAM, which can become one of the pillars of regional security, especially considering the GUUAM countries' involvement and bilateral ties with the

Alliance, and also the role that this dialogue can play in solving the matters of energy pipeline security.

One more thing, which I absolutely have to mention, is the situation in North Caucasus. Hostilities in Chechnya, as well as the complicated political climate in the neighboring republics not only lead to outbursts of brutality and suffering by civilians, but also, according to Moscow, justify concentration of Russian troops along the borders with Georgia and Azerbaijan. By refusing to discuss any limitations as far as these troops are concerned, as alleged sub-limits, Russia makes it clear that it has little intention of curbing its military presence in the region of Caucasus as a whole.

All of our five countries have yet another commonality which I wanted to discuss now. It is settlement of conflicts and conflict-resolution related activity. The problem is that we, all of us, have conflicts to deal with, either internal, or external in nature. These conflicts, in all their dimensions-political, economic, security, and social-drive the GUUAM participants to even closer cooperation, be it on conflict-resolution, or peace-keeping. That cooperation includes studying the nature of conflicts and decrying their roots and influence, as well as bringing together a peace-keeping force in Kosovo. By 2001-2002, we hope to achieve a new level of interaction, a joint peace-keeping training facility, and a peace-keeping force of a battalion. And our defense minister has already discussed the practical aspects of these issues during the recent meeting of ministers of defense in Kiev, Ukraine.

I would like to make a reference to an article written by Professor Stephen Blank, and published in the Fall Issue of *World Affairs*. Called, "American Grand Strategy and the Transcaspian Region," this article states that (and I quote), "the disproportion between Russia and the smaller Transcaspian states means that no natural equilibrium is possible there. Although this local disproportion in Russia's favor hardly means that Russia can succeed at will across Central Asia, it does mean that if any regional balance, on energy or other major security issue, is to be achieved, someone else must lend power to the smaller littoral states to anchor that balance. The analysts who argue against any major American involvement fail to understand the tragic situation of the region."

Based on that insightful quotation, I want to urge you, U.S. scholars, to play your significant role in guiding the U.S. Government towards a greater support of the states of the region, and of GUUAM in particular.

Historically, our nations have been passively subjected to the Great Game played out among the powers. Now, to turn the Great Game into Great Gain, it is time for us to become rightful players and we can do so only if united. This is yet another rationale for the GUUAM.

We have to understand that the perspectives for our future are inter-linked, and that our effort too, must be a coordinated one, which also means that to go through the transition period I have mentioned earlier, we have to necessarily think about the security of all, not just individual states.

"GUUAM: Genesis and Growth of a Group"
Presentation at the Black Sea Regional Security Program
Harvard University
May 31-June 1, 2001

I have been asked to speak on a very interesting and challenging topic, covering both [the] dimensions of security, economic, military, and other cooperation among the members of GUUAM, and more specific issues, including energy security and the problems of energy transportation, including pipeline security.

Allow me to start with a general observation. Periodically, resurfacing rumors about GUUAM's demise have been greatly exaggerated. This CFE-born group of four (at the moment of its establishment) was a product of close cooperation among delegations of Azerbaijan, Georgia, Moldova and Ukraine, which started during the Flank Agreement Talks in Vienna. In 1997, at the Strasbourg Council of Europe Summit, the Presidents of the four nations made a precise definition of the group's then-objectives, which remain unchanged now, realizing how important it is to develop the interaction "for the sake of a stable and secure Europe guided by the principles of respect for the sovereignty, territorial integrity, inviolability of state frontiers, mutual respect, cooperation, democracy, supremacy of law and respect for human rights."

In 1999, at the NATO-50 Summit in Washington, Uzbekistan joined the group. It was at this time that GUUAM's nature started being perceived by the international community as something wider than merely a group of nations sharing a similar agenda of arms control regime. It had become an important structure for enhancing regional economic cooperation through the development of the Europe-Caucasus-Asia transportation corridor, and a forum for discussion on various levels of existing security problems, promoting conflict resolution and the elimination of other risks and threats.

In the year 2000, this development continued further, turning GUUAM into a very effective forum for interaction, at least from an Azerbaijani perspective. Along with on-going regular meetings of the Committee of National Coordinators, a number of other significant and high-level events took place. In May of 2000, a seminar was held on GUUAM in the U.S. Senate under the aegis of the Foreign Relations European Affairs Chairman, Gordon Smith, concentrating on the approach of the participating countries to the future of this group. GUUAM's contribution to the counter-proliferation of weapons of mass destruction and sensitive technologies was specifically emphasized. As yet another proof of GUUAM's growing visibility on Capitol Hill, the U.S. Senate passed the Defense and Security Assistance Act of 2000. This legislation contains one whole section dealing with GUUAM and provided $8.5 million in fiscal year 2001 and $37 million in fiscal year 2002. I highly appreciate efforts of the many senators who fought for this bill and also for providing better assistance to GUUAM. At the same time, I have to mention that none of the $8.5 million has been appropriated up to now. I can only hope that in the coming year, the situation will change for the better.

In Vienna, on November 26, the Ministers of Foreign Affairs of all five members adopted the Joint Communiqué, approving the Perspective Plan of Development of GUUAM for 2000-2001, discussing the possibility of establishment of the Public Consultative Council and drafted an agreement on the free trade zone. A meeting of the Ministers with the U.S. Secretary of State also took place there, reiterating the ever-growing American interest in GUUAM.

U.S. universities have started showing considerable academic interest in GUUAM, covering multi-faceted interaction within the group. A number of events, including the GUUAM workshop at Stanford and discussions at Washington University in St. Louis, also took place in 2000. A current Harvard initiative on GUUAM, being pursued within the framework of the Black Sea Security Program, is an excellent example and an indicator of the American public's growing attention.

GUUAM shares the international community's goals and tasks of peaceful settlement of conflicts and crises on the basis of respect for sovereignty, territorial integrity and inviolability of the internationally recognized borders of states; combating ethnic intolerance, separatism, extremism and terrorism in all their manifestations, including illegal arms deliveries, organized crime, illicit drug and human trafficking as well as other illegal activities that flourish in the conflict zones.

If asked which areas of cooperation within GUUAM are the most important from an Azerbaijan's perspective, I would outline the following top priorities:

First, political interaction within the framework of integration into Euro-Atlantic and European structures of security and cooperation; this includes the establishment of interaction with the UN, OSCE, European Union and other international organizations, as well as dialogue with NATO based on mutual interests. It is fully acknowledged by the GUUAM countries that developing a safe and reliable infrastructure comprised of well-trained and well-equipped forces and institutions will undoubtedly make a considerable contribution to the European and world security architecture. In this regard, special efforts are being made to strengthen regimes of non-proliferation of nuclear and other weapons of mass destruction, as well as sensitive technologies, and the prevention of arms transfer to conflict zones and drug-trafficking.

Second, economic cooperation. First steps were made on the path towards establishing the Europe-South Caucasus-Central Asia transit corridor, in which the GUUAM countries will play a very important role because of their geo-strategic location.

Cooperation in the energy sector includes working together on several major goals which include minimizing the effects of external financial crises in the GUUAM countries, supporting each other against growing challenges to regional security and stability, accelerating the development of Caspian oil deposits, and constructing multiple pipelines to the international markets. The Main Export Pipeline, which will lead from Baku in Azerbaijan through Tbilisi, Georgia, and over to the Turkish Mediterranean port of Ceyhan, is in the finishing stages of the basic engineering and a detailed engineering study, will start this fall. This pipeline will become a backbone for the whole transportation corridor. In my mind, it is high time for all of us, including our Western partners, to think about pipeline security issues.

A recent seminar (May 2-5, 2001) on cooperation among the Chambers of Commerce of GUUAM member-states, held in Baku and attended also by representatives of Czech Republic, Slovakia, Latvia, Bulgaria, Romania, and Kazakhstan, became another vivid demonstration of the commonality of economic interests, as confirmed during a meeting of the participants with President Heydar Aliyev of Azerbaijan. The seminar also reaffirmed that these interests do not lie solely in the field of energy. A number of recommendations were adopted by the participants, including establishing a Co-ordination Committee of the Chambers of Commerce of GUUAM, creating an inter-parliamentary group for economic cooperation, simplification of customs procedures and formalities, harmonization of customs-related legislation, support for creating a free-trade zone, etc. Establishing several new entities was also recommended [including] a Congress of Entrepreneurs' Unions of GUUAM, a Joint Bank of GUUAM, [and] also joint transportation, insurance, leasing, and tourist and business structures.

And, finally, third, [the] cooperation in opposing ethnic and religious intolerance. The GUUAM states believe that both religious extremism and ethnic terrorism are among main reasons of numerous regional conflicts. And we in Azerbaijan, with 20 percent of our territory under foreign military occupation and approximately 1 million refugees and displaced persons, attach special importance to the peaceful settlement of regional conflicts based on respect for sovereignty, territorial integrity and inviolability of the frontiers of all states. This is, as mentioned earlier, one of the key GUUAM objectives.

My country considers that by acquiring additional experience, as was gained through participating in the peacekeeping operations in Kosovo, GUUAM countries will not only make a contribution to settling regional conflicts, but will also further strengthen their own stabilizing roles on the international arena. In the context of all the aforementioned tasks, NATO-GUUAM cooperation, activities in the framework of PFP programs and relations with the United States are of significant importance to my country. Azerbaijan views the potential of these contacts as one of the crucial elements in further promoting GUUAM's role as that of a force for peace in Eurasia.

In the recent year, cooperation and mutual support of the five countries at the international forums became even closer, with the GUUAM members not only coordinating their positions, but undertaking joint initiatives as well, with the intercultural dialogue and common statement on terrorism being the two most explicit examples at the United Nations.

We also attach great importance to institutionalizing GUUAM by further promoting the existing consultation mechanisms on the level of Heads of States, foreign and defense ministers, as well as among the national coordinators for GUUAM. A recent May 17-18, 2001 meeting of the coordinators in Kiev became a step towards the upcoming summit of Presidents in Yalta, to take place next week. We expect that this summit will bring the efforts to a fruitful conclusion.

On numerous occasions, we have witnessed that many in Moscow view GUUAM as something either very fragile and on the verge of dissolving, or a menacing threat to the very foundations of Russia's policy; all that, only because of the perceived "anti-Russian" nature of this group. As recently stated by *Nezavisimaya Gazeta,* even the most innocent efforts aimed at coordinating policies of the former Soviet republics are sometimes viewed as dangerous and unacceptable by politicians in Moscow, if Russia is not part of this process.

We see GUUAM as a structure that should bring security and stability to our part of post-Soviet space, by constructively engaging former Soviet republics into relationships of cooperation, replacing rivalry and animosity. This example of cooperation in a region known for its deep political, as well as other divisions, sets a very positive precedent of inclusion, not exclusion, in a new age of globalization. Interest shown by other nations (namely, Bulgaria and Romania) to interacting closely with GUUAM and maybe even going further in their relations with this group than just cooperation, has shown the potential for future development.

In conclusion, I would like to express my utmost gratitude to the organizers, especially Ms. Huntington and Mr. Konoplyov, for their efforts to make this event happen.

Thank you all for your interest to GUUAM [and] I hope this interest will grow just as this group's role and importance grow, too.

Speech at the Ceremony Dedicated to the Twenty-Fifth Anniversary of Baku-Houston Sister Cities Association
January 2001

It is a genuine pleasure to be here to help celebrate the twenty-fifth anniversary of the Sister City relationship between Houston and Baku. I suppose some would say there is nothing unusual about this event because anniversaries come and go every day; but, to me, this is a significant event and a significant day because it causes me to think about what was before, what is today, and what might be in the future.

For most of our Sister City relationship, Baku and Azerbaijan have not been free. We were merely pawns in the Soviet Empire. We existed to serve others. Our great farms fed the empire's masses. Our oil fueled the Soviet industrial and war machine. Our sons served, usually as privates, in the Soviet army. Our poets and writers and musicians were little recognized, and our nationhood was denied.

Today, we are a free and sovereign nation. We have now had a series of elections in which we freely chose our own President and Parliament. We are free to come and go when we please; we have a free and open media. We are developing our own oil industry-with the help of many companies based right here in Houston. We now celebrate our great Azerbaijani artists in all cultural fields. Most important of all, we are a free people. We do not belong to anybody else's empire-we control our own destiny. As a result, I believe [that] our Sister City relationship will flourish and [that] we will be able to do many great and wonderful things together in the future.

Economics and trade, of course, first come to mind. The energy sectors of Baku and Houston will, in my opinion, become closely associated and create great wealth and thousands of good jobs in both countries. This will lead to the founding of support and service industries, many cultural exchanges, and the formation of lasting friendships between individuals, as well as our two great cities.

At the turn of the century, Baku was the oil capital of the world, and when you visit our lovely seaside capital, you will see that the most beautiful architecture in Baku resulted from oil revenues. Our great tradition of opera and both classical and traditional music received enormous support from the wealth created by oil. The entire culture was improved and somewhat Westernized at that time.

My prediction is that our future will be closely connected with the United States as we use our new freedom and our new wealth to blend the best of Azerbaijani tradition and culture with the newly-discovered cultural, economic, and educational opportunities of the West.

We will grow richer together, both economically and culturally. We will learn from each other. We will work together, and we will play together. It will become common for Americans to speak of their Azerbaijani friends, and vice versa, and we will become true partners and genuine Sister Cities.

"Nagorno-Karabakh: The Key West Negotiations and the Prospects for Peace"
Speech Delivered at the Forum Organized by the Central Asia-Caucasus Institute
John Hopkins University
April 16, 2001

In April 2001, the United States attempted to facilitate the Karabakh peace process and hosted several rounds of talks between President Heydar Aliyev and his Armenian counterpart, Robert Kocharian in Key West, Florida. U.S. Secretary of State Colin Powell was present at the event for the opening ceremony. Both Presidents also met with President George W. Bush following the talks. Unfortunately, the parties failed to agree on major principles and the negotiations collapsed soon after. The Central Asia and Caucasus Institute organized a forum with the participation of the Armenian and Azerbaijani ambassadors, as well U.S. special negotiator for the conflicts, Ambassador Carey Cavanaugh.

Thank you for the invitation to speak at this institute on a very important topic, the recently concluded round of peace talks in Key West. Your institute has sponsored numerous discussions around the Armenia—Azerbaijan conflict and I remember very well that I was invited as one of the first speakers immediately after the inauguration of the Central Asia Institute in 1996. Since that time, many people have spoken here on the issue of the Nagorno-Karabakh conflict, including the President of Azerbaijan.

So, you have an extensive history of discussions on this conflict, but the process of negotiations, obviously, has an even longer history. In my opinion, it would be appropriate to remind you of the most crucial stages in those efforts aimed at bringing peace to the region.

As many of you know, the Minsk Group activity started nine years ago, with the CSCE defining the mandate of the Minsk Conference and, in doing so, establishing the framework for the negotiations process. It was an extremely important decision, since it has created a venue for international mediation to settle this lasting conflict.

Later in 1993, the United Nations Security Council raised the issue of Armenia's aggression against Azerbaijan several times, demanding immediate and unconditional withdrawal of the Armenian occupation forces from Azerbaijani territories as well as creating conditions for the return of refugees and internally displaced persons to their homes. Four resolutions to that effect were adopted that year, but none of these resolutions has been implemented.

In December of 1994, during the CSCE Budapest Summit, a decision was adopted to intensify the activities of the CSCE on the Armenia-Azerbaijan conflict. The CSCE Heads of State agreed on the step-by-step settlement and instructed the CSCE Minsk Conference Co-Chairs to work out an agreement on the cessation of the armed conflict. The agreement was to become the basis for convening the Minsk Conference. A decision was also adopted to deploy the CSCE multi-national peacekeeping forces into the conflict zone. At the OSCE Lisbon Summit in December 1996, another important step was made, and a basic formula for settlement of the conflict was defined. All the OSCE Member States, with the exception of the Republic of Armenia, supported three main principles of the settlement, which ensures the territorial integrity of the Republic of Azerbaijan, granting the highest degree of self-rule within Azerbaijan to the Nagorno-Karabakh region of the Republic of Azerbaijan and security guarantees for its whole population. Unfortunately, Armenia's position made it obvious that this nation was not about to give up its territorial claims.

Since the OSCE Lisbon Summit, Russia, the U.S. and France have been the Minsk Group Co-Chairs. We had great hopes and expectations for them, counting on their efforts to achieve resolution of the conflict, restore territorial integrity of Azerbaijan and return refugees to their homes, but unfortunately, until now, it hasn't happened.

The Minsk Group Co-Chairs have put on the table three proposals on the settlement of the conflict. The first proposal was submitted in June of 1997, and contained a package solution for the conflict. The second one, in October 1997, was based on a step-by-step solution. In November of 1998, the Co-Chairs made a new proposal, this one being on the "common state."

Azerbaijan accepted the first and the second proposals of the Co-Chairs as a basis for the negotiations, despite being fully aware that they in part contradicted some principles of international law, specifically as far as the territorial integrity of Azerbaijan was concerned.

We did not accept the proposal of the Co-Chairs on the "common state;" the term "common state" has no international law basis. It implies that the Nagorno-Karabakh is an independent entity, and grants it equally with Azerbaijan, the status of a subject of the "common state." This proposal not only fully deprives Azerbaijan of a part of its territory, but also de-facto legitimizes Armenian aggression against Azerbaijan.

At the early stages of the Co-Chairs' activity, the approaches of both Russia and the U.S. were bearing obvious traces of a "double-standard policy." In the case of Russia, it was dictated by what I should call a "special relationship with Armenia." In the case of the United States, the approach was championed by the Armenian Diaspora, exploiting American politics.

Azerbaijan considers that the Co-Chairs of the OSCE Minsk Group, guided by the principles of international law, had to exert a positive influence over the negotiation process and promote settlement of the conflict, restoration of my country's territorial integrity and return of the refugees to their homes.

Now, finally, to the Key West summit. As many of you know, it was the most recent of the series of meetings between President Heydar Aliyev of Azerbaijan and Robert Kocharian of Armenia in their ongoing effort to find a peaceful settlement of the conflict. These direct negotiations started in April 1999 in Washington, DC, at the initiative of the U.S. Secretary of State, and it is very symbolic that the new format was introduced during the recent round of talks also held on the U.S. soil and hosted by the new Secretary of State, Secretary Powell. The very fact that new U.S. Administration reacted in such a "hands-on" manner so early in President Bush's tenure is significant.

Once again, here I would like to thank the organizers, especially Ambassador Cavanaugh and his team. As you are aware, there was an extensive opening statement by President Aliyev, which was made available by the press. Let me share with you my understanding of why it was necessary to make such a statement at a point when the history of mediation has already spanned many years and the positions of the sides are well-known. I believe that the international community is not focused enough on the violations of the principles of international law perpetrated by Armenia. We still have to fully inform the international community of the injustices inflicted upon my people, and an obvious example is the continuing harm done by the infamous Section 907.

In Key West, active participation of the OSCE Minsk Group Co-Chairs made it quite visible that the international brokers are not relenting in their efforts to mediate the conflict. We appreciate their activity, despite the fact that in the past the Co-Chairs were often waiting for something to happen between the sides and standing ready to accept it, whatever it would be.

Absence of peace is devastating for both Armenia and Azerbaijan, and also for the region as a whole. Azerbaijan, with almost one million refugees and IDPs, and about 20 percent of its territory occupied, has an imminent interest in bringing about peace and returning the affected persons to their homes. The two Presidents have shown good will in working together to end the conflict, for the better of both peoples and of the whole region of the South Caucasus. In the past, we have been very close to achieving a compromise (for example, in 1999), but then the shooting in the Parliament in Yerevan took place and Armenia renounced the agreement.

Now, as you know, details of the negotiations are kept confidential by both sides and also by the mediators. But, according to the press coverage, there may be more than one opinion on what was achieved in Key West, what was not, and what to expect in the future.

To close with, what are the ways out of this situation, which continues to exist? Of course, there is the idea of renewing hostilities. As you are aware, after the discussions on the Co-Chairs' proposals, which took place in my country's Parliament, the Milli Majlis, public discourse in Azerbaijan became quite heated. A considerable part of the Azerbaijani public does not accept any compromise, considering it inadmissible to allow the other side to use military occupation of the Azerbaijani territories as leverage. Still, I can confirm to you that the Azerbaijani leadership is committed to solving the dispute by peaceful means.

Then, there is a possibility to continue "freezing the situation." This is nothing new to us. We have lived under the current conditions for about a decade now, managing in the meantime to strengthen our economy and solidify Azerbaijan's position in the world.

The third option is to reach a settlement, acceptable to both sides, through mutual compromises. We consider this to be our priority, and hope that Yerevan decides it is in Armenia's best interest, too, to achieve lasting peace.

In October of 1996, during the opening event at this Institute, I said that "what we do have a problem with is the lack of consistency and political will on issues like Nagorno-Karabakh." Now, it is different, and we seem to have awareness, consistency, and political will. This situation creates some hope.

Letters to Members of the U.S. Congress and the U.S. Administration

Although an oil contract had been signed in 1994 which granted the Russian oil company, Lukoil, a 10 percent share of the contract, Moscow still opposed the agreement on the basis that it violated the legal regime of the Caspian Sea. Obviously, Azerbaijan did not agree with the Russian position, as it was an indirect infringement on Azerbaijan's right to its natural resources and sovereignty over its sector of the Caspian Sea. Below is my letter to U.S. Vice-President Al Gore, who met President Aliyev during a U.S.-Russia summit in Cairo.

October 17, 1994

Dear Mr. Vice-President:

Let me express my appreciation for your recent meeting in Cairo with President Aliyev and for your attention to the concerns of Azerbaijan during the recent summit between the United States and Russia.

In particular, we are pleased that you and the President expressed support for the recently-concluded $7 billion oil contract between Azerbaijan and major Western oil companies, including Amoco, Unocal, Pennzoil and McDermott.

As you know, Russian Foreign Minister Kozyrev has raised questions at the United Nations about the legality of the contract; however, Russian Energy Minister Shafrannik supports the contract and Prime Minister Chernomyrdin told President Aliyev any problems are reconcilable.

We do not seek controversy or confrontation on this matter. We wish only friendly relations with Russia, but we must stand firm on issues of sovereignty over our natural resources and our independence. We urge your continued diligence on this matter.

Please, let me thank you for all you efforts on behalf of my country and assure you of my highest respect.

Sincerely,

Hafiz Pashayev

Ambassador

Below is a letter sent to U.S. Ambassador to the United Nations, Madeleine Albright, thanking her for her assistance to and interest in Azerbaijan. Ambassador Albright played an important role in arranging a meeting between President Aliyev and his Armenian counterpart President Ter-Petrosian. The meeting took place at the UN General Assembly in New York, in September of 1994. The letter also highlights some controversial issues raised by the Russian government con-

cerning Azerbaijan's right to oil exploration in the Caspian
Sea.

October 18, 1994

Dear Madam Ambassador:

*First, let me express my appreciation for your recent visit to Baku
and for participating in the meeting between President Aliyev and President Clinton. We are also appreciative of the role you played in arranging a meeting in New York between President Aliyev and President
Ter-Petrossian. President Aliyev was very impressed and grateful.*

*The Azerbaijani government has been greatly encouraged by the re-
cent interest and attention that the United States has paid to the problems and issues affecting my country. We believe this has led to a new
stage in the relationship between the United States and Azerbaijan. We
are particularly pleased with the active role and involvement you have
taken in these matters because increasingly, the United Nations has become a forum where issues of concern to Azerbaijan are discussed and
dealt with by the international community.*

*One of those issues is the recently signed $7 billion oil contract which
Azerbaijan has signed with eleven companies, including Amoco, Unocal,
Pennzoil and McDermortt from the United States, and British Petroleum from the United Kingdom. Under this contract, the consortium will
recover oil from Azerbaijan's offshore reserves in the Caspian Sea over a
thirty-year period. As you are probably aware, the Russian Government
recently submitted to the United Nations a document entitled "Position
of the Russian Federation regarding the legal regime of the Caspian
Sea".*

*In summary, the Russian representative argues that the Caspian
Sea is landlocked and thus "the norms of international maritime law"
do not apply to the Caspian. Further, he argues that laws enacted under
the Soviets prohibit the unilateral development of the energy resources offshore the littoral states of the Caspian. Such an interpretation, of course,
would nullify the recently concluded contract.*

Needless to say, Azerbaijan does not agree with this interpretation, and neither, I might add, do significant segments of the Russian government. In order to promote good will and avoid just such misunderstandings, Azerbaijan awarded 10 percent of its consortium share and expected revenue to Lukoil, the Russian oil company. This was done following amicable negotiations with Lukoil, and assures both Russian participation and Russian benefits.

On the day of the signing ceremony, the Russia's Deputy Energy Minister participated in the ceremony and signed the document on behalf of the Russian Federation. However, the next day Russian Foreign Minister Kozyrev announced that Russia does not recognize the contract. Then came the submission of the document to the United Nations.

Subsequent to that, Russian Energy Minister Yuri Shafrannik was quoted on October 12 by Itar-Tass as saying [that] Russia should not object to the contract and that Russia should actively participate in the project.

The historical record is clear, and can be seen in the well-known book, The Prize, which documents the role Baku and Azerbaijan have played in the development of the oil industry. At the beginning of the twentieth century, 50 percent of the world's oil was produced in Azerbaijan. Developers included the Nobel brothers (of the Nobel Prize family) and the French branch of the Rothschild family.

Indeed, most of the famous buildings, which you saw in Baku, including museums and symphony halls, were built with this early oil money. Much of our modern culture was made possible by the wealth generated from oil. All of this began and was in existence long before Azerbaijan was conquered and then absorbed into the Soviet Union.

Oil development and Azerbaijan's sovereignty over its reserves in the Caspian long pre-date the imposition of Soviet rule, and during the brief period of independence between 1918 and 1920, no one questioned Azerbaijan's continued development of its energy resources in the Caspian. So Azerbaijan's rightful "ownership" of these reserves was universally accepted by the international community from the late 1800s, and has never been questioned before.

In 1970, the then Soviet Union authorities established sectors in the Caspian Sea, whereby Azerbaijan had the right over the offshore oil fields to be developed under the signed contract.

We do not seek confrontation on this matter. Russia is our neighbor and we seek both friendly and cooperative relations with her.

It is our hope that the United States will vigorously resist any effort by Russia's foreign ministry to place restrictions or otherwise limit the contract, which we recently signed with American oil companies. I understand that President Clinton and Vice-President Gore both raised the issue with President Yeltsin during the recent summit. We are grateful for U.S.' attention to this matter, and we urge you to remain firm. This affects not only our economic future, but our independence and sovereignty as well.

Thank you for your concern for Azerbaijan, and I urge you to visit Baku again in the near future.

Sincerely,

Hafiz Pashayev

Ambassador

The year 1994 was also a historical one for the Republican Party. After spending forty years in the minority, Republicans came to control the majority of the House. Representative Newt Gingrich became the new Chairman of the House. The following is my response to one of the letters I received from Representative Gingrich.

November 18, 1994

Dear Congressman Gingrich:

Thank you very much for your letter of November 3, which clarified your views on matters relating to Azerbaijan. Our government is very gratified to know that the assertions made in the memos by the Armenian National Committee of America (ANCA) do not represent your views regarding my country.

Relations between the United States and Azerbaijan have improved dramatically in recent months. We signed a $7 billion oil contract with major Western oil companies-including Amoco, Pennzoil, Unocal and McDermott from the United States-on September 20. On November 15, our Parliament ratified that contract.

President Heydar Aliyev had a meeting with President Clinton during the recent opening of the United Nations, the first meeting ever between the President of the United States and Azerbaijan, and I am pleased to report that the American government has supported Azerbaijan and the Western oil companies in opposing Russian objections to this oil contract.

In fact, the only unfortunate aspect of relations between our two countries today remains Section 907 of the Freedom Support Act, which prohibits any assistance to Azerbaijan. Certain members of Congress have supported this provision despite objections of President Bush and Clinton, former Secretary of State Baker, and many other prominent Americans. My hope is that the 104 Congress will remedy this error by repealing Section 907.

Finally, let me congratulate you upon your pending election as Speaker of the House of Representatives. That is indeed a high honor, and Azerbaijan looks forward to working with you to further the friendship of our two countries.

With warmest personal regards,

Sincerely yours,

Hafiz M. Pashayev

Ambassador

P.S. I read today your remarks concerning Ataturk. I was very impressed that the new Speaker of the House is so well versed on the history of our region. Ataturk is a hero to all Turkic peoples who support secular, democratic government. He was a decisive and determined leader, and you chose an excellent model.

Despite some positive developments in energy relations between Azerbaijan and the United States, Section 907 remained the biggest obstacle for improving U.S.-Azerbaijani relations between 1994 and 2001. While the U.S. Congress awarded Armenia $75 million per year, Azerbaijan still received no assistance. Unfortunately, the U.S. Congress preferred to turn a blind eye to the ongoing humanitarian tragedy in Azerbaijan and made no attempt to repeal Section 907. Below is my letter to Senator Mitch McConnell in which I highlighted the importance of rescinding this unjust provision and its detrimental impact on American energy interests in the region.

January 10, 1995

Dear Senator McConnell:

I have carefully read the announcement of your proposed bill to revise the current United States foreign aid system, and I write to commend your leadership in putting forward bold, new ideas on relations with the nations that have emerged from the former Soviet Union. However, I am disappointed that your bill does not call for the repeal of Section 907 of the Freedom Support Act, despite your previous opposition to it.

That amendment was imprudent to begin with, and, as the situation of the region has changed drastically since its enactment, it is even more inappropriate now. Therefore, I ask that you consider including a provision in your bill to repeal Section 907.

Not only does Section 907 hurt my country, but it runs counter to the philosophy of your new foreign aid bill. You have stated that foreign aid "must preserve political and regional stability." This commitment is evidenced by the prohibition of assistance to Russia if the Russian government "directs, supports, or encourages any action which violates the territorial integrity or national sovereignty of any other state [...]" You wisely introduced similar language in the FY1994 Foreign Operations Appropriations Act, which was applied to all the republics of the former Soviet Union.

However, despite this legislation, the goals of your new bill, and America's interest in the region, the Republic of Armenia continues to receive United States foreign aid assistance, while continuing to violate the principle of respecting the territorial integrity of its neighbors. Indeed, your proposed bill contains a $75 million earmark for Armenia. This is all the more shocking considering that Section 907 prohibits direct American assistance to Azerbaijan, even though Azerbaijan respects the sovereignty of its neighbors and is itself a victim of military occupation by Armenian forces. Such patent injustice must no longer be allowed to occur.

You yourself recognized this during the consideration of the Freedom Support Act in 1992, when you joined with senators Lugar, Sanford and Kassebaum to oppose the amendment, suggesting in a joint statement that "by imposing sanctions against a specific country in the former Soviet Union, this amendment would establish a potentially dangerous precedent of choosing sides in conflicts which have deep historical roots." Your conclusion that, "We simply do not believe that this provision will have any positive effect on resolving the conflict. The effect, regrettably, is more likely to be counter-productive," has proven to be prophetic.

In the time since the passage of Section 907, the realities of the Nagorno-Karabakh conflict have changed dramatically:

(1) Armenian military forces now occupy nearly 20 percent of Azerbaijan territory.

(2) In an October 1994 response to the FY1995 Senate Foreign Operations Appropriations requirement, U.S. AID described Azerbaijan as "one of the world's worst refugee/internally displaced persons situations" and reported that Section 907 had a substantial negative impact on the provision of humanitarian assistance.

(3) Azerbaijan has taken numerous demonstrable steps toward the resolution of the conflict, which might lead to the restoration of normal communications and transportation in the region, including rail and pipeline links to Armenia.

(4) Azerbaijan has abided by a cease-fire mediated by Russia and the CSCE since May 1994, two months prior to its acceptance by the Republic of Armenia.

(5) At the December 1994 CSCE meeting in Budapest, member nations agreed in principle to send a multinational peacekeeping force to the region.

Learning from the Georgian civil war, President Heydar Aliyev has stood fast in his decision not to allow unilateral Russian involvement in Azerbaijan, refusing to permit the stationing of Russian troops and rejecting offers of a unilateral Russian peacekeeping force. In light of this, and given the progress made toward a peaceful settlement of the Nagorno-Karabakh conflict this year, Section 907 is outdated and serves only to punish hundreds of thousands of refugees and displaced persons in Azerbaijan.

There have been other important recent developments in Azerbaijan which have enhanced the direct national interest of the United States. In September 1994, a consortium of international oil companies, including four American firms-Amoco, Pennzoil, UNOCAL, McDermott International-concluded agreements with Azerbaijan to develop three Caspian Sea oil fields with estimated reserves of 3.6 billion barrels of oil. The thirty-year year production sharing agreement, valued at more than $7.5 billion, was ratified by the Parliament of Azerbaijan in November. This marks the beginning of a new, vitally important commercial link between the United States and Azerbaijan. The repeal of Section 907 will help Western companies seeking to do business in Azerbaijan. The Azerbaijani public docs not understand nor like the United States policy. [The] Repeal of this law will serve to restore confidence and trust in America and American companies.

I can assure you that the Republic of Azerbaijan is working hard to end the conflict with the Republic of Armenia peacefully and promptly, to care for its refugees and displaced persons, to maintain its independence vis-à-vis Russia, and to build a growing, free-market economy. These are the goals of your new approach to American international assistance.

The sanctions of Section 907 run counter to all of these goals and to the new direction in U.S. foreign aid proposed in your bill. Ending these sanctions will directly complement the national security and economic interests of the United States. The removal of that amendment would send an important signal to the countries of the region that the United States respects and appreciates nations which pursue policies to develop independent, democratic, free-market republics in the midst of the chaos of the region. Further, the removal of Section 907 would restore American neutrality as it seeks to play the role of an honest broker. This is especially important when you consider that this is the only instance in which the United States has a direct role in negotiating conflict resolution within the territory of the former Soviet Union.

I respectfully request that you add a section to your bill to repeal Section 907. I would be happy to discuss this request with you at your convenience.

Sincerely yours,
Hafiz M. Pashayev
Ambassador

By early 1995, some U.S. congressmen had started to pay close attention to developments in Azerbaijan. Some of them, including Representative Bill Emerson (R-MO), were interested in visiting Azerbaijan, which I welcomed and encouraged.

February 16, 1995
Dear Congressman Emerson:
Thank you very much for your letter about a possible trip to Azerbaijan by representatives of the House and Senate "Breakfast Groups."

Having attended this year's annual Congressional Prayer Breakfast, I am pleased that your group has an interest in visiting Azerbaijan. We would, of course, welcome your delegation, and we will be happy to work with you to facilitate such a visit.

I know that you have a great interest in agriculture, and it is our most important industry other than energy. Cotton, grapes, tobacco, livestock and vegetables are all grown in Azerbaijan.

I also understand that Congressman Hall is interested in issues of hunger and refugees. As you might know, we now have over one million refugees in Azerbaijan due to the conflict with Armenia. That represents one of every seven citizens.

Relations between the United States and Azerbaijan have improved tremendously since we gained our independence after the collapse of the former Soviet Union. We are always happy to have Americans visit our country. Such visits contribute, as you say, to better understanding and greater friendship among the nations of the world.

Please have Mr. Miller or Mr. Heyn contact the Embassy for any assistance they need.

Sincerely,

Hafiz M. Pashayev

Ambassador

On February 14, 1995, Representative Christopher Smith (R-NJ), then Chairman of the House International Relations Committee's Subcommittee on International Operations and Human Rights, introduced the Humanitarian Aid Corridor Act. In his statement, Representative Smith remarked, "Americans open their hearts to refugees and displaced persons in countries less fortunate than their own," but for the U.S. Congress, Azerbaijan with its refugees and internally displaced persons did not make the list of "less fortunate countries," even as efforts to guarantee the delivery of U.S. humanitarian assistance to Armenia continued. Nonetheless, I used this as an opportunity to write Representative Smith, Representative Joseph Kennedy (D-RI) and Representative Frank Pallone (D-NJ) concerning some misleading points in their statements and urging them to extend U.S. humanitarian aid to Azerbaijan.

In 1994, Representative Robert Livingston (R-LA) played an important role in achieving some modifications to Section 907, but the adjustments by no means adequately addressed the humanitarian needs of Azerbaijan or the limited operability of U.S. energy companies there. Thus, in 1995, understanding that a repeal of Section 907 was nearly impossible, I decided to urge the U.S. Congress to at least modify it further. The Clinton Administration supported the rescinding or modification of Section 907, but it was not among its priorities. So while there was little possibility for rescinding Section 907, there remained a chance to change it gradually. During hearings in the Senate Foreign Operations Appropriations Subcommittee, Ambassador James F. Collins, then Senior Coordinator for the U.S. State Department Office of the Ambassador at Large for the New Independent States, did not even mention Section 907. In my letter to Ambassador Collins, I expressed my disappointment at his failure to stress the position of the U.S. Administration on the matter.

March 1, 1995
Dear Jim:

I have just finished reading the testimony that you, Tom Simons and Tom Dine gave before the Senate Foreign Operations Appropriations Subcommittee on February 22. I was extremely disappointed that, unlike last year's testimony by Strobe Talbott, there was no mention of Section 907 of the Freedom Support Act in any of the three statements.

Section 907 is, without doubt, harmful to relations between the United States and Azerbaijan, and I believe it is helping to prolong the conflict by giving the Armenians (and more particularly the American Armenian lobby) the impression that the United States will continue to support them despite their offensives and military occupation, which have created more than one million refugees.

Repeal or even modification of Section 907 would be a clear signal to Armenia and its supporters that the conflict cannot be settled militar-

*ily and that the United States wants and expects both sides to end hos-
tilities, negotiate and reach a compromise solution. As long as Armenia
believes the U.S. will acquiesce in its military operations, they will never
stop them.*

*I know that the Administration opposes Section 907, and tried to
modify it last year. I also know of your personal concerns about this provision inhibiting the ability of the U.S. to play the role of honest broker.*

*Given those views, it is especially disappointing that the Admini-
stration did not take advantage of the opportunity before the Senate subcommittee to advance the cause of repeal or modification.*

Sincerely,

Hafiz Pashayev

Ambassador

Below are my two letters to Representative Sonny Calla-
han, then Chairman of the House Foreign Operations Appropriations Subcommittee, explaining to him why the modification of Section 907 was critical.

June 2, 1995

Dear Mr. Chairman:

*Last year, Congressman Livingston was very helpful in seeking a
modification of Section 907 of the Freedom Support Act, which bans direct U.S. assistance to Azerbaijan-even for humanitarian assistance.
Unfortunately, there was not enough support at that time to achieve success.*

*I am writing to ask for your help to seek modification, not repeal, of
Section 907. I have enclosed language recently proposed by senators
Lugar and Helms, which would make exceptions for humanitarian assistance, programs to promote democracy and free markets, and work
with the Organization for Security and Cooperation in Europe
(OSCE). Both the Bush and Clinton Administrations have urged repeal of Section 907, and last year and this year the Administration
supported modification of Section 907 (See attached State Department
Position Paper).*

Section 907 greatly complicates efforts of the Western oil consortium, which will eventually produce 700,000 barrels oil daily. More importantly, Section 907 implies a lack of political support by the United States for Azerbaijan, whose independence has been jeopardized on more than one occasion since the collapse of the former Soviet Union. Those who would destabilize Azerbaijan believe Section 907 indicates a lack of American support for Azerbaijan.

I urge you to support a modification of Section 907 in the Foreign Operations Appropriation Bill that will be considered next week.
Sincerely,
Hafiz M. Pashayev
Ambassador

June 16, 1995

Dear Representative:

Permit me to briefly discuss with you an amendment that was added to the House Foreign Operations Appropriations Bill, which will come before the House of Representatives on Wednesday.

When Congress passed the Freedom Support Act in 1992, Azerbaijan had neither a U.S. Ambassador, Embassy or Washington representative. As a result, domestic ethnic lobbies successfully persuaded Congress to ban all direct U.S. assistance to Azerbaijan (a provision known as Section 907).

The House Appropriations Committee provided an exception from that ban for funds "to be used solely for humanitarian assistance or democracy-building purposes."

This provision is important because on November 12, Azerbaijan will hold its first-ever parliamentary elections. The government of Azerbaijan is committed to independence, democracy and free markets. We would very much like the advice and assistance of the United States in planning and carrying out these elections and other democratic reforms. We had no opportunity for democracy-building during seventy years of Soviet communist domination.

My arrival to Washington Dulles International Airport (February 6, 1993). I was greeted by the officials from U.S. Department of State, including Ms. Maria Germano. She was very helpful during my first days in Washington.

The first reception on May 25, 1993 at Hay Adams Hotel. Speaking is the first Ambassador of the United States to Azerbaijan, Richard Miles. On the left, Undersecretary of State, Peter Tarnoff.

With Ms. Zuleykha Asadullayeva-Weber, a descendant of one of the first oil barons of Azerbaijan in the early 20th century, Shamsi Asadullayev (1840-1913). In 1922, as a child, Ms. Asadullayeva-Weber and her family were forced to leave Azerbaijan when the communist regime came to power. She was very excited to see the openning of the Embassy of an independent Azerbaijan in Washington, DC. She used to say "My dream has come true!"

With President Bill Clinton and Mrs. Hillary Clinton during the presentation of my Letter of Credence. (April 14, 1993).

Washington is a place for unexpected encounters. During a reception at the house of Ambassador Joe Pressel I met a Nobel Prize winner physicist, Pierre-Gilles de Gennes (and his wife), whose research in the field of superconductivity has inspired many physicists, myself included. This was a field of physics in which I had spent many years studying while at the Academy of Science of Azerbaijan. On the right, Ambassador of Azerbaijan to the United Nations, Yashar Aliyev.

With Baku-born American scientist Lotfi Zadeh, who is a professor at the University of California, Berkeley. He is the founder of the theory of "Fuzzy Logic." On the left, his wife Fay Zadeh; on the right, my daughter, Jamila.

With the legendary singer, Mr. Joe Williams, at Blues Alley jazz club.

With special U.S. negotiators for the Nagorno-Karabakh conflict, Ambassador John J. Maresca (top), Ambassador Steven Mann (middle) and Ambassador Joseph Pressel.

With Dr. Zbigniew Brzezinski in our home in Baku, with my wife Rana and son, Mir Jamal (Dec. 2003).

Visiting Dr. Henry Kissinger in his New York office.

Discussions with Chairman and President of National Democratic Institute, Madam Madeline Albright and Kenneth Wollack.

With Turkish Ambassador, Nuzhet Kandemir (left) and Russian Ambassador, Yuli M. Vorontsov.

Left: With Ukrainian Ambassador, Yuri Sherbak (far left) and Georgian Ambassador, Tedo Japaridze.

Speaking before the constituency of Senator Sam Brownback during a tour for foreign Ambassadors to State of Kansas.

Briefing Congress-
man Dan Burton (R-
IN) about develop-
ments in the U.S.-
Azerbaijan relations.

With President of Amoco
Eurasia, Robert Blanton (far
left) and Congressman Greg
Laughlin (D-TX).

President Heydar Aliyev and Vice-President Al Gore witnessing the signing of an
agreement on energy cooperation between the United States and Azerbaijan during
President Aliyev's official visit in 1997. Co-signers are Foreign Minister of
Azerbaijan Hasan Hasanov (left) and U.S. Secretary of Energy Federico Peña; other
witnesses me, on the far left, Secretary of State Madeline Albright and Secretary of
Commerce William Daley.

Azerbaijan's delegation at the United Nations General Assembly session in 1995: (first row) President Heydar Aliyev, Foreign Minister Hasan Hasanov, Ambassador Eldar Quliyev; (second row) Presidential Adviser Vafa Quluzade, me, Assistant to President Eldar Namazov, and Consular Yashar Aliyev.

President Aliyev meets with Speaker of House Newt Gingrich. On the far left, Congressman John Boehner (R-OH) (1997).

After meeting with President Clinton, President Heydar Aliyev talks to the press (1997).

Lunch at the Blair House (1997). Invitees were Richard Armitage, Alexander Haig, Brent Scowcroft, James Schlesinger, Colin Powell, Zbigniew Brzezinski, Richard Cheney, Anthony Lake.

President's last instructions to Ambassador before leaving the United States (1997).

Secretary Powell speaking at the reception hosted by Secretary Donald Rumsfeld on September 10, 2004.

With Richard Armitage, a good friend and long-term colleague in Washington.

With Richard Cheney before his keynote address at luncheon organized by the U.S.-Azerbaijan Chamber of Commerce (1997).

At the White House Dinner Honoring the Chiefs of Diplomatic Missions hosted by President George Bush and Mrs. Laura Bush (March 2005).

At the residence of Chairman of the Joint Chiefs of Staff Gen. Peter Pace. Mr. and Mrs. Pace hosted a dinner in honor of Azerbaijan's Ambassador and military attaché, Col. Dashdamir Mammadov.

With President Ilham Aliyev and Foreign Minister Elmar Mammadyarov.

During his 2003 visit to Washington, then Prime Minister of Azerbaijan Mr. Ilham Aliyev met with U.S. National Security Adviser, Stephen Hedley.

Meeting with Senator Chuck Hagel (R-NE).

Modification of Section 907 would send an important message to the world community that the United States supports Azerbaijan's independence. During our long history, we have only known five years of true independence and U.S. diplomatic and political support is important to help maintain our independence.

Both the Bush and Clinton Administrations have strongly opposed Section 907, and the State Department recently stated that "The U.S. has a long tradition of providing assistance to the needy, but Section 907 has hindered our efforts to aid almost one million refugees and displaced persons in Azerbaijan. It has also undermined our efforts to help the conflicting parties find a peaceful solution to the Nagorno-Karabakh dispute and to promote democracy and a free market economy in the region."

I urge you to resist any effort to remove or change this modification of Section 907 from the Foreign Operations Appropriations Bill.

Thank you in advance for your consideration of our views.
Sincerely yours.
Hafiz M. Pashayev
Ambassador

As much as I wanted to believe that the U.S. Congress did not have a double standard or discriminatory policies against countries in need, my belief had proven to be wrong over and over again. Even the slight modifications to Section 907 in 1995, which were aimed at allowing humanitarian assistance to and democracy building efforts in Azerbaijan, received great opposition from some U.S. congressmen. My frustration can be sensed from the following letter to Representative Robert E. Andrews (D-NJ).

July 12, 1995

Dear Congressman Andrews:

Please permit me to comment on the views you and other members of Congress expressed in opposing a small modification of the current congressional ban on assistance to Azerbaijan.

(1) Most members ignored or glossed over the fact that the exception proposed by the committee was very narrow in scope-only for humanitarian assistance and democracy building. It is a source of amazement to me that members of the United States Congress would want to be identified with an effort designed to deny humanitarian assistance to more than one million refugees, or to prevent efforts to build democracies in the former Soviet Union.

(2) It was stated over and over again that the Armenians suffer a terrible plight. I do not disagree. Armenians face severe problems, but they are in large part problems of their own making. Azerbaijan has not invaded Armenia. Azerbaijan has no soldiers in Armenia. Azerbaijan did not start the war. The fact is that Armenian forces occupy 20 percent of Azerbaijan. Armenian forces have looted, burned and destroyed hundreds of villages in Azerbaijan.

(3) Armenian forces have created over one million Azerbaijani refugees. If Armenia had not invaded Azerbaijan, occupied 20 percent of our territory, and ethnically cleansed the western part of the country, the social and economic disaster facing both countries would not have occurred. As Chairman Livingston stated, "The hepatitis cases in Azerbaijan among the IDP's and refugees have increased 144 percent since January 1993. Water-borne diseases among children are up 15 percent. Salmonellosis is up 70 percent in the first 8

months of 1994 compared with all of 1993. The leading cause of infant mortality and their main reason for hospitalization in Azerbaijan is acute respiratory infections. Drugs supplied by the former Soviet central system have decreased from 75 percent of the country's needs to 5 percent." I can only conclude that the compassion expressed by Members of Congress for Armenians does not extend to innocent, hungry and homeless Azerbaijanis.

(4) Over and over, members talked about the so-called "blockade" of Armenia. If Mexico invaded the United States and occupied Texas, would the U.S. send fuel to Mexico that could be used to further its aggression? Of course not. Why should Azerbaijan supply fuel to Armenia so long as it occupies 20 percent of our country? Would you have us transport fuel across Armenian occupied territory to Armenia? As Congressman Wilson said, "They (Armenians) now occupy 20 percent of the territory of Azerbaijan. I say to my colleagues, it is not normal when you have wars, and one country occupies 20 percent of the other country, that the country which is occupied opens its borders to the occupier." Furthermore, there is no way in the world right now, for Azerbaijan to carry on commerce with Armenia because the occupying Armenian forces have destroyed all transportation and communication links in the western part of the country. When you talk of blockades, what about the blockade by the Armenians against Nakhchivan, a non-contiguous region of Azerbaijan? Why is one blockade justified and another not? Is the morality of a blockade determined by who has the most votes, or who has the most powerful domestic lobby?

Perhaps the most eloquent statement in the debate was that of Congressman Smith, who stated that "A refugee is a refugee, Mr. Chairman, regardless of nationality or religion. Democracy building, including the facilitation of free and fair elections, is important to U.S. foreign policy, regardless of the nationality or religion of the country in question."

However, after dealing with this matter for three years, I am forced to conclude that a majority of Congress does not agree with that assessment, or that domestic political considerations take precedence over humanitarian needs. In either case, I find it to be a sad commentary on the role of Congress in the formulation and execution of American foreign policy."

Unfortunately, the situation in my country reminds me too much of Bosnia. An ethnically-based nationality engages in aggression in its quest for territorial expansion (Greater Serbia, Greater Armenia), carries out ethnic cleansing, creates huge numbers of refugees, thumbs its nose at repeated United Nations condemnations, portrays its actions as Christians against Muslims, and receives de facto Western support through inaction. Unlike Bosnia, however, Azerbaijan does not even receive moral or humanitarian support from the U.S. Congress.

I would welcome the opportunity to discuss these matters with you at your convenience.

Sincerely,
Hafiz Pashayev
Ambassador

Another issue debated on the Senate floor was the so-called "blockade" of Armenia by Turkey and Azerbaijan. Some U.S. senators disapproved of Turkey closing its border with Armenia, although Turkey did so in protest of Armenia's continuous occupation of Azerbaijani lands. Not a single U.S. Senator objected to Armenia's occupation of Azerbaijani territories, but many criticized Turkey for its stand. Senator Byrd was one of the few U.S. senators with a clear understanding of the reality of the region.

September 27, 1995

Dear Senator Byrd:

I have just finished reading your statement on the Senate floor during consideration of the so-called Humanitarian Corridor Amendment by Senator Dole.

During my almost three years as Azerbaijan's first ambassador to the United States, I have found an appalling but understandable lack of knowledge about Azerbaijan and its conflict with Armenia. Your statement showed greater understanding of the true facts and the underlying issues than any I have seen from other members of the Senate. Unfortunately, too many members only know what they have been told by the Armenian lobby, or they choose to ignore the facts.

Regarding the Humanitarian Corridor Amendment, why should Turkey or Azerbaijan reward an aggressor by supplying materials with which to continue the aggression? Why should Azerbaijan supply energy to Armenia when it occupies a major portion of country, and yet the Congress says we should have normal commerce with the very ones who caused the refugee crisis?

Again, let me commend you on behalf of my small but independent, democratic country. We are extremely pleased that you have attempted to set the record straight.

Finally, I hope that you will do me the honor of meeting with me to discuss our nations' mutual concerns.

Sincerely,

Hafiz M. Pashayev

Ambassador

By 1996, the Organization for Security and Co-operation in Europe (OSCE) was the main mediator in the Nagorno-Karabakh conflict and the U.S. had appointed a full-time envoy to participate in the negotiations on behalf of the U.S. Government. As the OSCE were holding negotiations between the parties, the Congressional Caucus on Armenian Issues, which mainly consists of pro-Armenian congressmen, sent a letter to President Bill Clinton urging him to favor Armenia and separatists in the Nagorno-Karabakh region. Below is my letter to President Clinton clarifying some of the allegations in the Congressional Caucus' letter.

April 5, 1996

Dear Mr. President:

Please permit me to comment on the letter (March 29, 1996) that was sent to you by the Congressional Caucus on Armenian Issues concerning negotiations on Nagorno-Karabakh under the auspices of the OSCE.

As we have done previously, we join the caucus in commending the administration both for its appointment of a full-time U.S. Special Envoy and for the time and attention the Administration has spent recently in seeking a fair and just settlement of the issue. However, I must take very strong issue with several points these members have made in their letter.

(1) These members incredibly seem to be saying that the United States should not initiate or pursue a settlement unless it is a one-sided solution for Armenia and its surrogates in Nagorno-Karabakh. The essence of negotiations is that both sides must compromise, and Azerbaijan has repeatedly expressed its willingness to do so. Indeed, President Aliyev has expressed his willingness to grant some form of enhanced autonomy for Nagorno-Karabakh, but that does not mean Azerbaijan should or will compromise its territorial integrity. That will not happen.

(2) The suggestion that Armenia be allowed to provide "security guarantees" for Nagorno-Karabakh is totally out of the question. What sovereign country would give another country the right to intervene militarily in its

own territory? Such a concept is totally alien to international law, the very principle of state sovereignty, and common sense. Would the United States give Mexico or Canada the right to provide security guarantees to Texas or Minnesota?

(3) This letter also suggests that the United States begin "official" contacts with the so-called "government" of Nagorno-Karabakh. International law, the United Nations, the OSCE, the Commonwealth of Independent States (of which Armenia is a member), and the United States Government have rightly recognized that Nagorno-Karabakh is part of the sovereign territory of Azerbaijan. It is not an independent country. For the United States to carry on bilateral relations with this unofficial "government" would do grave damage to relations between the United States and Azerbaijan. That has been fully recognized and respected by the U.S. Government in the past, and we trust that policy will be continued.

(4) I must comment on that portion of the members' letter, which contends that the conflict was instigated by mistreatment of Armenians in Azerbaijan. Objective observers know that atrocities have been committed on both sides, but they also know that the origin of the conflict was a desire by Armenia to create a Greater Armenia, in much the same way that Serbia used the Bosnian Serbs in an attempt to create a Greater Serbia. This is a conflict about territorial expansion, pure and simple.

Perhaps most appalling of all is that members of Congress said not one word about the fact that Armenia occupies 20 percent of Azerbaijan, has killed thousands of our peoples, destroyed hundreds of towns and villages, and created more than one million refugees. And some, but not all, of these same members have steadfastly opposed direct American humanitarian assistance to these refugees.

Again, Mr. President, we commend you and the State Department for the sincere efforts you are making to reach a just and fair settlement, but proposals and propositions such as those contained in the March 29 letter do not represent a basis upon which progress can be made.

Mr. President, in my opinion one of the biggest impediments to solving this problem has been the extremist, intransigent opposition to any reasonable solution by the Armenian American lobby. They are more hard-line than the Government of Armenia. Unfortunately, I believe the members' letter is reflective of that hard-line position.

Sincerely,

Hafiz M. Pashayev

Ambassador

The two letters below address the issue of illicit weapon deliveries from Russia to Armenia in violation of the Conventional Forces in Europe (CFE) agreement.

April 25, 1997

Dear Madam Secretary:

It is axiomatic that one must live dangerously in the Caucasus, but for Azerbaijan the danger and pressure have increased tremendously in recent months. Consider the following:

> *(1) The Russian Defense Ministry and the Defense Committee of the Russian Duma both revealed that about $1 billion in illegal arms shipments were made from Russia to Armenia between 1993 and 1996. These shipments started at a time of Armenian offensives which resulted in a million refugees and Armenian occupation of 20 percent of Azerbaijan, which is still in effect. These arms shipments probably violated the CFE treaty and have created a huge military im-*

balance in the region, threatening not only Azerbaijan but Armenia's other neighbors as well.

(2) *Former Soviet Premier, now deputy of the Russian Duma, Nikolay Ryzhkov gave a speech in Yerevan condemning President Yeltsin's decision to launch an investigation of these arms shipments, and bragged of his role in approving the January 1990, Soviet attack on Baku in which hundreds of civilians were killed. He urged a closer union between Armenia and Russia. About the same time as Ryzkov's speech, two Russian ultranationalist analysts wrote a prominent article in a Moscow newspaper urging the Russian government to de-stabilize foreign governments that take an "anti-Russian" position.*

(3) *The Iranian Parliamentary Speaker and presidential candidate told the Russian Duma that Azerbaijan made "nothing less than an historical mistake" by allowing Western oil companies to develop its offshore oil deposits. The Baku newspaper Panorama said that "Throughout the entire five-year history of Azerbaijani-Iranian relations, the authorities in Iran would not have countenanced such an attack upon their northern neighbor." The paper said the recent "cooling" of relations between Azerbaijan and Iran "was taking place against a background of increasing cooperation between Iran and Armenia."*

(4) *The Republic of Armenia recently appointed as its Prime Minister Robert Kocharyan, heretofore leader of separatist forces in Nagorno-Karabakh. It was under Mr. Kocharyan's leadership that the Armenian offensives and the illegal Russian arms shipments were made.*

(5) *Armenian lobby groups in the United States have announced they will seek legislation providing direct U.S.*

assistance to Nagorno-Karabakh. They hope Congress will draw a distinction between Azerbaijan and its region of Nagorno-Karabakh, thus furthering the objective of dismembering Azerbaijan either through independence or the annexation of Nagorno-Karabakh. Such legislation would do great damage to U.S.-Azerbaijani relations, as did Section 907 of the Freedom Support Act.

(6) *It seems obvious that many in our region, including several ultra-nationalist groups in various countries, seek to destabilize Azerbaijan in an attempt to interrupt or destroy relations between the United States and Azerbaijan, or to achieve other objectives such as territorial expansion or influence over vital oil development in the region. They want American oil companies out of Azerbaijan, and more importantly, American influence out of the region (please see my attached op-ed piece in The Boston Globe and the article on illegal arms shipments from Russia to Armenia).*

(7) *That being the case, it is very important that the United States give strong support and diplomatic recognition to Azerbaijan. Consideration has been given to a summit meeting between Presidents Clinton and Aliyev. In my opinion, such a meeting would be extremely helpful at this time to counter the pressure being placed upon Azerbaijan's government.*

Sincerely,
Hafiz Pashayev
Ambassador

May 6, 1997

Dear Senator Helms:

During Senate consideration of the CFE Treaty, I hope members of the Senate will address security issues affecting the Government of Azer-

baijan. We are concerned about the possibility of a large arms buildup in the "flank" area, which could pose security risks for Azerbaijan. Let me mention four specific concerns:

(1) Senate should recognize that countries like Azerbaijan, which were republics of the former Soviet Union when the treaty was signed, do not belong to either of the two groups of state parties envisaged by the treaty.

(2) Senate should stipulate that the treaty in no way nullifies provisions of the Tashkent Agreement on Principles and Procedures for Implementation of the CFE treaty as it relates to obligatory consultations among all interested states as the only way to approve reallocation of quotas.

(3) Senate should also stipulate that provisions allowing Russia to increase its armaments in the "flank" area, even on a temporary basis, do not apply to the territory of Azerbaijan.

(4) Senate should explicitly state that any presence of armed forces on the territory of the Republic of Azerbaijan against her will, and without her legalized consent, is unacceptable to the United States of America.

I would also remind you that the Russian Government recently revealed that from 1993 to 1996 some $1 billion in illegal arms were shipped from unofficial sources in Russia to Armenia, which has already created a strategic imbalance in the area for Azerbaijan. These shipments probably violated the CFE Treaty.

Without the support of the world community, small countries such as Azerbaijan face the danger of overwhelming military forces being stationed on its borders, creating an unstable security situation.

Azerbaijan has only known eight years of independence in its long history, the last six only since the collapse of the Soviet Union. There is nothing more important to Azerbaijan than the preservation of that in-

dependence, and the stipulations enumerated above would be very helpful in maintaining our independence.
Sincerely,
Hafiz Pashayev
Ambassador

Chapter 3
From Cooperation and Partnership
to a Strategic Relationship
(2002-2006)

Undeniably, the most shocking and horrific development of 2001 was the 9/11 terrorist attacks. This tragic event changed the United States and the rest of world overnight. Azerbaijan was among the first states to offer its help to the United States and the American people. The Azerbaijani government granted an unconditional blanket over-flight clearance for U.S. planes long before Operation Enduring Freedom began in Afghanistan. However, in this critical moment for U.S. national security, it was Section 907 that blocked the U.S. military from cooperation with Azerbaijan. Ironically, only after the 9/11 tragedy did the U.S. Government and U.S. Congress realize how damaging and detrimental Section 907 had been to the U.S. national interest for all these years. President George W. Bush waived Section 907 in January 2002, thus removing, albeit still not permanently, the major obstacle in the path of strengthening U.S.-Azerbaijani relations.

Suddenly, the U.S. media started to publish articles highlighting the critical position of Azerbaijan and the South Caucasus region for the U.S. national interest. On December 23, 2001, an article titled, "The Importance of Armenia and Azerbaijan" appeared in the Washington Times. It read, "Americans may not be too familiar with far-away countries like Armenia and Azerbaijan, but in this post-9/11 world, these neighboring former Soviet republics will be increasingly important to U.S. counterterrorist initiatives."

Yet, the author was clearly careful not to say anything that might offend the Armenian lobby and its supporters, who

even at this critical moment for U.S. national security opposed the waiver of Section 907. As if deeply disappointed,
the author wrote, "The White House recently asked Congress
to institute an annual waiver of the U.S. sanctions against
Azerbaijan, and Congress has appropriated $4.3 million in
military training and assistance to Armenia. Though neither
Azerbaijan nor Turkey has relaxed the embargo on Armenia,
the government [in Armenia] has demonstrated admirable restraint in response to the administration's request for a waiver
on U.S. sanction on Azerbaijan and has expressed understanding of the administration's need to enlist allies in this
ongoing struggle."

The newspaper argued that Armenia did not oppose the
waiver of Section 907, as if it was the Armenian Government
who passed the laws in the United States or whom the
American people should thank for showing "admirable restraint." It quoted the Director of Government Relations for
the Armenian Assembly who "was pleased to see that the
waiver on the sanctions would be renewable, rather than
permanent" and stated, "It's hard to argue that you're not going to give the president some flexibility to counter terrorists." In other words, even after terrible terrorist attacks on
the United States, the Armenian lobby was happy that Section
907 was not removed permanently and that the lobby and its
friends could still use it against Azerbaijan in the future as
"blackmail."

I responded to this article and my letter was published on
December 28, 2001, titled, "History Sheds Different Light on
U.S. Sanctions Against Azerbaijan." Below is the passage
from that letter:

> Lack of knowledge is the main reason why the powerful
> Armenian lobby has succeeded in misrepresenting the cessation
> of normal trade relations, quite natural between two warring par-
> ties, as a blockade. Thus, it misled the U.S. Congress into adding

insult to injury and passing Section 907 of the 1992 Freedom Support Act, containing sanctions against Azerbaijan. Despite the opposition of successive U.S. administrations to 907, it was only after 9/11 that U.S. policy on this matter was reconsidered.

As far as Armenia's "admirable restraint" and "gracious response to the relaxation of U.S. sanctions against Azerbaijan" are concerned, I would like to set the record straight. After 9/11, the President of Armenia himself went on record viciously opposing any modification of Section 907. At the same time, a high-ranking Armenian delegation was dispatched to Washington to enforce this position.

In my letter, I welcomed the Bush administration's engagement in the Karabakh peace process and applauded the congressional decision to provide the president with the authority to waive Section 907. It was an important step towards making U.S. involvement in the peace process "truly unbiased"—a step that was "needed to counter the aggressive separatism that merged with international terrorism threatening to destroy our values and way of life."

The waiver of Section 907 was a critical step in removing the last obstacle in the building up of military relations between the United States and Azerbaijan. In 2003, the Pentagon launched a $100 million Caspian Guard program that was aimed at strengthening Azerbaijan's Coast Guard and establishing a maritime border control regime in the Caspian Sea. Also, within the U.S. Defense Threat Reduction Agency's Cooperative Threat Reduction program, both states actively cooperated against the proliferation of Weapons of Mass Destruction (WMD). Thanks to these initiatives, the Caspian Guard Command Center and two radar stations were set up in Azerbaijan in 2005. These installations elevated the Azerbaijani security agencies' ability to better monitor and intercept illegal trafficking in the Caspian Sea.

The global war on terrorism and international security were among other major issues that were at the center stage of U.S.-Azerbaijan cooperation. Azerbaijan acceded to all twelve international counter-terrorism conventions and protocols and the Azerbaijani government strongly supported the U.S.-led fight against terrorism. Currently, Azerbaijani troops serve along with the U.S. soldiers in Afghanistan, Kosovo and Iraq, where they provide security on the ground and assist the international community's efforts in post-conflict reconstruction.

In the field of energy development, we also witnessed another historic event, the inauguration of the Baku-Tbilisi-Ceyhan (BTC) pipeline on May 25, 2005. There were many "behind the scenes" activities that made this project possible. I have to mention a special mission of Dr. Brzezinski in Baku in 1996, where he delivered a letter from President Clinton to President Aliyev. In this letter, President Clinton laid out his support for the Baku-Ceyhan pipeline and encouraged President Aliyev to pick the western route for the export of Azerbaijan's crude oil. In 1999, during the OSCE Istanbul Summit, President Clinton observed the signing of a legal framework agreement by the presidents of Azerbaijan, Georgia, and Turkey, committing themselves to the construction of the BTC pipeline. Presidents of Kazakhstan and Uzbekistan witnessed the accord. Three years later, on September 18, 2002, following a ceremony held at the Sangachal Terminal near Baku, the construction phase of the BTC pipeline began.

There were many officials whose insights helped to formulate the policy of establishing the East-West Energy Transport Corridor. I personally believe that without the strong and relentless work of Ms. Sheila Heslin, a former National Security Council aide, the issue of BTC would not have been the central focus of the Clinton administration's energy policy. Moreover, the roles of the U.S. special envoys on Caspian energy diplomacy were important in moving this project forward. In particular, I would like to note the contributions of Richard Morningstar, John Wolf and Steven Mann, who understood very well how vital this pipeline was for the regional states and the rest of the world.

This project could not have been made possible without the presence of three key components: private business interests, the pipeline's geo-strategic aspect, and strong regional leadership. The private U.S. and international energy companies were instrumental in the financing and implementation stages of the project. Initially, the energy companies were reluctant to support the BTC route, as there were many risks and challenges involved, including political instability in the region and the project's economic viability, but it was British Petroleum's involvement and leadership that moved the BTC project forward from a standstill. By 2000, BP had successfully completed a merger with the U.S. oil company, Amoco, and took over another U.S. oil firm, ARCO. As a result, the interests of the U.S. Government and BP regarding the BTC pipeline converged. Furthermore, BP became the main operator and the largest shareholder (with 34.1 percent of shares) in the AIOC consortium of international energy companies developing Azerbaijan's major oil and gas reserves. This meant that BP would lead the construction efforts, which it did starting in 2002.

Ironically, in 1994-1995, BP was not even interested in considering any routes for oil from Azerbaijan other than the existing Baku-Novorossiysk pipeline through Russia. Here again, President Aliyev's personal conviction in the necessity of an alternative route for the Caspian oil made it possible for the Baku-Supsa early oil pipeline via Georgia to be in operation by 1997.

I should also point out strong regional leadership of President Heydar Aliyev, and two other Presidents, Eduard Shevardnadze of Georgia, and Süleyman Demirel of Turkey that made the BTC pipeline a reality. It will not be an overstatement, if I say that President Aliyev's vision and his ability to maneuver in a volatile region of the South Caucasus and his never-ending energy to carry on, despite constant external pressure, particularly from the Yeltsin government, were behind the successful BTC strategy.

The BTC pipeline was a project with a geopolitical dimension. It involved multiple players with diverging interests. While Azerbaijan, Georgia, Turkey and the United States supported the project and its route, Russia and Iran opposed it. Particularly, the opposition from Russia was a challenge, since Moscow still had considerable leverage over internal politics in Azerbaijan and Georgia, which it occasionally used to undermine the pro-Western course of Baku and Tbilisi. However, when Vladimir Putin became the President of Russia in 2000, many things changed. Unlike President Yeltsin, President Putin and his pragmatic approach brought stability to the Azerbaijani-Russian relations. Gradually, Moscow tuned down its opposition to the BTC and bilateral relations between the two states improved. In general, Azerbaijan's foreign policy in its dealings with Russia has been noticed in Washington.

I have often been told by U.S. officials that when it came to U.S.-Russian relations, Azerbaijan was not a "headache" to the United States. They just wished that the neighboring states in the region would follow the example of Azerbaijan. I should admit that one of the main reasons why our foreign policy has been successful is self-reliance. Since our independence in 1992, "thanks to Section 907," we have had only ourselves to rely on while trying to rebuild the country, but since then, we have come so far. The BTC pipeline opened a new door to future transportation projects between Europe and Asia and has made Azerbaijan a pivotal state in the Caspian region.

Finally, the elections in Azerbaijan and the promotion of democracy were two topics that dominated my discussions with U.S. officials and U.S. congressmen during this period. There were two major elections in Azerbaijan in the last four years, the presidential elections in October 2003 and the parliamentary elections in November 2005. It was the timing of these elections and the events that took place between 2003 and 2006 that made the two elections significant but very different from each other.

In the run up to the October 2003 Presidential Elections, there was speculation about the health of the late President Heydar Aliyev, who had previously undergone bypass surgery at the Cleveland Clinic in Ohio in April, 1999. His health condition deteriorated when he suffered another heart attack during a live televised speech in April 2003. Soon after, he was hospitalized and flown to Turkey and from there to the United States for further treatment. He died on December 12, 2003. It was a critical time in the history of Azerbaijan, as many feared that the decade long stability could be jeopardized and the country could be headed back into civil war. Fortunately, the majority of Azerbaijanis chose stability over chaos. Although the results of October 2003 presidential elections were questioned by some western observers, the majority, including U.S. officials, agreed that Ilham Aliyev gathered more than two-thirds of the votes. Nonetheless, the aftermath of the elections was marked with disturbances and riots by members of opposition groups who sought to overthrow the government. The law enforcement agencies intervened and prevented further civil unrest and bloodshed.

In November 2003, opposition groups in Georgia ousted the government of President Eduard Shevardnadze through peaceful demonstrations-an event that later came to be known as the "Rose Revolution." It was the first in a series of "color revolutions" that took place in the former Soviet republics. In 2004, Ukraine had its own "Orange Revolution" followed by a "Tulip Revolution" in Kyrgyzstan in 2005. At the time, these political events drew much attention from the Western media and excited many in the United States. The opposition groups in the other former Soviet republics, including Azerbaijan, were inspired by these "color revolutions" and planned one in Azerbaijan. This was the pre-election spirit in the country in the run up to the November 2005 parliamentary elections.

Despite the fact that the parliamentary elections of November 2005 had many novelties that were implemented for the first time such as the allocation of free airtime on state television to all candidates, the marking of fingers with invisible ink and the conducting of exit polls; opposition parties and some members of the Western media were preparing themselves for an Azerbaijani "color revolution." I was therefore not at all surprised to read articles published in some U.S. media outlets that expressed disappointment over the fact that they did not see a "color revolution" in Azerbaijan. I also could not stop wondering about the whole idea of "democracy promotion," as the U.S. Administration was propounding.

The idea of spreading democracy and freedom in today's world is a genuine and natural thing. I could not agree more with President Bush's remarks from his meeting with President Ilham Aliyev at the White House in April 28, 2006, when he said that "democracy is the wave of the future." I share and applaud his personal commitment and desire to see the rest of the world free and democratic. However, President Bush's current "democracy promotion doctrine" and the way it is pursued around the world sometimes remind me of Leonid Brezhnev's doctrine of spreading communism. Too often we forget that democracy-building is a gradual process that requires time. Revolution will not resolve the chronic problems of a country if that country lacks a strong institutional basis or basic understanding about democracy itself. I think many staunch "color revolution" supporters began to have second thoughts about this method of change, after seeing that the situation in some "revolutionized" countries had not changed much, and had even worsened in some cases.

I am glad that the April 2006 visit of President Ilham Aliyev to the United States convinced Washington that he genuinely shares the same values and aspirations for freedom and democracy and sees the future of Azerbaijan, in his own words, "as a modern, secular, democratic country." In that sense, his visit was a significant step in gaining U.S. support for further democratic reforms in our country. I believe that we would have made more progress in this area, had he been invited to visit the United States earlier. The visit of President Aliyev further upgraded the strategic partnership and alliance between the United States and Azerbaijan. It was my "last accord" as an Ambassador of Azerbaijan to the United States. Today U.S.-Azerbaijan relations are firmer than ever before and I am proud and elated that my years of service have contributed to building up these relations.

Remarks at the Reception Dedicated to Tenth Anniversary of the Restoration of Azerbaijan's Independence
October 25, 2001

I would like to extend a special welcome to our distinguished guests from the U.S. Government, both the Congress and the Executive Branch, as well as to the representatives of many nations who have joined us tonight.

Today, we celebrate the tenth anniversary of the restoration of independence of my country. I fully realize that to some of you, ten years may sound like a short time, but for a nation with a previous experience with independence of only

less than two years and that over eighty years ago, it is a milestone. I am not going to speak long, but let me very briefly
tell all of you what Azerbaijan has achieved in those ten years.

We have managed, under most difficult conditions in the
volatile region of South Caucasus, to consolidate and
strengthen our sovereignty and independence and to incorpo-
rate our nation into the world community.

We have built the infrastructure for political and economic freedom, while facing the hostility from those who
have been our good neighbors, and to our regret, indifference
from many of those we looked to for friendship and inspira-
tion.

We have followed, without deviation, a pro-Western path,
transforming our society according to the ideals of openness,
transparency, democracy, and human rights' protection.

We have attracted considerable foreign investments to
transform our economy from state-regulated to market-
oriented, while paying special attention to inviting the biggest
companies to participate in the energy development of the
Caspian. The energy policy of Azerbaijan's leadership has become both a tool for re-structuring the economy and also a
means to achieve our ultimate goal of transforming the society.

We have succeeded in becoming a genuinely independent
force for peace and regional cooperation. GUUAM, an organization which encompasses also Georgia, Ukraine, Uzbekistan, and Moldova, is a good example of that. It is a
qualitatively new group among the former Soviet republics,
one that is based on commonality of interests, not on somebody's bidding.

Now, in the wake of [the] 9/11 heinous terrorist attacks
on the United States, Azerbaijan has unconditionally an-
swered the call to join the broad international coalition, and

we feel like our rightful place in the world community has been re-emphasized again in these trying days.

On a more personal note, my almost nine years in office have made me believe that the foreign and domestic policy of President Aliyev has brought bilateral U.S.-Azerbaijan relations to a point where, regardless of whether the White House Administration is Democratic or Republican, my nation is a constant on the landscape on the political map they use in Washington. It is non-partisan since the strategic partnership between our two countries is in the national and national security interest of us both. This was once again confirmed yesterday by the Senate voting to give President Bush waiver authority on Section 907 of the FSA, thus eliminating the last remaining obstacle to the rapidly growing U.S.-Azerbaijan relations. We are grateful to the U.S. Administration and to Senator Brownback for acknowledging the importance of our bilateral relations and look forward to many years of cooperation.

"Azerbaijan's Foreign Policy Priorities in the Relations with the United States: 9/11 and the Perspective" Presentation at USACC Fifth Annual Conference and Exhibition March 7, 2002

It is a real pleasure for me to speak here, at the Fifth Annual Conference of the USACC. This event is more proof of how much we have progressed in our ties with the United States since the starting point exactly ten years ago when we established diplomatic relations.

Indeed, ten years is not a long time when you look at it in the historical perspective. Actually, it is such a short time that some people still refer to us as a newly independent state.

On the other hand, in my view our accomplishments in these ten years are truly historical. We made progress from relative obscurity to being "of some interest" to the U.S., later of "significant importance" to the U.S., and, finally, of "strategic importance" to the United States. I have heard these definitions on many occasions during the Capitol Hill testimonies presented by high-ranking U.S. Administration officials.

It gives me real pleasure to say that the contribution of the USACC to this evolution has been crucial. It is sufficient to take a look at the topics of the annual conferences sponsored by the Chamber and also at the list of speakers those events attracted and fully comprehend, without doubt, the importance of the USACC for promoting Azerbaijan's image in the U.S., bringing it closer to the American businesses and public.

Our relations are being developed in full accordance with the proclaimed U.S. foreign policy objectives in the region of South Caucasus and Central Asia. In fact, Azerbaijan is the most edifying example of how these goals are being implemented within the framework of bilateral ties. These relations are also defined by their consistency and continuous progress. Despite the turbulent developments in the region, including conflicts, both legal and armed, despite assassination attempts, despite severe external pressure on Azerbaijan, and despite lingering effects of domestic politics in the U.S., the relations between our countries continue to develop and broaden steadily.

Progress of the bilateral ties with the U.S. will be eventually to the benefit of not only our two nations, but of the whole region. I can name numerous success stories, but the most impressive ones are, obviously, the projects underway in energy development and transportation. These ventures have proven that the oil strategy of Azerbaijan under the leadership of President Aliyev is correct and viable, proven by how we've gotten multi-billion investments, including $1.3 billion worth from American companies. Later in the afternoon, you will hear more about energy development in Azerbaijan [with] first-hand information from other panelists.

Now, my country puts special emphasis on developing the sectors of its economy beyond the energy sector. Our cooperation with the World Bank, the IMF and with U.S. agencies aims to improve the environment for investors and diversify the economy. Attracting investments, both domestic and external, to small and medium-size businesses is a special priority for the Government of Azerbaijan. My country's agriculture also has great potential; land privatization is almost completed and an extensive farm system is rapidly growing.

We demonstrate a very careful and attentive approach to developing our banking infrastructure and the creation of capital and security markets, but you have already heard about that from the most competent speakers.

When we embarked on the path of independence, we were proclaiming that our choice was in favor of the Western model of democracy and we have come a long way to now calling our relations with the United States a "strategic partnership."

It is our belief that the climate of cooperation will also positively influence the development of democracy in the region. We in Azerbaijan are pleased that in spite of the occasional criticism voiced by the human rights watch-dogs, we are not judged by the pretty liberal standards developed specifically for the post-Soviet states. As a member of the Council of Europe, we are now experiencing how it feels to have full-scale European norms applied to you, and we hope that the promotion of human rights will continue to improve thanks to the growing public awareness in Azerbaijan and broadening educational ties with the United States and other

Western nations, which allow us to look in the future with optimism.

In the months since the tragedy of 9/11, the interaction between our two nations has acquired a new dimension. Of course, what I mean is Azerbaijan's participation in the anti-terrorist campaign. Azerbaijan was one of the first of the post-Soviet states to offer, unasked, its assistance to the United States, and not only because we decided that our part-nership with America demanded that we act that way. It was in part because we are well aware of the problem of terrorism and its negative effects in the modern world.

Long before 9/11, we experienced what aggressive na-tionalism and separatism look like when they assume their most radical form and turn into terrorism; and we are not the only ones dealing with this problem. Separatism in the Cauca-sus is the reason for the current situation in Georgia. There is no question, as far as I'm concerned, that this country needs U.S. assistance. We have dealt with the problem I mentioned not only on individual basis, but also as a group, on the level of GUUAM, trying to work on common approaches and co-ordinated policies to negate terrorism's possible impact on the emerging societies.

We are very pleased that the U.S. constantly upgrades its cooperation with GUUAM as a whole, also pushing its bilat-eral contacts with its individual participants. And, once again, Azerbaijan is a good example, with its well-developed interac-tion with the United States in the area of border security, in-cluding both border and customs control, and growing ties in law-enforcement.

While Azerbaijan is devoted to the principle of develop-ing its cooperation with foreign countries, it is quite obvious that there is an issue which we can not neglect and that is the continued occupation of our territories by Armenia. I have to be quite emphatic and unequivocal on that we cannot and will not agree to any cooperation projects that involve interaction with this nation as long as the conflict between the two countries remains unsolved and the Armenian troops hold what they have occupied by force during their aggression against Azerbaijan. I doubt it very much that any of you will be able to name a situation in the world when two nations, at war by all definitions, trade or otherwise cooperate with each other.

Talking about the Armenia-Azerbaijan conflict, I have to underscore that it remains not only the biggest problem the region experiences, but also a big impediment in the path of the broad international campaign that the U.S. is waging against international terrorism. Think tanks and experts throughout the world try to get to the very essence of terrorism, to its roots, if you will. I agree with those who say that terrorism is rooted mostly in international conflicts. It feeds on the emotions of those who are deprived of their lands and normal way of life.

Without any doubt, settlement of the Armenia-Azerbaijan conflict over Nagorno-Karabakh will have a great positive impact on the situation in the region, both in dealing with the above-mentioned problem, and also in the sense that it will allow to eliminate the so-called gray areas, uncontrollable to the international community, which having become spreading grounds for international terrorism, drug-trafficking, weapons proliferation, etc.

This is yet another reason why we value so much the U.S. involvement in brokering a peaceful and just solution to the problem, and it's Co-Chairmanship of the OSCE Minsk Group.

I believe that after ten years of close cooperation, the level of understanding and appreciating the importance of Azerbaijan for promoting the U.S. interest in the region has grown enough to make it difficult to mislead members of Congress on issues related to my country. I think the time —

when destructive elements in Armenian Diaspora could instigate anti-Azerbaijani moves has passed.

Now it is even more obvious that it was only the lack of
knowledge about Azerbaijan and the region which gave free
hand to those who advocated the adoption of Section 907.
The moment is right to remind those members of the U.S.
Congress that the most active champion of this unfair legislation was Mr. Mourad Topalian, now a U.S.-convicted criminal
with close ties to terrorists, who at the time was a prominent
leader of the Armenian National Committee of America.
Anyway, now, with Section 907 finally removed, be it through
waiver and not repeal, as we were hoping, the relations between Azerbaijan and the United States are moving towards a
qualitatively new stage. I am confident that in another ten
years, an Azerbaijani Ambassador will be standing here in
front of you reporting new accomplishments in what we can
call a beautiful friendship between our two nations.

"Azerbaijan: Economic Development and Business Opportunities"
Address at the Ambassadors' Roundtable
Organized By BISNIS
May 1, 2002

It is a pleasure to appear here today before such a determined audience intent on doing business in Azerbaijan. And
my sincere thanks to our friends at BISNIS, who are doing
such a tremendous job at establishing closer economic links
between our countries.

Since restoring its independence, Azerbaijan has aimed
for both Western-style democracy and also for implementing
transition towards the market economy. Back in 1992-1993,
while the main issue was the survival of Azerbaijan as a sovereign nation, we at the same time did our best to overcome
crisis and stabilize the economic situation. At that time, this

work was challenged by the disruption of traditional economic ties and the division of labor which existed in the former Soviet Union [due to] a lack of internal stability in my country, as well as by the ongoing Armenian aggression and plight of the refugees and displaced. It was at the end of that period that the rate of inflation reached its absolute high of 1600 percent, as did unemployment. Production plummeted in both industry and agriculture. This was the reality when we started our efforts to transform our economy.

I would remind you that in contrast with the image of Azerbaijan as an energy-producing country in 1993-1994, then we actually imported energy. By that time, it had been well understood in Azerbaijan that without Western technology and investments, it would be impossible to develop new oil-fields in the Caspian Sea. Overcoming internal and external obstacles, Azerbaijan managed to sign its first contract in 1994 and to create a consortium of twelve companies representing eight countries. Today, the Azerbaijan International Operating Company (AIOC) has accomplished the so-called "early oil" stage of the development and is producing now more than expected-about 130,000 barrels per day. The first contract proved that the chosen legislative background, the format of Production Sharing Agreement (PSA), created the best possible conditions for foreign investors. The energy strategy of the President and the Government aimed at restructuring the economy was thus put into action. Flow of major foreign investments started.

The foundation laid in the initial years enabled us to proceed with the transformation proper since 1995-1996. In these two years, Azerbaijan started its privatization programs, the most obvious precondition of moving to the market economy from the centralized, directive-driven economy of the Soviet time. Land privatization can be a very positive example here. Having completed land privatization (with over

95 percent of land privatized and farmers emerging as a social group), we now have achieved production growth in certain food articles of up to 45 percent in the last five years with the share of food products declining steadily in Azerbaijan's imports, from 42 percent in 1995 to just 16 percent last year. Where are the roots of this breakthrough?

The August 1996 Land Reform Law has created momentum for the revival of the sector. This legislation paved the way for transfer of land ownership from State to private enterprises and established the rights to sell, lease, inherit, and mortgage the land. For future development of Azerbaijan's agriculture and rural entrepreneurship, my country will need foreign credits and additional investments, since the internal "reform resources" are mostly exhausted.

After the privatization of the small and medium state-owned businesses (close to 100 percent privatized), we are now successfully proceeding with the privatization of larger enterprises. Altogether, 24,000 small and over 1,500 medium and large enterprises have been privatized.

It was at that time that we began capitalizing on the growing attention to my country's geographical location, which makes it the regional and international hub.

To show the dynamics of progress, let me give you some figures: 4.7 million tons of goods were transported within the framework of the TRACECA program in 1999, with this figure growing constantly and reaching 5.2 million tons in 2000 and 8.7 million tons in 2001.

Azerbaijan also started its program of creating a new legal basis for the economic transformation, updating, and in many cases, adopting brand-new pieces of legislation. Our ultimate goal here is to create similar levels of trust among foreign investors in the non-energy sector, as we did for the oil companies through the PSAs. Now, we can proudly refer to the new Civil, Tax, Customs Codes, as well as a number of lesser acts, which were passed in these years, including the Law on Trade Marks and Service Marks, Law on Protection of Foreign Investments, Budget Systems Law, Public Procurement Law, and the recently adopted Law on the Chamber of Accounts.

As a result of the abovementioned facts, the stagnation tendency has been reversed and the economy started growing steadily (9.9 percent GDP growth in 2001, equaling $500 million). Overall GDP growth since 1996 has been 55 percent, averaging over 9 percent a year. There has also been considerable growth of total investment as Azerbaijan has been looking more and more promising to foreign investors, with total foreign investments in the economy exceeding $7 billion in the last six years; including $3 billion in the non-oil sector. It is well-known that from 1994 to 2000, Azerbaijan received more foreign direct investment, per capita, than any other of the NIS countries (in 1996-1999, FDIs in the Azerbaijani economy comprised 15 percent of the NIS FDI portfolio).

On equal pace, we have been dealing with the internal problems of development, bringing the level of inflation down to 1.4 percent in 2001, and cutting budget deficit to 0.4 percent. Tax collection has grown considerably, in yet another reflection of the Azerbaijani leadership's attention to creating a favorable economic climate in the country.

Still, we obviously have to overcome the passive approach by many foreign companies outside the energy sector, who have continued to "fence-sit"-first waiting for the legal groundwork to be completed, and later to see how the infrastructure develops.

I would also like to say a few words on the role of multilateral credit institutions in Azerbaijan's transition towards a new economic model. Those lenders support institution building while also providing financing for new projects. The multinational corporations active in my country include the International Monetary Fund, the World Bank, the Asian Development Bank, the European Bank for Reconstruction and Development, and others. The IMF, with its highly-developed system of economic leverage, has become a prominent force in Azerbaijan's development. It has become an arbiter of the development, using the economic criteria it set for aid disbursement. As an example, Azerbaijan has met and even exceeded all the criteria set by the IMF for its 2001-approved $100 million poverty reduction and growth facility, including real GDP growth and the amount of net foreign reserves of the Central Bank.

The Government has to take into account the social situation in the country while pursuing the strategy of economic transition. This is imperative and inevitable. We managed to achieve full understanding with the World Bank, despite the latter's urgings, for example, that we raise the energy tariffs on the domestic market, which would have led to burdening individual consumers.

Under the leadership of President Heydar Aliyev, Azerbaijan has progressed along the path of economic restructuring using the energy sector as both a driving force behind those changes and the core of the newly-established market economy.

Privatization and creation of an investor-friendly climate being inseparable pillars of Azerbaijan's economic reforms, the continued attention paid by my Government to economic restructuring is bearing fruit. Major structural reforms and macroeconomic transformation have been pursued to create a modern structure of economy. The results are obvious, with growth in key sectors far exceeding the overall industry growth figures. For example, with an average figure here being only 5.1 percent in 2001, growth in engineering was over 25 percent, and in construction materials production, almost 85 percent.

The April 25 meeting of Azerbaijan's President with the nation's business people has become yet another crucial point documenting my Government's dedication to promoting business development. The President pledged his full support to entrepreneurs, vowing to remove the remaining bureaucratic obstacles to their activity. We have a similar meeting scheduled with foreign businesses in Azerbaijan early this month. The government of Azerbaijan is going to revise existing regulations and rules, paying special attention to the licensing process, with the number of areas of entrepreneurship requiring licensing from the Government to be reduced from over 250 to 70 and further reductions to come.

Yet another of the recent developments was April 24-26's Interfood, the Eighth Azerbaijan International Exhibition for Food and Drink, Packaging and Food Technology, which focused on bringing my nation's still restructuring agriculture closer to the world. Despite a history of being the main exporter of fresh, as well as canned, fruits and vegetables to all the former republics of the USSR, as I have already mentioned, we turned into an importer, largely because of the outdated equipment we inherited after the Soviet Union's collapse. Now Azerbaijan seems to be making a comeback in agriculture.

Finally, let me once again emphasize the energy projects, which play a significant role in shaping the geopolitical image of the whole region. It is obvious that Azerbaijan's oil and gas development is not merely an issue of energy production and delivery. Azerbaijan has developed and persistently implemented its own oil strategy with the major goal of strengthening its independence and integration into with the international community. Now, with numerous PSAs signed on oil and gas fields, we see the multi-billion investments changing Azerbaijan's future.

In a relatively short period of time, we were able to put in operation two pipelines (Baku-Novorossiysk and Baku-Supsa). Again, the decision and implementation were not easy. Now, we are facing construction of the Main Export Pipeline, which will run from Baku through Tbilisi to the Turkish Mediterranean port of Ceyhan. The MEP will become one of the components of an extensive infrastructure to foster the economic development of Azerbaijan and the entire region becoming one of the key elements of the regional cooperation, as well as an instrument of ever-growing integration with the West.

The efforts of the Government of Azerbaijan are aimed at utilizing the petrodollars, via the recently-established Oil Fund (created in January 2001), to change the balance in favor of the non-oil economy, despite the fact that, as they say, "oil rules."

This year is a very significant one for my country, because in 2002, several projects are becoming reality. First and most important, the Azeri-Chirag-Guneshli oilfield project. Phase 1 of its development, a $3.4 billion project, will take Azerbaijan beyond the "early oil" stage. In early 2005, we expect the first "big" oil to flow. Also, this summer we expect the MEP detailed-engineering stage to be complete, marking the start of the physical construction of the pipeline in order for it to be ready in time to carry the increased volumes. Parallel to this, the Shah Deniz gas field will be developed, and we already have the trilateral agreement with Turkey and Georgia to build the Baku-Tbilisi-Erzurum pipeline to carry Azerbaijan's gas to the ever-growing Turkish market. The idea of further expanding my country's gas supplies to include Greece and other European nations has recently been explored during the visit of an official Greek delegation to Baku, and we will be able to sell up to 1.5 billion cubic meters of gas to Greece by the year 2007.

Azerbaijan's aspiration to fully liberalize trade can be well-served by our bid to join the World Trade Organization. We hope to see this happen with the assistance of the TDA, which as recently as March awarded my country a $1 million grant to assist with WTO accession.

Availing myself of the opportunity to talk in front of the gathered U.S. Agencies' representatives, I would like to express how appreciative we in Azerbaijan are of their assistance, including OPIC, TDA, Ex-lm Bank, as well as that of U.S. AID. Despite limitations of Section 907 of the Freedom Support Act, which existed until recently, these agencies have managed to provide considerable assistance, including help with micro-lending ventures and seed capital.

Last but not least is the contribution of the U.S.-Azerbaijan Chamber of Commerce, which for a number of years since its inauguration in 1996, pursued its objective of developing closer business ties between the two nations. If you only take a look at the topics of their yearly conferences, you will see how much they have done in familiarizing the U.S. business community and public with Azerbaijan. The Chamber has the full support of the President of Azerbaijan, who has himself been a speaker at those conferences a couple of times.

In closing, I would like to say that I am fully confident, in my country's case, that its economic performance will be one of the pillars supporting its revival. We have done our utmost to achieve that, and, in my opinion, succeeded in the most crucial task-to make the economic transition irreversible. As for the rest, including specifics of development, I don't know who could have done better especially considering the realities in the region for most of this time, and now, I invite you to play your role in Azerbaijan's further economic re-emergence.

"Caspian Oil Windfalls: Who Will Benefit?"
Remarks at the Conference Organized By Open Society
Institute and Center for Strategic and International
Studies (CSIS)
May 12, 2003

First of all, I would like to express my appreciation to the organizers of this Conference-Open Society Institute and CSIS for their initiative aimed to overview the impact of energy revenues on Azerbaijan and Kazakhstan. I am particularly thankful to the CSIS for the continuing interest to the political and economic processes in Azerbaijan. With utmost pleasure, I am recalling my previous presentations at several CSIS events, as well as an appearance here of the Executive Director of the Oil Fund of Azerbaijan, Mr. Samir Sharifov, last year. Currently, he is in London participating in British Government-sponsored Extractive Industries Transparency Initiative (EITI), which is immediately interconnected with the topics that we are addressing here.

Development of hydrocarbons in Azerbaijan has been influenced by two rather ironic paradoxes.

First, despite a century and a half of experience with oil production, Azerbaijan has never been able to manage its oil assets and, especially, the oil revenues. At almost all points of its development, the decision on what portion of the dividends we could keep and spend on our internal needs, were being made by an outside power. As a matter of fact, besides obvious negative effects of such injustice on the society, it had a positive side [for] unlike in many other energy-producing countries, in Azerbaijan, social processes have never experienced excessive influence of the "oil money."

In yet another paradox, after the collapse of the Soviet Union in 1991, my nation, despite its internationally-established image of an oil-producing country, was actually importing energy. Thus, any greater-scale tasks of reforming society were quite naturally preceded by the need to restore energy production and accumulate, after covering the production-related expenses, the dividends, to be used for general infrastructure related development, for concrete projects in economic transition, as well as country-specific projects like alleviating the suffering of refugees and IDPs.

In my country, the job of accumulating and managing those dividends in a most open and transparent way is performed by the State Oil Fund. The State Oil Fund of the Republic of Azerbaijan (SOFAZ) has been established in accordance with the Presidential Decree of December 29, 1999. It is a mechanism whereby energy-related windfalls will be accumulated and efficiently managed; in so doing, the government is demonstrating its over-riding desire and determination to avoid the inherent inclination for any nation in the midst of an oil and gas boom to spend excessively and create macroeconomic distortions.

The Oil Fund has as its main objective the professional management of oil, and gas related revenues for the benefit of the country and its future generations. Statutory Regulations of the State Oil Fund of the Republic of Azerbaijan were approved by the President of Azerbaijan on December 29, 2000. The major sources of income for SOFAZ are: revenues generated from the country's share of sales of crude oil and gas (after deductions envisaged by the appropriate legislation); bonus payments; royalties (acreage payments from all PSA operators in Azerbaijan);rental fees for the use of state property by foreign companies under oil and gas contracts; revenues generated from the sale of assets that are transferred to the Azerbaijan's ownership under contracts signed with foreign companies; other revenues from joint activities with foreign companies; and revenues generated from investment of the Fund's assets.

SOFAZ adopts a prudent strategy for the management of its assets. Full use is made of the security offered by keeping the funds offshore with internationally reputable financial institutions and fund managers. According to the Fund's rules, it can only invest into at least double-A-rated banking deposits with foreign banks or debt.

Azerbaijan Oil Fund's assets are not the biggest compared to other countries' stabilization Funds. Thus, according to the figures officially published on May 1, 2003, SOFAZ has accumulated $920 million, including $886 million from oil and gas contracts and $34 million earned by Fund through its own activity.

With the establishment of the Oil Fund, Azerbaijan, like many other countries blessed with rich natural resources aspires to achieve several goals, namely: to create a buffer reserve against oil price volatility; to amass funds that can be used to offset depletion of natural resources; to control expenditure and safeguard against excessive spending; and to fund [the] diversification of the economy.

Unlike Government Petroleum Fund of Norway, which originally served as its model, SOFAZ, besides accumulating financial assets for future generations, is also playing a major role in providing funds for the economic development, including key infrastructure projects. Taking into account the specifics of transition in Azerbaijan, social development agenda is also high on SOFAZ's list of priorities.

One of the most important elements of the Fund's rules and regulations is how and when the money and revenues of the Fund are to be spent and what is the decision-making process.

Up until today, SOFAZ has been involved in a few development projects: First, financing of 6741 housing and infrastructure facilities for refugees and internally displaced persons, who were driven from their homes as a result of aggression and armed occupation by Armenia. There are $75 million appropriated for these purposes, including $50 million already spent. This involvement is one of the key elements in Government's poverty reduction program and socio-economic progress in a broader context.

The second area of SOFAZ expenditures is partial involvement into financing of the commercially beneficial Baku-Tbilisi-Ceyhan main export pipeline. The pipeline is strategically important to Azerbaijan's economy. According to the BTC financing concept, Azerbaijan should cover $850 million out of total project-related expenditures of $3.4 billion (project cost of $2.9 billion, plus credit interest). Our immediately payable share is $250 million, with $70 million corning from SOCAR and $180 provided by SOFAZ, out of which $118 million has already been transferred by the Fund.

Third, SOFAZ is going to transfer $100 million to the 2003 budget of Azerbaijan for financing investment projects. To bring more public control to Oil Fund, the Government of Azerbaijan, after intensive consultations with the International Monetary Fund (IMF) and World Bank (WB), agreed to make changes in the Law on the State Budget and include SOFAZ expenditures, as part of the State Investment Program, into the consolidated Parliament-approved budget of Azerbaijan.

SOFAZ publishes quarterly reports on its revenues and expenditures, undergoes annual audits and makes their findings publicly known. Its activity is subject to the audit by the Parliamentary Chamber of Accounts, which is a supreme audit institution of the country. Besides that, internationally acclaimed companies conduct tender-based yearly audits of the Oil Fund and publish reports on the Fund's web-site: www.oilfund.az. The 2002 audit is being carried out by Ernest and Young.

As pointed, challenges on Azerbaijan's path on transition are many and my nation's financial resources are scarce. We have to mobilize our capacity both material and human, to speed up the development of the country, and that's where the role of SOFAZ along with SOCAR cannot be overrated.

My personal experience convinces me that broad public discussions on and around energy-related projects promotes the development of civil society in Azerbaijan; thus furthering the progress of my nation towards democracy.

"Azerbaijan and the Situation in and Around Iraq"
Remarks at the Conference Titled "Iraq and the Cauca-
sus: How Will War Affect the Region?"
Organized by the Center for Strategic and International
Studies (CSIS), Caucasus Initiative
May 27, 2003

It is a pleasure to appear here before you, speaking on a topic of such paramount importance to the international community. Being well aware of the debates that still concentrate on this issue, it will be my honor to present Azerbaijan's vision.

Escalation of stand-off around Iraq posed a dilemma for many nations, and my country seemed to be no exception. Azerbaijan, located in a volatile region of the world and being a secular Muslim country, seemed to be in a rather precarious position from the very beginning. Yet, there was no major contradiction between the decision we made and my country's long-term goals and policy principles. On the contrary, it was a logical continuation of the basics of our foreign policy and a reflection of public opinion.

From the very moment of restoration of its independence in 1991, Azerbaijan has thrived to become a rightful member of the world community, a law-abiding international citizen. As such we always proceeded from the necessity to endorse and support supremacy of the norms and principles of international law, to which we adhere without deviation.

My country's position on Iraq and decision to be a part of coalition are reflected in two statements by the Foreign Ministry. Our approach was based on the conviction that Iraq should "fully fulfill all the demands, resulting from the appropriate UN Security Council resolutions 678, 687, 1441." Azerbaijan was one of the ardent proponents of the UN-based course of action and only when the latter became impossible and having expressed our "deep regret over the UN Security Council's absence of unity on actions towards Iraq" did we support alternative steps; thus becoming a member of the "coalition of the willing." While doing so, Azerbaijan never lost its belief that the operation in Iraq would promote the United Nations' role in maintaining international peace and security.

As you are aware, for over a decade now, my country has been under armed aggression from neighboring Armenia which led to military occupation of about 20 percent of Azerbaijan's territory and emergence of nearly one million of refugees and internally displaced persons in my country. Despite UN Security Council resolutions 822, 853, 874, 884 adopted in 1993, which called for immediate withdrawal of the occupational armed forces, the conflict between Armenia and Azerbaijan is still unsolved, and none of the resolutions is fulfilled yet.

The international community should react and add practical steps to condemnation of Armenia's aggression against Azerbaijan, just like it did in case of Iraq's annexation of Kuwait. So far, unfortunately, we have faced rather hypocritical double standards.

I was very interested to hear that the Armenian Ambassador confirmed territorial integrity of Iraq. I hope that some day, Armenia will openly recognize territorial integrity of its immediate neighbor too. That would be the most valuable contribution of Armenia to the stability of our region.

Secondly, there were other reasons that dictated our policy decision on Iraq. Azerbaijan's position doesn't differ from that of international community, with respect to the twin threat of WMD proliferation and international terrorism as the most acute challenge to international peace and security.

While being a party to Comprehensive Nuclear Test Ban Treaty (CTBT), Nuclear Non-Proliferation Treaty (NPT), Chemical Weapons Convention (CWC), [a] member of International Atomic Energy Agency (IAEA), and undertaking practical measures, Azerbaijan has always put its every effort for prevention of WMD proliferation. We were expecting the same approach from other countries. Unfortunately, Saddam's Iraq was not eager to do so, thus undermining stability of the region and posing risk to the global security.

As far as international terrorism is concerned, having been among the first to express its support to the United States after the heinous crime of 9/11, my country has been an active member of the U.S.-led international coalition combating terrorism in all its forms and manifestations. We provided "whatever needed" to coalition forces to fight terrorists in Afghanistan and later sent peacekeepers to International Security Assistance Forces (ISAF) as a support to Operation Enduring Freedom. We are also actively cooperating with international community aimed at extirpating the menace of terrorism. Regrettably, the regime in Baghdad was ignoring the international efforts to eliminate terror from international relations. Azerbaijan's participation in NATO's Partnership for Peace program has always meant more for my country than just a formal pledge. Our position that active engagement into Euro-Atlantic partnership structures has to be followed by concrete steps on the international arena was behind my nation's involvement in Kosovo, Afghanistan, and Iraq.

Thirdly, the decision-making was influenced by Saddam's policy of suppression. Of all the realities of the Iraqi dictatorship, I was especially shocked by *The Washington Post's* reports about oppression for the last thirty years of Shiites in Iraq, who have been even deprived of their right to worship. Here, an obvious parallel in my memory can not be escaped. The list of wrongdoings of the Communist rulers in Moscow was endless; yet, even at their crudest, they never managed to completely suppress the religious roots of Azerbaijanis.

Looking at all facts surrounding the pre-war situation, we can say without any doubt that Saddam Hussein's regime was fully outlawed. Thus, it came as no surprise that my Government's decision on Iraq met with no disagreement whatsoever from either Azerbaijani political groups or public as a whole.

In implementing this decision, we supported the efforts of the coalition aimed at soonest resolution of the Iraq crisis, while at the same time urging strict adherence to the norms of the international humanitarian law, both during the military operation in Iraq, as well as within the framework of upholding law and order and pursuing relief efforts currently underway.

Azerbaijani leadership has adopted a decision to send 150 peacekeepers to Iraq to help implement the principles we have been advocating all along. The decision has already been approved by our Parliament and Azerbaijani soldiers and officers will be on duty in Iraq very soon. Our peacekeepers will serve in the cities of Karbala and Najaf, where holiest shrines of Shiites are located. This factor could play a significant role in ensuring stability and security in these cities.

My country's willingness to play a role in the stabilization force is not limited to the peace-keeping only. We also stand ready to render assistance in other areas, where Azerbaijan has expertise, considering humanitarian rehabilitation of post-conflict Iraq to be among the important tasks for the foresee-able future. Health care and infrastructure specialists, Arabic translators, as well as oil development experts-of all those Azerbaijan has abundance.

We believe that providing such assistance is crucial not only for the humanitarian reasons but because of the role that should be played by the international community in bringing Iraq back on track in terms of economic restoration. It is my country's position that the Resolution 1483, recently passed by the UN Security Council will be of utmost importance in establishing "conditions of stability and security in Iraq." Ensuring close and effective cooperation between the United Nations and the occupying powers will allow the transition process to be relatively swift and painless.

Speaking about the effects of the war on Azerbaijan and the Caucasus, we should note that, fortunately, worst-case scenario (protracted war) did not take place, mainly due to the well-calculated strategy and precision of Operation Iraqi Freedom. At the same time, the outcome of reconstruction, both political and otherwise, of Iraq, [a] country with a mixture of ethnic and religious groups, is of concern to us. How this outcome will influence policies of neighboring Turkey (vis-à-vis Kurdish issue) or Iran (with its Shī'a population) has to be watched carefully and addressed through persistent diplomatic efforts.

We consider that establishment of a viable representative Government of Iraq could both significantly contribute to establishing a more stable region and also bring a new positive element to the Middle East peace process. We already have first signs of that.

In general, the policy against terror and any forms of oppression in modem worlds dictates that the international community be very aware of and attentive to any conflict, including those that, for the time-being, appear to be of lesser significance. No conflict should be "forgotten" and the world will not have to deal with their consequences in the future.

"En Route to a Strategic Alliance"
Ten Years of the U.S.-Azerbaijan Diplomatic Relations
Published in 2002 USACC Investment Guide

I often recall my sentiments after having arrived to the U.S. almost ten years ago as the first, newly-appointed ambassador of sovereign Azerbaijan. As a physicist, I can't help but to try and put development of the bilateral relations in scientific terms. So, parts of the equation called "bilateral relations" were set by that time. My nation's priorities were set and its choice in favor of the pro-democracy development made clear and irreversible. The full-scale economic and political interaction with the United States became both basic principle of and the driving force behind our orientation. Reflecting on the achievements of those ten years of relationship, on the difficulties we've overcome together, inevitably brings me back to the times immediately following collapse of the USSR, when we were laying groundwork for our future bilateral partnership.

It is then, prior to opening Azerbaijan's Embassy in Washington, that the biggest blow to the emerging relations was dealt. I mean the unfair provision of the U.S. law, [the] infamous Section 907 of the Freedom Support Act. It considerably hampered the development of the bilateral U.S.-Azerbaijan cooperation during most of these ten years. Nevertheless, my first experience of dealing with the U.S. legislative branch, which came almost immediately after my arrival to America, was a positive one. I comprehended that a voice of reason can be and always will be heard. I came to that conclusion in early 1993 after yet another piece of anti-

Azerbaijani legislation was introduced on the Capitol Hill, the 1993 "Bonior Amendment," blaming my country for [its] so-called hostile approach to the Armenian side. It is then that I have witnessed firsthand, that the newly-opened Embassy alone was able to change many members' minds and prevent this legislation from passing.

In general, the first years of the U.S.-Azerbaijan relations were spent under the "Russia First" principle, which, at that time, dominated American foreign policy vis-à-vis former Soviet republics. My task was to bring Azerbaijan closer to the American decision-makers, convincing them that recognition of my country's place in the regional and world affairs was not only inevitable, but also to the U.S.' benefit.

In 1994 a new stage began. At that point, the U.S.-Azerbaijan ties received a huge impetus in the economic field, which, thanks to the wise oil strategy of President Aliyev, also became the moving force for our economy in general.

The commonality of approaches between the United States and Azerbaijan is especially obvious in the field of development and transportation of the Caspian energy resources. Despite considerable pressure from elsewhere, Azerbaijan succeeded in bringing the American oil producers into the region; thus raising its visibility on the world energy map.

After the discoveries in Azerbaijan's off-shore sector of the Caspian, which resulted in signing of the "Contract of the Century" [in] 1994, huge amounts of hydrocarbons were also found in Kazakhstan, turning the Caspian, in the words of Ambassador Steven Mann, into the potential major non-OPEC source of energy. The perspective was also confirmed in last year's National Energy Plan of the U.S. Administration.

It is also at this point that the U.S. started a more active engagement in the process of search for a lasting settlement to the Armenia-Azerbaijan, Nagorno-Karabakh conflict. Earlier American involvement was more or less going along the lines of trying to pass (and, sometimes, passing) Congressional resolutions, at times insensitive and even irrelevant. In 1995, the U.S. started, in its capacity as a member and, later, Co-Chair, of the Minsk Group, to work closely with the sides to the conflict.

After President Aliyev's 1997 official visit to the United States, the bilateral relations entered a qualitatively new phase-the one defined by creation of basis for future development through signing a package of bilateral documents. It is at this point that the U.S. started getting actively engaged in securing the independence and prosperity of the countries in the region. Joint efforts in this area led both sides to thinking more about regional stability and security-be it in the form of a pan-regional structure or individual arrangements.

Azerbaijan, with no foreign military bases or troops on its soil, pursues a policy of integration into European and global security architecture. Our active cooperation with NATO-especially within the framework of the Partnership for Peace-is yet another factor, bringing us closer to fulfilling the mentioned goal, underscoring our nation's strategic importance, and also further cementing our ties with the United States. We view future development of the region as a process that should move along the lines of demilitarizing the area around Caspian Sea.

East-West energy transportation corridor is at the core of our economic relationship. It will serve as both means of diversification of the energy transportation options, and as a catalyst for further overall economic development of the region. It also becomes yet another channel of political unification in the region, bringing Caspian energy-producing states closer to the Western consumers of energy. [The] Groundbreaking of the Baku-Tbilisi-Ceyhan pipeline in September became a milestone for the emerging transportation corridor.

The U.S. support to the independence of the former Soviet republics is well-reflected in its approach towards
GUUAM, a group of five, comprising of Azerbaijan, Georgia,
Ukraine, Uzbekistan, and Moldova. We hope that this support will be becoming more and more resolute.

The United States also continued the policy aimed at enhancing business opportunities beyond energy sector for
companies from the U.S. and other countries. Here the direction and tempo of reforming Azerbaijan's economy remain
vital elements. We believe that the steps undertaken by the
Government of Azerbaijan, including creation of the oil fund
and restructuring of the Cabinet of Ministers, will lead to
making Azerbaijan ever more attractive to foreign investors.
My country values contribution of the Bilateral Task Force,
which has done a lot in this direction.

After the tragic events of 9/11, our comprehensive and
multi-faceted relationship has acquired another dimension.
Azerbaijan has long been warning about dangers of international terrorism, which has done enormous damage to my nation as well, and now we are with the United States in this
campaign, unequivocally and unconditionally, and it also
brings us closer together as two allies. President Aliyev's February 2003 visit to the United States, meetings with President
Bush, Vice-President Cheney and a number of other high-
ranking Administration officials proved that our relations of
partnership are for real- the last, but not least. For a number
of years, Azerbaijan has strived trying to deal away with the
unjust sanctions contained in Section 907. Finally, early in
2002, President Bush, exercising Congressionally-provided
waiver authority, suspended those restrictions. Relations between the two nations have entered a brand-new stage, out-
growing previously-established framework of mutually beneficial cooperation and acquiring the nature of a true alliance.

**"Elections in Azerbaijan and U.S. Interests
in the Caspian Sea"
Remarks at the Heritage Foundation
October 27, 2005**

It is a pleasure to participate on this panel addressing "Elections in Azerbaijan and U.S. Interests in the Caspian Sea." It is a particular honor to speak to you at this critical moment in our country's history. We are well on the path to becoming a democratic, free market economy. We are proud of the progress we have made over the last fourteen years and recognize the challenges before us. We welcome the support we have received from the United States and know that continued commitment from you is integral to our future progress.

Since Azerbaijan became independent in 1991, it took the decision to pursue policies of a pro-Western, democratic country with a free market economy. Azerbaijan has continued to develop in accordance with those objectives. As you know, this is a process, which needs to be nurtured and protected.

Azerbaijan has also been closely cooperating with the United Nations, the OSCE, the Council of Europe, and other international organizations to undertake democratic reforms necessary to fulfill the aspirations of the Azerbaijani people. In just thirteen years, Azerbaijan conducted four presidential, two parliamentary elections as well as two municipal elections in a timely manner. Azerbaijan never deviated from the electoral timetable and ensured that they were open to international observers.

We appreciate the recommendations that have been expressed after all previous elections and we used them for implementing reforms. This process allowed people unfamiliar with the tradition of democracy to gain an appreciation for full participation in the political process.

Still, we understand that this is a difficult path to follow, and the Government of President Ilham Aliyev has pursued many steps to meet international electoral standards.

We are now less than ten days away from parliamentary elections. Indicative of the appeal democracy has gained in our young country, there are almost two thousand candidates for 125 seats in our multi-party system.

In 2003, a unified election code was adopted which incorporated recommendations by international organizations and established standards in accordance with international practice. Additionally, two major presidential decrees on elections were announced-one on May 11th, and the latest just this week on October 25.

The May 11 executive order instructs regional executive authorities to ensure freedom of assembly, equal access to the media, create conditions for exit polls, and prohibits any intervention in the electoral process.

Following this decree, Baku hosted several high level visitors from the U.S., including Under Secretary for Global Affairs Paula Dobriansky, senators Richard Lugar, Chuck Hagel and Barack Obama, Assistant Secretary of State Daniel Fried, former Secretary of State and Current NDI Chairman Madeline Albright, and Congressman Darryl Issa and Congresswoman Loretta Sanchez. During these visits, steps taken by the government were praised as well as democratic and economic reforms. The visitors expressed belief that Azerbaijan will fulfill its promise for free and fair elections.

Azerbaijan has been subject to commentary by a variety of international organizations on these developments. On September 30, the OSCE issued an Interim Report on the electoral process in Azerbaijan acknowledging the achievements like the May 11th presidential decree, orderly registration of candidates, technical preparations of the Central Election Commission, and the opening of public television.

Sixty days before the elections, candidates launched their campaigns. Azerbaijan has witnessed five round table discussions among the government and opposition candidates, many opposition rallies in Baku authorized by the authorities (and peacefully conducted), and numerous others throughout the country. Even [the] U.S. media covered the town hall style campaign events where Azerbaijani citizens engaged candidates in platform and policy discussions.

In August, the first public television station was launched which has provided free and equal air time for all the candidates. This is in addition to state television allotting time.

Azerbaijanis have expressed their views on this process through various means, such as a public opinion survey among 1,200 Azerbaijanis conducted in June by the International Republican Institute, and the Agency for International Development, which revealed: a decisive majority of the voters think Azerbaijan is headed in the right direction; resolving the conflict in Nagorno-Karabakh, creating new jobs, reducing inflation and corruption are of significant importance to the voters; a majority of Azerbaijanis disapprove of the job Parliament is doing and few citizens believe Parliament or their Members of Parliament share the same priorities as they do; and voters would prefer seeing candidates and/or parties doing more TV commercials and personal outreach than holding demonstrations or protests.

The U.S. Congress paid special attention to the elections and made a constructive contribution, which we appreciated. Both the House and Senate passed resolutions calling for free and fair elections [including] House Resolution 326 in August and Senate Resolution 260 last Friday.

Less than two weeks prior to the election, President Aliyev, taking into account concerns received from the regions and precincts about election code violations, issued a decree on October 25 taking additional steps to ensure successful elections. These steps also addressed concerns and recommendations raised by the U.S. Congress and other international organizations. [The] Decree of October 25 was extremely well received, both in the country and outside of the country.

Highly controversial issues were resolved with this executive order such as lifting restrictions on election observation by NGOs with more than 30 percent foreign funding, use of invisible ink on the finger of voters, guaranteeing political parties and blocs the right to demonstrate freely, and issuing identification cards for citizens lacking necessary documents.

The President was motivated not by outside pressure, but by the desire to fulfill promises made to the voters. President's insistence on free and fair elections in November is also based on the idea that Azerbaijan's secular government can co-exist with its Muslim traditions.

In parallel with democratic reforms, Azerbaijan has undertaken economic and social initiatives. Azerbaijan is blessed with energy resources, but other countries' experiences have proven that the effective management of energy related resources and revenues are crucial. For this purpose, we established a State Oil Fund in 2001, whose Executive Director was recently in Washington for the Extractive Industries Transparency Initiative, sponsored by the World Bank. The Fund was established to meet the needs of future generations, manage the macroeconomic effects of the infusion of energy revenues into the economy, and fund infrastructure and social projects. The Fund has received high praise from even the most skeptical observers who recognize that its resources are being used to create favorable living conditions for the entire population. We acknowledge that without stable economic development, it would be difficult, if not impossible to achieve the democratic aspirations of the people.

Azerbaijanis have experienced an improvement in their quality of life. In the last two years, the minimum wage has increased three fold. Azerbaijan's macroeconomic performance in recent years, as reported by the IMF, "has been impressive with strong growth, low inflation and a stable exchange rate." Real GDP grew by an annual average of over 10 percent during last seven years. GDP growth is expected to reach 18 percent in 2005.

The crown jewel of our energy policy is the Baku-Tbilisi-Ceyhan main oil export pipeline which, again, despite overwhelming skepticism, is almost completed, and will start providing up to 25 percent of new oil to the world markets by early 2006.

This pursuit of democratic ideals and economic reforms are even more impressive given the fact that roughly 20 percent of Azerbaijan is occupied by Armenia, and almost one million refugees and internally displaced persons are waiting to return to their homes. For the first time, the Central Election Commission established two precincts for Nagorno-Karabakh and is encouraging the citizens of Azerbaijan in that region to vote for their representatives.

We know that on November 6, the eyes of the world will be on us, and that events will be scrutinized and analyzed for some time. We expect 1,500 international and 9,000 local observers. We are the first to recognize that stability and prosperity depend on successful democratic reform. President Aliyev wants orderly transition, as our last few years of unprecedented economic growth would be jeopardized by political instability. It is our intention to hold free and fair elections with a transparent process not because of international opinion, but because our citizens deserve it and the future of our country and region is at stake. This responsibility is shared by all of the stakeholders in the electoral process. President Aliyev has done more than his share to ensure an enabling environment for democratic progress and economic reforms.

We expect that the opposition will also act responsibly and refrain from any destabilizing activities.

"The Future of U.S.-Azerbaijan Relations after Parliamentary Elections" Remarks at the Conference Organized by the Nixon Center November 14, 2005

Thank you for organizing this conference and providing the opportunity to speak on recent parliamentary elections in Azerbaijan. For the last three-to-four pre-election months, Azerbaijan was under an international microscope because Azerbaijan is now recognized as an important country in the region. Azerbaijan's accomplishments achieved with close cooperation with the U.S. and other Western countries in strengthening its independence, energy developments, security cooperation, and diversification of the economy are pretty impressive.

We recognize that our future stability and prosperity depend on the successful implementation of democratic reforms. That is why the President of the country took a number of steps to ensure free and fair elections. More than two thousand candidates have been registered and they had an opportunity to conduct more than 26,000 meetings with their voters in a transparent manner.

Obviously, Parliamentary elections in Azerbaijan on November 6 represent a very important step towards democratic reforms in the country. The President's commitment to conduct free and fair elections played a crucial role throughout the entire process, from the preparation stage up to Election Day. This commitment continued after Election Day as well. Currently, the Government and the Central Elections Commission (CEC) are sorting out all complaints and irregularities.

I am not going to remind you of all of them but would like to emphasize only that steps taken during this period were praised by many domestic and international observers. The President said (and I quote), "We took all these actions because I did not want any questions to be raised and I wanted to remove any doubts that may remain."

Regarding Election Day, almost half of Azerbaijani voters came to polling stations to express their will. The general atmosphere was calm and positive. More than fifteen hundred international and over seventeen thousand local observers monitored the elections and noted orderly process. At the same time, they registered a number of irregularities, especially in the counting and tabulation processes.

On Election Day, for the first time exit-polls were used. 85 percent of their results matched the preliminary official results. Only around 10 percent of the results showed that there are differences beyond the margin of error. According to these results, YAP won sixty-two seats, twenty seats went to opposition, and independent candidates gained forty seats in the Parliament.

The views of international observers are important for us. The day after [the] elections, the President promised that the Government will seriously consider and analyze all the criticism coming from the international organizations. We recognize that cooperation with the CE, OSCE, and human rights organizations is vital for further democratization of our country.

As you know, CEC is working hard in accordance with the provisions of our country's laws to address all concerns. For now, the results in three constituencies (that is Sumgait, Binagadi, Zagatala) were annulled, and recounting in two other constituencies have resulted in [the] declaration [of] two opposition leaders as winners.

President Aliyev fired three regional Governors (Sura-khani, Sabirabad, Zagatala). Four election officials were charged and investigations have begun.

Every single fraud case will be thoroughly examined. I have to emphasize that [it was] for the first time in the history of independent Azerbaijan [that] so many officials were fired or indicted for election fraud.

Regarding "color" revolutions, I have the impression that the majority of foreign reporters (204 in general) representing fifty-two international media outlets came to Azerbaijan with the expectation of witnessing the next "color" revolution in the post-Soviet space, although everybody, except a small group of radical opposition leaders, predicted an easy win for the government party. The great majority of the Azerbaijani people reject the notion of a revolution. They still remember very well what disastrous consequences it brings to people. During the early nineties we already experienced some sort of "color" revolution. Now, people want to see an evolutionary process which can drive Azerbaijan towards real and genuine democracy. Every nation has a right to choose its own pace in that direction.

Azerbaijan has already made its choice towards western democratic values. It is the first country in the Muslim world to establish a democratic republic. We have our own history and experience in this area. Therefore, special attention should be given to this country. A special policy should be worked out. It should be taken into account that Azerbaijan is located in a fragile region. If properly approached, Azerbaijan with its religious tolerance and secularism can serve as a model for other Muslim countries.

With the reality of complexity and geopolitical risks, I do not believe in any "absolutes" being it the doctrine of democracy or anything else. I firmly believe that parliamentary elections became a watershed in the life of Azerbaijan.

First and foremost, these elections had a great educational impact on Azerbaijani voters. People gained a lot of new experiences. I consider these as the most important achievement of elections.

Letters to Members of U.S. Congress and U.S. Administration

By 2001, the situation in the South Caucasus had changed. In addition to the active U.S. involvement in the Karabakh peace process, the major issues on the U.S. agenda were democratization efforts, energy projects, human rights and the fight against corruption. Some of the questions raised by the U.S. Congress were legitimate concerns and I always welcomed constructive proposals. Yet, there were certain statements and letters that were solely aimed at damaging the reputation of Azerbaijan as a country. The following letter is my response to the author of one of these, Representative Joseph R. Pitts (R-PA).

June 25, 2001

Dear Congressman Pitts:

I have recently been made aware of your letter, co-signed with Congressman Tancredo, to President Bush about Azerbaijan. As I have told you earlier, I am very appreciative of your interest in Azerbaijan and its efforts to settle the conflict with Armenia over the Nagorno-Karabakh region of the Republic of Azerbaijan. However, I trust you will permit me to make several observations concerning the ideas contained in the abovementioned letter:

> *(1) You make the point that the vast majority of Azerbaijani citizens live in poverty because of the conflict and the fact that over one million persons are either*

refugees or internally displaced persons. Let's call a spade a spade; this is not conflict we are talking about but Armenian aggression, of which Azerbaijan is a victim and which has resulted in the military occupation of 20 percent of Azerbaijan. Can you imagine the economic consequences to the United States if one-eighth of your population consisted of either refugees or internally displaced persons? The extent of poverty is also a result of transition from totalitarianism to a free society with a market economy.

(2) *You state that the U.S. has failed to achieve its goal of creating an "Independent secure, democratic and prosperous Azerbaijan," but despite the obstacles already mentioned, Azerbaijan is today the most stable country in the Caucasus and has no foreign troops stationed on its soil (unlike Armenia, by choice and Georgia, by duress). What you could have mentioned is the negative impact on my nation's stability of one certain piece of U.S. Congress adopted legislation (Section 907), which has kept unjust unilateral sanctions for more than nine years, despite the opposition of three U.S. Presidents.*

(3) *You further state that President Aliyev has held onto power through "a series of falsified elections." I would point out that Azerbaijan has had a series of national elections, each one [being] an improvement over the previous election, as stated by the Office of Democratic Institutes and Human Rights of the OSCE. In fact, it was the parliamentary re-election in several districts in January of 2001 where irregularities had occurred that won the praise of the Council of Europe and led to Azerbaijan's admission into that organization. Azerbaijan would not have been admitted to the*

Council of Europe without making steady progress toward a true Western-style democracy.

(4) With reference to your statement regarding corruption, much of it is a carryover from previous Soviet times, and President Aliyev has made a determined effort to remove it. The most vivid case is the one of former Speaker of the Parliament, Mr. Rasul Guiliev, who stands accused of stealing over $60 million in oil revenues when he headed the state oil refinery. It is ironic that when writing about corruption in my country you rely upon such people and their paid lobbyists, whose bias threatens to embarrass anyone using them as a source.

(5) Azerbaijan has an improving human rights record. We have a free press, freedom of religion, constitutional guarantees of human rights, and we have abolished the death penalty. This is not an empty claim; check what the Council of Europe has to say about each of these issues. Azerbaijan suffers the same problems other former Soviet republics do in making the transition to true democracy. After all, it was yourself who acknowledged my country's achievements in this field.

Finally, let me urge you to exercise caution when pronouncing judgment on developments in Azerbaijan. From my own years-long experience, I can tell you that any unbalanced U.S. congressional criticism of Azerbaijan is being used for the purposes of destabilizing my country, which, obviously, does not comply with the U.S. goals you mention in your letter.
Sincerely,
Hafiz Pashayev
Ambassador

In October 2003, Ilham Aliyev was elected President of Azerbaijan. Following the October 16 Election Day, some members of the opposition groups in the country called on their supporters to stage riots and instigate violent clashes against the law enforcement. Soon, some of the protestors started to hurl rocks at the police and move through the streets of the capital city, breaking windows and rampaging along the way. The law enforcement agencies interfered to stop further escalation of the violence. Nonetheless, the extensive use of force on the part of some local law enforcement officers drew criticism from international community and some U.S. congressmen. While I acknowledged the deficiencies of the October 2003 elections and events that took place afterwards, I also knew that the actions taken by law enforcement agencies to stop further bloodshed were not completely unjustified. Below is my letter to Representative Tom Lantos (D-CA) with an attached fact-sheet about the election and its aftermath.

February 10, 2004

Dear Congressman Lantos:

It is with utmost concern that I have read your February 3 remarks regarding the Human Rights Watch report on Azerbaijan's elections.

First of all, while recognizing that there is some justification to the accusations about irregularities in the process and conduct of the elections, I should emphasize that no observer expressed doubt on the final outcome, including the opposition proper. The latter being aware of imminent defeat as a result of the vote, has decided in favor of the planned stand-off with the authorities, hoping that ensuing confrontation would cast a shadow of doubt over the polls outcome.

The Government of Azerbaijan is doing its best to rectify the violations which took place. At the same time, we do not bear any responsibility for the claims that are not documented. Unfortunately, as you will see from the enclosed fact-sheet, those unsubstantiated allegations are many.

Remembering our past conversations and your interest in the developments in my country, I believe that after receiving my letter you will look deeper into the issues you touched upon in your remarks.

It will be my pleasure to have a meeting with you at your convenience to respond to any questions you might have.

Sincerely,

Hafiz Pashayev

Ambassador

Fact-Sheet: Some Aspects of the January 2004 Report by Human Rights Watch

Some of the critical issues voiced by the Human Rights Watch with respect to the presidential elections of October 15, 2003, and the events that ensued, have to be addressed, especially the basic premise of peaceful unarmed protesters being attacked by the law-enforcement employing "excessive force.

While recognizing that there is justification for some criticism, it must be emphasized that many of the claims made in the Report, including the allegation of "massive and brutal campaign of arrest and torture," are unfounded.

The following are some of the counterpoints to the claims contained in the mentioned Report.

"The first clash, on the night of October 15, involved an unprovoked attack by the security forces on peaceful protesters gathered in front of the Musavat headquarters" (p.21).

Those gathered in front of the opposition headquarters were not there for the purposes of peaceful protest or even civil disobedience. As evident from the opposition newspapers in the days and weeks before the election and immediately after it, the opposition has been making plans for employing violence as a tool of achieving their political goals. Here are just a few quotes to document that.

On September 30, 2003, Mr. Rauf Arifoglu, Deputy Chairman of Musavat, has written in the party newspaper Yeni Musavat, of which he is also Editor-In-Chief, "Our people who live in villages and far regions [...] should go to the polling stations with food and specially-made truncheons at the end of the election day. Should there be anyone among the polling station staff who'll try to falsify, try to steal one's vote or future, that man should be beaten as a donkey! Just a dozen of such active and truncheons-equipped men in every village can assure the objectivity of election in that polling station."

One week prior to the election Almaz Alikizi, an activist of the pro-Musavat "Bizim Azerbaijan" bloc called for the people to "get ready for a revolution" ("Cumhuriyyet," October 7, 2003). So did Mr. Arifoglu in [the] October 5 issue of "Reyting."

Chairman of [the] People's Party Panah Huseynov stated in the same newspaper, "Stability has to be necessarily taken away in Azerbaijan. Yes, we are against the stability. If we wish to accede to power, we will go for a revolution."

Chairman of the "Umid" Party Igbal Agazadeh [stated], "We will fight till our last drop of blood in order to bring Isa Gambar to the Presidential Chair" ("Xalq Qezeti," October 13, 2003). Similar is the case of singer Flora Karimova, who is described on page twenty-five of the Report as pleading with the police "not to attack their brothers" and who actually instigated the violence by shouting, before the clashes began, slogans like "it is either our way or death" and "Baku's streets will be washed in blood," both very well-documented in the newspapers and on video.

One more statement by the mentioned above Mr. Arifoglu. In Yeni Musavat, dated September 11, 2003, he writes about two of the candidates for the Presidency, Ilham Aliyev and Hafiz Hajiyev: "That dog of his will also get its head smashed [...] I would love to see the head of that dog smashed right in the Gelebe square. If someone wishes to take this job on, let him not wait for an urging [...] It is, indeed, a national duty of each and every one of us to make those mad dogs, those Armenians step down [...] at some point a reporter working for the pro-government Lider TV was attacked by unknown assailants " (p. 21).

The identity of the man who attacked Sahil Kerimli, a Lider TV reporter, is well-documented. His name is Mehdi Mehdiyev and he is yet another of the Musavat leaders, an advisor to Isa Gambar. [The statement], *"Opposition supporters who had commandeered a military truck rammed the vehicle into the advancing security forces, but were quickly overwhelmed" (p.23)* creates a false impression of a desperation act by outnumbered demonstrators, while in reality it was a series of concerted efforts to run down a single unarmed law-enforcement representative, as documented by video tape and numerous media representatives present.

A significant number of harshest accusations against the Government of Azerbaijan (pp. 24, 31, 42, 43, 44 etc.) so eagerly taken up by the Human Rights Watch, admittedly makes reference to people identified by made-up names. As such, they are nearly impossible to verify and refute.

There is a preposterous claim made on page twenty-four that *"a group of protesters, when chased by security forces, fled towards the Caspian Sea (on the eastern border of the Azadliq Square), some [...] jumped into the water to escape the violence."* This outrageous statement has been never documented by any source, including the oppositional, and they surely would have been the first to jump on such a tempting accusation. The only proof the authors of the Report could find was somebody using the alias of Saidali Muradov and insisting that he was among that group: *"Among those detained and abused were more than one hundred election officials and observers who, after witnessing fraudulent practices, had refused to sign their voting stations' protocols which certify the station's vote count, or who had made official complaints about the fraud that they had witnessed" (p. 36).*

Among the persons included by the Election Observation Mission and the U.S. Embassy in Baku into the lists of detained (not arrested!) only twelve were election officials. The reasons for their detention had nothing to do with their duties on the polling day, but dealt directly with law violations that ensued. Also, even those detained were in custody very

*briefly (October 16-18). None are incarcerated as of now. Azerbaijani
authorities have shown ample willingness to thoroughly investigate all accusations and violations [as] in nearly seven hundred precincts, the results were announced null and void, [and a] majority of those detained
have been released, including all the journalists. As for those against
whom specific evidence is present, their cases will go before court.*

From time to time, the Armenian lobby has used Representative Frank Pallone, Jr. and Representative Joe Knollenberg to push its own agenda on the Hill. The offices of these
congressmen distributed "Dear Colleague" letters asking fellow representatives and the President to support numerous
Armenian causes. Most of these letters contained falsehoods
and misleading information about Azerbaijan and the Karabakh conflict. The following letter was sent to all members of
Congress presenting true facts about Azerbaijan and the
Karabakh conflict urging them not to fall under the influence
of the misleading statements distributed by supporters of the
Armenian lobby in the U.S. Congress.

August 17, 2005
Dear Representative:

*On August 3, Representatives Frank Pallone, Jr. and Joe Knollen-
berg circulated a "Dear Colleague" requesting support for a letter to
President Bush about the Nagorno-Karabakh (NK) region of Azerbaijan.*

*This letter provides inaccurate information regarding the situation in
the region and the international community's position on the status of
NK. We urge you to consider the following before determining whether
you will support this initiative:*

*(1) [The] NK was never independent-nor a part of Ar-
menia. It was always an indigenous part of Azerbaijan. It was recognized as such by the United States,*

the United Nations, and other international organizations. Armenia is the only country that has not recognized Azerbaijan's territorial integrity. Any political actions by the U.S. or economic assistance to NK should occur within the legal, political and economic development context of Azerbaijan, of which it is an integral part. The Knollenberg/Pallone letter is asking your support to change U.S. policy on this issue.

(2) *Seeking independence for NK or its unification with Armenia, Armenia initiated the armed conflict with Azerbaijan in 1988 and waged a full fledged military action in 1991.*

(3) *Armenian aggression resulted in the occupation of not only NK, but seven additional regions of Azerbaijan, creating a million refugees and internally displaced Azerbaijanis. In 1993 the UN adopted four Security Council resolutions demanding the unconditional withdrawal of Armenian forces from the occupied territories. NATO, OSCE, and other international organizations also repeatedly called for the restoration of Azerbaijan's territorial integrity. Armenia ignored all of the appeals. A Russia brokered cease-fire in 1994 remains in place, yet it was the military assistance from Russia, including $1 billion in illegal arms transfers, which significantly contributed to Armenia's military occupation. The absence of internationally recognized authority in the region created fertile ground for illegal narcotics and arms trafficking.*

(4) *After initiating the conflict, expelling all Azerbaijanis, and ethnically cleansing NK and the seven regions of Azerbaijan, Armenia and NK authorities started the process of legalizing their actions. They tried to create a "democratic" image by staging elections which were never recognized by any international*

organization or entity. The United States position has always been firm in stating that these actions are illegal and don't help the peace process.

(5) *On October 29, 2004, acting on the recommendations of its General Committee, the UN General Assembly decided to include a special item on its current agenda entitled "The Situation in the Occupied Territories of Azerbaijan." Only Armenia opposed this decision.*

It is essential that the United States Congress acknowledge and respect existing U.S. policy regarding the territorial integrity of Azerbaijan as recognized by the rest of the world. At the current tenuous stage of negotiations between the Foreign Ministers of Azerbaijan and Armenia regarding the NK conflict; it would be counterproductive to the Minsk Peace Process for you to support Knollenberg-Pallone initiative. Shift in U.S. policy would represent an unfortunate acquiescence to special interests who disregard broader U.S. foreign policy priorities in the strategically vital South Caucasus.

Azerbaijan has already suffered the economic and political impact of these types of initiatives. In 1992, Congress imposed Section 907 of the Freedom Support Act which prohibited direct assistance to Azerbaijan, making Azerbaijan the only country in the world denied all direct U.S. assistance, including humanitarian Since September 11, the Administration has waived Section 907, an indication of where U.S. interests lie.

Please keep these points in mind as you consider your position. I would welcome the opportunity to discuss this further with you and respond to any questions you may have.
Sincerely,
Hafiz Pashayev
Ambassador

Hurricane Katrina was probably one of the worst natural disasters in the recent history of the United States. While watching the images of displaced Americans and hearing the hopeless cries of victims, I was too often reminded of the Azerbaijani refugees and displaced persons. The government of Azerbaijan donated $500,000 for Katrina relief. Below is my letter to Senator Daniel Akaka (D-HI), in which I also thanked him for his interest in the upcoming 2005 Parliamentary Elections in Azerbaijan, and the Washington Times article on the elections in Azerbaijan.

September 14, 2005

Dear Senator Akaka:

Please accept my sincere condolences for the loss of life and property resulting from Hurricane Katrina. The hearts and minds of Azerbaijanis are with all Americans who are struggling to cope with one of the worst natural disasters your country has ever faced.

As a country which has also grappled with a million refugees and internally displaced persons as a result of Armenian aggression, the Azerbaijani government was quick to provide much needed financial assistance to the victims of Katrina.

For its part, Azerbaijan is working to ensure that the upcoming parliamentary elections in November will meet expectations of our people and the international community. We recognize that independence, stability and prosperity depend on successful democratic reforms.

We appreciate U.S. interest and encouragement in Azerbaijan's democratic processes. The House of Representatives recently passed H. Resolution 326 calling on Azerbaijan to "hold orderly, peaceful, and free and fair elections in November 2005 in order to ensure the long term growth and stability in the country." The recommendations in the resolution have been carefully considered for implementation.

As a follow up, the attached editorial in the Washington Times provides an update on recent developments for your review.

I look forward to the opportunity to discuss any other issues affecting U.S.-Azerbaijan relations with you.

Sincerely,
Hafiz Pashayev
Ambassador

Once again, the Armenian Caucus Co-Chairs, Representative Pallone and Representative Knollenberg, undermined all acceptable norms of public diplomacy and showed their disrespect and disregard for principles of international law. They sponsored an event commemorating the self-declared and unrecognized independence of an entity, which is a part of another internationally recognized country. Clearly, by celebrating and promoting secessionist and military regimes, Representatives Pallone and Knollenberg were not sending a positive message to the eight million Azerbaijanis and other U.S. allies around the world who have struggled against secession and occupation for years. I felt the need to bring this to the attention of Speaker Dennis Hastert in my following letter.

September 29, 2005

Dear Speaker Hastert:

On September 28, the Armenian Caucus Co-Chairs Frank Pallone and Joe Knollenberg, along with other groups, held an event on the Hill entitled "14 years of Nagorno-Karabakh Independence: Progress Toward Freedom, Democracy and Economic Development." The entire event was a farce, paying tribute to, playing the national anthem of, and displaying the flag of a country which does not exist.

Mr. Speaker, as an Ambassador representing a close U.S. ally in both the war against terrorism and in the economic field, I find these activities tremendously offensive. Nagorno-Karabakh (NK) is a region of Azerbaijan currently occupied by Armenian forces.

(1) [The] NK was never independent nor a part of Armenia; it was always an indigenous part of Azerbai-

jan. *It was recognized as such by the United States, the United Nations, and other international organizations. Armenia is the only country that has not recognized Azerbaijan's territorial integrity.*

(2) *Armenian aggression resulted in the occupation of not only NK, but seven additional regions of Azerbaijan, creating a million refugees and internally displaced Azerbaijanis.*

(3) *In 1993, the UN adopted four Security Council resolutions demanding the unconditional withdrawal of Armenian forces from the occupied territories. NATO, OSCE, and other international organizations also repeatedly called for the restoration of Azerbaijan's territorial integrity. Armenia ignored all of the appeals.*

(4) *A Russian brokered cease-fire in 1994 remains in place, yet it was military assistance from Russia, including $1 billion in illegal arms transfers, which significantly contributed to Armenia's military occupation. The absence of internationally recognized authority in the region created fertile ground for illegal narcotics and arms trafficking.*

(5) *After initiating the conflict, expelling all Azerbaijanis, and ethnically cleansing NK and the seven regions of Azerbaijan, Armenia and NK authorities started the process of legalizing their actions. They tried to create a "democratic" image by staging elections which were never recognized by any international organization or entity. The United States position has always been firm in stating that these actions are illegal and don't help the peace process.*

The United States Congress should acknowledge and respect existing U.S. policy regarding the territorial integrity of Azerbaijan as recog-

nized by the rest of the world. At the current tenuous stage of negotiations between the Foreign Ministers of Azerbaijan and Armenia regarding the NK conflict, it is counterproductive to the Minsk Peace Process for members of Congress to be engaged in activities counter to U.S. policy.

Azerbaijan has already suffered the economic and political impact of these types of initiatives. In 1992, Congress imposed Section 907 of the Freedom Support Act which prohibited direct assistance to Azerbaijan, making Azerbaijan the only country in the world denied all direct U.S. assistance, including humanitarian. Since September 11, the Administration has waived Section 907, an indication of where U.S. interests lie.

Mr. Speaker, no doubt you have a full agenda and cannot know about every meeting held on the Hill. This is my effort to let you know that some activities run counter to U.S. policy and damage U.S. interests in the region. These activities create a distorted view in Azerbaijan of U.S. intentions in the South Caucasus.

I would welcome the opportunity to discuss this further with you and respond to any questions you may have.

Sincerely,

Hafiz Pashayev

Ambassador

Chapter 4
Published Articles
and Letters to the Editor

The Boston Globe
January 3, 1994
"Armenians Talk Peace and Wage War"

One who reads George Keverian's article (on Dec. 13) would come away with the impression that "threatened Armenians" are under savage attack by Azerbaijan. Let me tell your readers some of the facts that Keverian failed to mention:

- Armenian forces now occupy 25 percent of the territory of Azerbaijan, while Azerbaijan occupies no territory in Armenia.
- Armenian offensives have created more than 1 million refugees; by UN estimates, that constitutes one out of every seven citizens in the country.
- These Armenian offensives—all inside Azerbaijan—have been condemned repeatedly by the United Nations, the Conference on Security and Cooperation in Europe, the United States, Russia, and Turkey, European countries and others, all to no avail. Armenians talk peace and wage war.
- More than 18,000 Azerbaijanis have been killed and 50,000 more wounded by these Armenian offensives.

Armenia has long cultivated an image as the world's greatest victim. A Nov. 29 *Newsweek* article ("When the Victim Becomes Bully") stated, "Armenians have traditionally been cast, as history's victims, but they seem intent now on rewriting the script. For the past seven months troops and tanks have swept across rival Azerbaijan—a land grab exceeded only by what the Serbs have accomplished in the past year. Last month they pushed south all the way to the Iranian border, driving more than 60,000 Azerbaijani civilians across the Araz River into Iran and looting and torching vacant villages in their wake."

The truth is that these Armenian forces are, as *Newsweek* stated, engaged in a land grab in pursuit of their objective of creating a "Greater Armenia." This is not new; Armenia in the past has also made territorial claims against Georgia, Turkey and other neighboring countries.

The territory Armenia seeks to annex is part of the sovereign territory of Azerbaijan and is recognized as such by the United Nations, the United States, Russia and every other international organization.

Armenians seek to achieve through force of arms what they cannot justify through reason or logic or diplomacy, because the world knows better.

The Christian Science Monitor
January 26, 1994
"Azeris Don't Merit Aid Ban"

NEWLY-RISEN concerns about Russia's future should not obscure the tragedy taking place in another independent nation of the former Soviet Union.

Americans would be dumb-founded if they were aware that their Congress has mandated a legal bias against Azerbaijan and in favor of Armenian aggression condemned by the United Nations Security Council. This tilt against the Azeris' struggle to maintain their homeland comes at the same time when the United States supports the seeking of oil contracts in Azerbaijan's Caspian Sea oil fields and opposes Serb aggression in Bosnia.

In pursuit of a "Greater Armenia," Armenian ultranationalists have conquered one-fourth of the Republic of Azerbaijan and driven 1.1 million Azeris from 700 towns and villages that have been laid waste. At the same time, not an inch of Armenian territory has been attacked or sought by Azerbaijan during six years of conflict totally within the territory of secular, multiethnic Azerbaijan, which strictly observes the rights of more than 70 ethnic groups—including Russians, Armenians and Jews.

On Oct. 23, 1993, a month-long-cease-fire was violated by Armenian troops which, with artillery support from the territory of Armenia, forced another 60,000 Azeri refugees to flee. The seventeen thousand death toll rises daily as half a million new refugees are exposed to the freezing Trans-Caucasus winter, without adequate food and shelter.

On Nov. 12, the UN Security Council condemned the continuing Armenian aggression and called for "unilateral withdrawal of occupying forces." On Nov. 20, as the Armenian offensive continued, U.S. Deputy Secretary of Energy William White met in the Azeri capital of Baku with Azerbaijan's elected President Gaidar Aliyev concerning the participation of the Amoco, Unocal, Pennzoil, and McDermott oil companies' possible $7 billion oil-production contract involving other Western firms and Russia's Lukoil.

Urgently needed now are:

- Vigorous efforts by the Clinton administration to convince Armenia to halt the senseless killing, looting, and burning; to resume the aborted cease-fire; and to negotiate in good faith.

- Additional emergency assistance from the UN, the U.S., and other donor countries. The $8.4 million, six-month UN World Food Program effort announced Nov. 18 and the existing U.S. Government assistance through. Non-governmental organizations will not begin to cover the needs.

- Application by President Clinton against Armenia of an appropriations bill for fiscal year 1994 covering the 1992 Freedom Support Act, which denies U.S. aid to "any government of the New Independent States of the former Soviet Union—which directs any action in violation of the territorial integrity or national sovereignty of other New Independent States."

- A formal presidential determination to allow direct aid to Azerbaijan through the Freedom Support Act "to stabilize democratic forms of government and foster economic growth;" thus ending the congressional prohibition against aid to Azerbaijan, the only country so treated among all of the former Soviet republics.

Some Americans, including Senator Dennis DeConcini (D) of Arizona, are recognizing that continuation of the ban on aid to Azerbaijan is not appropriate to the circumstances. Ambassador at Large Strobe Talbott testified before Congress that "the restriction under the Freedom Support Act does, indeed, hamper our foreign policy objectives."

The Freedom Support Act mandates that no government-to-government U.S. aid may go to Azerbaijan as long as there are "blockades and other offensive uses of force against Armenia and Nagorno-Karabakh"-a predominantly ethnic Armenian enclave within Azerbaijan—recognized by the international community as Azerbaijani territory since the 1919 Versailles Conference.

Clearly the terms "blockade" and "offensive uses of force" do not apply to Azerbaijan in this one-sided conflict. Azerbaijan, understandably, has ceased normal commercial trade with Armenia, including petroleum sales because of the brutal acts of Armenian ultranationalists. For example, 200,000 ethnic Azeris have been deported from Armenia, and the entire 60,000 member Azeri community has been exiled from Nagorno-Karabakh.

No "blockade" exists, as Armenians forcibly have extended the territory under their control lying between Nagorno-Karabakh and the frontiers with Armenia and Iran. Armenia itself is not "blockaded," as it shares frontiers with Turkey, Georgia, and Iran as well as Azerbaijan.

It is time for principled and self-interested fairness on the part of the U.S. in this disastrous conflict.

The Boston Globe
February 19, 1994
"The Facts Counter Globe Editorial on Karabakh"

I was shocked when I read the Feb. 9 editorial "The Invisible War in Karabakh." It sounds as though it had been written by the U.S. Armenian lobby.

Let me cite a few facts:

To read the editorial, you would think Azerbaijan is the aggressor in this conflict. Armenian forces occupy about 25 percent of Azerbaijan. Most of this occupation occurred in the past year and has been accompanied by killing, looting and burning of villages.

The editorial implies that while the suffering is occurring on both sides, it is the Armenians who are the primary victims. Because of the Armenian offensives, the United Nations estimates that there are 1 million Azerbaijani refugees-one of every seven people in the country. More than 18,000 of my countrymen have been killed [and] another 50,000 [have been] wounded.

The most egregious statement refers to the ethnic cleansing of Karabakh by Azerbaijan. When the conflict began there were about 50,000 Azerbaijanis in Karabakh. Today there are none. The Armenians are doing the ethnic cleansing-not only of Karabakh but also of Armenia. There were 200,000 Azerbaijanis in Armenia when the conflict began; within weeks all were forced out. Armenian officials have bragged that their country is now 99 percent pure.

The editorial implies that the United States and other Western governments have been too solicitous of Azerbaijan. In fact, the U.S. Congress, at the urging of the Armenian lobby, imposed a ban on any assistance to Azerbaijan in the Freedom Support Act. Thus, with 1 million refugees and Armenians occupying 25 percent of my country, the U.S. Government is prohibited even from providing humanitarian assistance to Azerbaijan. Rather than being too solicitous of Azerbaijan, the American government has been a prisoner of the Armenian lobby.

The editorial implies that the boundaries of Azerbaijan are not legitimate. But the United Nations and other international bodies recognize Karabakh as part of the sovereign territory of Azerbaijan.

I recognize that there is a large Armenian Diaspora in Massachusetts, but that should not blind Globe editorial writers to the basic facts.

The New York Times
February 23, 1994
"Secular Muslim Countries Watch Bosnia"

The United States and the West often show little understanding of the impact of their actions or inaction on other countries. Take Bosnia. While there has been much concern—and little action—about the atrocities committed daily against the citizens of Bosnia by the Serbs and Croats, Americans do not stop and think how their actions affect countries other than the former Yugoslavia.

My country of Azerbaijan is, like Bosnia, a secular Muslim country. The same is true of several other former republics of the Soviet Union. All of these countries, having been freed of Soviet bondage, immediately looked to the West and the United States as models for democracy and free market reforms. We looked to the West for its history of defending human rights, territorial sovereignty and independence. We remember the West's role in the World Wars, the Cold War and the Persian Gulf War.

But these former Soviet republics—all of them secular and most of them emerging democracies, concerned about their independence and sovereignty—feel great disappointment with the way the West has reacted to the horrors of Bosnia. Some wonder if the West believes Muslim democracies and independence are less worthy than Christian ones.

If these countries come to believe the West does not care about their freedom and independence, it can only encourage the growth of radical Muslim fundamentalism, which is spreading in other parts of the world. This radical fundamentalism is probably the greatest threat to world stability over the next decades.

The United States and the West fervently hope that Muslim countries will follow the example of Turkey and maintain secular governments committed to democracy and free markets. That is certainly the desire of Azerbaijan and other emerging democracies of Central Asia. But the supporters of secularism are not helped when the United States and the West by deed or inaction indicate that they are unwilling to help Bosnia defend its basic right of survival.

More than just Bosnia is at stake.

The Los Angeles Times
March 19, 1994
"Armenia's Bid for U.S. Aid"

I cannot help but respond to the article by Raffi K. Hovannisian (Commentary, Feb. 25), arguing that Washington has not given sufficient consideration to the needs of Armenia.

Armenia might find more sympathy in the United States and the world if it were not engaged in a war of aggression against Azerbaijan—a war in which Armenian forces have occupied 25 percent of my country, looted and burned hundreds of villages, created a million refugees, killed more than 16,000 and wounded another 50,000.

When you take actions like that, you should not expect sympathy or support. The current Armenian government is now supporting:

- A war of aggression for territory, in violation of all international norms of behavior. Armenia is seeking through force of arms to create a Greater Armenia. I believe this action is the result of a small group of ultranationalists, not the Armenian people as a whole, with whom Azerbaijanis have lived and worked for centuries.

- The premise that borders and territorial sovereignty can be violated through force, again in violation of international law and contrary to the principles upheld by the United Nations, the Conference on Security and Cooperation in Europe and every major world power. What Armenian forces are attempting is no different from the Iraqi attempt to conquer Kuwait through force.

- A series of Armenian offensives that have made one in every seven citizens of Azerbaijan a refugee. On top of that, the Armenian government's American lobby persuaded Congress to enact a ban on direct aid—even for refugees—in Azerbaijan. Armenians are indeed suffering terribly because of their government's actions, but nothing in comparison to the tens of thousands of innocent Azerbaijanis who lost their homes and are now living out the winter in open camps beside the roads.

So, please, Mr. Hovannisian, spare us the crocodile tears. When Armenia starts acting like other civilized countries, it will gain more sympathy throughout the world.

The Wall Street Journal
March 22, 1994
"The War That Shouldn't Be"
Felix Corley's article, "The Forgotten War" (editorial page, March 3), provides a very narrow view of the conflict

between Armenia and Azerbaijan. It is similar to the views of the Armenian-American lobby, which constantly portrays Armenia and Armenians of Nagorno-Karabakh as a beleaguered people under attack by Azerbaijan. The essential fact is the Armenian forces have effective control of one-fourth of the territory of Azerbaijan.

The United Nations estimates that there are now more than 1.1 million refugees in Azerbaijan as a result of this conflict. The U.S. cannot directly help these refugees because the Armenian lobby got Congress to enact a ban on assistance, including humanitarian assistance to Azerbaijan. While this U.S. law is being enforced, others have been neglected. Stipulations contained in the fiscal 1994 Foreign Operations Appropriations bill stated that no funds shall be made available to a "government of the New Independent States of the former Soviet Union which directs any action in violation of the territorial integrity of any other New Independent State."

Mr. Corley also makes the classic mistake of believing that this war is being carried out by Karabakh Armenians alone (100,000 Armenians against seven million Azerbaijanis). This is the same fiction put forward by Serbia. The Karabakh Armenians, like the Bosnian Serbs, do not have the heavy weaponry, artillery and helicopters to carry out a war of aggression. The war material all comes from Armenia itself, along with many of the military personnel. It is no coincidence that the same person serves as defense minister of Armenia and Karabakh. While Mr. Corley speaks of the massacre at Sumgait where "dozens" of Armenians were killed, he neglects to mention the Khojaly massacre of Feb. 25, 1992. In one night this town of 7,000 was overrun by Armenian forces, hundreds of civilians were killed, thousands were forcibly expelled, and the entire town destroyed. Other towns in the Armenian-occupied territory have experienced similar fates.

Without citing any evidence Mr. Corley confidently asserts that "mercenaries from Iran and elsewhere" are aiding the Azerbaijani war effort, while failing to discuss widely circulated reports that Armenian commanders have "received military training at secret facilities in Libya and Lebanon" (Eurasian Report, Winter 1992). Resolving the longstanding conflict between Armenia and Azerbaijan will require the best efforts of a U.S. that is committed to an evenhanded policy in our troubled region. One-sided reports, such as Mr. Corley's, however well-intended, do little to further the education of either the policy-making community or the public.

The Washington Times
April 5, 1994

"Dueling Ambassadors" by James Morrison

The ambassadors of Armenia and Azerbaijan plan to share the same stage this week to debate the six-year war that has torn apart their countries. As one Azeri diplomat said, "We are looking forward to it." He chuckled when asked if we can expect a frank and open exchange.

That, of course, is diplomatic code for a confrontation that stops just short of throwing things.

Ambassador Rouben Shugarian of Armenia and Ambassador Hafiz Mir Jalal Oglu Pashayev of Azerbaijan will appear Thursday at 3 P.M. at George Mason University in Fairfax.

Given the hostility, brutality, charges and countercharges surrounding the conflict, it will be interesting to see if both ambassadors can—as the program organizers hope—share common points for peaceful resolution" of the war.

Since the conflict erupted in 1988 over the predominantly Armenian enclave of Nagorno-Karabakh, Armenia has seized one-quarter of Azeri territory.

In Washington the conflict has taken the form of a public relations war, with the Armenian side mostly burning up the fax machines and warning against attempts to lift the U.S. ban on aid to Azerbaijan.

Just last week, the Armenian National Committee of America, in a fax, condemned Russia for "efforts to delay" the shipment of U.S. humanitarian aid to Armenia.

The committee applauded Deputy Secretary of State Strobe Talbott for "raising hell" with Moscow over the delivery, of the aid, which is chiefly a shipment of wheat.

In January the Azeri Ambassador complained, in an interview in The Washington Times, that his country is being overburdened by more than one million war refugees. "Our humanitarian situation is desperate," Mr. Pashayev said. "All our cities under [Armenian] occupation have been burned, destroyed and looted."

The Washington Post
April 29, 1994
"Aggression Against Azerbaijan"

As pointed out [on] April 21 by Steve LeVine ["Azerbaijan Throws Raw Recruits Into Battle," World News], Armenian forces have launched a new offensive against the Republic of Azerbaijan. Those forces are now moving toward the strategically located city of Yevlakh. Seizure of that city will effectively cut off Gyandzha, Azerbaijan's second-largest city. In a country already faced with a situation in which one of every seven people—more than one million individuals—is a refugee, this new Armenian offensive threatens to set off an unthinkable situation.

It is ironic given that as much is being written and spoken about the historical suffering of Armenians, forces of that country are furthering their ambitions of territorial aggrandizement and ethnic cleansing of proportions that threaten to make the Bosnian situation pale in comparison, there is no outcry over the recent offensive actions on the part of Armenians. Indeed, many speak as if Azeri forces were on the outskirts of Yerevan.

Armenian forces now control almost all of the Nagorno-Karabakh region, as well as more than 20 percent of the remaining territory of the Republic of Azerbaijan. The seizures of Azerbaijan's land have been repeatedly condemned by the UN Security Council. No Azeri soldier occupies Armenian lands, none of our troops have been trained in Libya, as has been widely reported about the Armenians, and no leader of our country is calling for expansion of our territory at the expense of our neighbors.

Congress has placed a ban on assistance to Azerbaijan, including humanitarian assistance, until it ceases "all blockades and other offensive uses of force against Armenia and Nagorno-Karabakh." With Nagorno-Karabakh having been "ethnically cleansed" of Azeri's and Armenian forces on the offensive, this policy might simply seem irrelevant if so many innocent civilians were not suffering under past and present brutal pushes by foreign invaders."

The United States remains to the world the model of democracy and freedom. This idealized image is particularly important within those nations such as Azerbaijan just emerging from some 70 years under the yoke of Soviet imperialism. As we face this brutal onslaught by our neighbors, we find ourselves puzzled by the one-sided nature of U.S. policy toward our region. Our continued pleas for balance have fallen on deaf ears. President Gaidar Aliyev has declared Azerbaijan's determination to maintain our sovereignty and our real independence. However, we find ourselves with no support from the West.

Perhaps when our refugees number two million—as they do in Bosnia—someone will speak up. Perhaps when the Armenians control three-quarters of our land, someone will acknowledge their role as aggressor. Perhaps then someone will speak of the atrocities leveled on the people of my country, but perhaps then it will be too late.

The Los Angeles Times
May 5, 1994
"Armenians in Karabakh"

The headline on your article "David and Goliath in Caucasus" (April 21) epitomizes the faulty premise of the article, namely that 120,000 feisty Armenians in the tiny enclave of Nagorno-Karabakh have successfully taken on the rich country of 7 million Azerbaijanis.

Karabakh Armenians are no more capable of carrying out this war of aggression by themselves than are the Bosnian Serbs capable of carrying out their war of aggression in Bosnia. In both cases, it is the motherland that provides all the war material and wherewithal to prosecute their wars of aggression. The Karabakh Armenians love to claim that all their material was captured from Azerbaijan forces.

Karabakh Armenians do not have the capacity to produce helicopters, tanks, armored personnel carriers, rocket launchers, etc. Probably 90 percent of it comes from Armenia itself, and some of that comes from Russian military units stationed in Armenia.

But the worse fiction perpetuated by your article and the Armenian American lobby is that Armenian soldiers are not involved in the fighting. I refer you to the April 16 article in the *New York Times*, "The Armenian Government has long considered that the only Armenian citizens fighting in Karabakh have been volunteers like Mr. Gevorkian and that no

Government troops have fought there. But the Martyrs' Cemetery tells a different story."

The article then reports on the burial of an Armenian soldier and quotes his commanding officer as saying "six more of his soldiers were killed in the battle." He then reports "All of them," Mr. Yeghoian (the commanding officer) said, "were members of the Armenian Government's Internal Forces, a special military branch of the Ministry of Internal Affairs!"

The truth of the matter is that this is not a fight between Karabakh Armenians and Azerbaijan. It is a fight between the Republic of Armenia and the Republic of Azerbaijan. Otherwise, it would have been impossible for Armenian forces to conduct a war of aggression that has resulted in the occupation of 25% of Azerbaijan, created one million Azerbaijani refugees and caused the deaths of more than 18,000 Azeris, and the looting and burning of dozens of Azeri villages and towns.

The Journal of Commerce
May 30, 1994

"Origins of Armenia's Energy Crisis"

The Reuters article you carried on Armenia's energy situation helps to perpetuate the myth that Armenia's energy crisis is caused by Azerbaijan ("Armenia Set on Reopening Controversial Nuclear Plant," May 9, Page 5B).

It states that four years ago, "Azerbaijan imposed an embargo on energy supplies across its territory to Armenia because of the undeclared war over the territory of Nagorno-Karabakh."

The facts are that in 1988, Armenians in [the] Nagorno-Karabakh territory—wholly within Azerbaijan and so recognized by the international community—unilaterally declared independence from Azerbaijan and started a war of independence at the instigation and with the support of Armenia.

Since then, a series of Armenian offensives have conquered and occupied 20 percent of Azerbaijan, created 1 million refugees, burned many towns and killed 18,000 Azeris. It is not logical to expect a country that is the victim of such massive aggression to reward its aggressor by helping supply the energy that fuels its war machine. Armenians are without energy because their government is engaged in a war of aggression and because the war effort gets energy supplies that could go to ordinary citizens. Also, it would be impossible to supply energy through Azerbaijan to Armenia because these offensives have destroyed the railroads and highways that would carry such commodities.

Rather than worrying about Armenia reopening an unsafe nuclear plant, the world community should be applying pressure on Armenia to halt its aggression against Azerbaijan.

The Washington Times
January 24, 1995
"Proposed Law on Aid Would Create a Double Standard of the Worst Kind"

I took great interest in your Jan.13 *World* article "Dole Targets Nations That Impede U.S. Aid." The thrust of the article is that the legislation would prohibit American assistance to any country that does not allow transshipment of U.S. humanitarian aid to a third country. While not stated in the legislation, the objective is to assure shipment of aid to Armenia and punish Azerbaijan's friends.

This is ironic because Armenia and the U.S. Congress are currently violating the letter and the spirit of the law being proposed on behalf of the Armenian-American lobby. In the current conflict between Armenia and my country of Azerbaijan, various Armenian offensives have resulted in the creation of 1 million Azerbaijani refugees and the Armenian occupation of 20 percent of Azerbaijan. One out of every seven

Azerbaijanis is a refugee in his own homeland. An equivalent percentage of refugees in the United States would number 37 million.

The non-contiguous Azerbaijani territory of Nakhchivan is cut off from the rest of Azerbaijan by an Armenian land corridor created by Josef Stalin and by Armenian military occupation of vast portions of Azerbaijan. Armenia does not allow humanitarian assistance from Baku—where the Azerbaijani humanitarian relief effort is coordinated—to cross either the occupied land or the territory of Armenia itself to Nakhchivan.

The U.S. Congress, at the same time, has enacted a prohibition on American assistance, including humanitarian assistance, to Azerbaijani refugees, again at the urging of the Armenian-American lobby. As far as I know, Azerbaijani refugees are the only refugees in the entire world denied direct assistance by the American government.

The Armenian-American lobby does not even acknowledge the hypocrisy of what it is asking of its friends in Congress.

The New York Times
February 27, 1995
"Let Aid into Azerbaijan"

As Azerbaijan's Ambassador to the United States, I have spent two years trying to persuade Congress to repeal Section 907 of the Freedom Support Act, which prohibits United States assistance to Azerbaijan.

Thus far, the Armenian-American lobby has prevented Congress from even modifying this provision, to allow direct assistance for the one million refugees caused by Armenian offensives.

"Azerbaijanis Try to Learn English, Under U.S. Handicap" (news article, Feb. 19) makes the case for repeal better than I could. Perhaps the situation is summed up best by the Azerbaijani woman who is quoted as saying of the Armenians: "They are occupying 20 percent of our territory, and you punish us. You Americans are strange people."

The Christian Science Monitor
April 10, 1995
"Conflicts With Soviet Roots"

I recently had the honor of hosting the Ambassador of Bosnia at the Azerbaijan Embassy, where we signed documents to establish diplomatic relations between our two countries.

Bosnia and Azerbaijan have much in common. We are both secular Muslim countries emerging out of the wreckage of the Soviet Union. Azerbaijan, of course, is a former Soviet republic that gained independence when Soviet communism collapsed. Bosnia was a captive nation both within Eastern Europe and within former Yugoslavia. With, the demise of the Soviet Union, each claimed its independence.

We are also alike in our desire to establish democracy and free markets. We both have highly educated work forces that, given the chance, will doubtless rebuild our countries and demonstrate the creativity and ingenuity that was subdued but not destroyed by communism.

Bosnia and Azerbaijan are multi-ethnic societies and wish to remain so. Both are primarily Muslim, but religious tolerance is extended to all.

Unfortunately, we also share another common characteristic: we are both embroiled in wars of ethnic origins that threaten the very future, and certainly the independence, of our countries. Both conflicts have been shrewdly and erroneously portrayed in the West as conflicts between Muslims and

Christians. The truth is that both are wars of aggression in which the aggressor seeks territorial expansion at the point of a gun. Both involve an internal ethnic group, armed and supported by an outside country, which seeks to expand its national homeland through conquest.

Just as Serbia armed and provoked the Bosnian Serbs, Armenia armed the Nagorno-Karabakh Armenians, and provoked them to declare unilateral independence. This was followed by a series of offensives that, as in Bosnia, have resulted in huge numbers of refugees (more than one million) and large areas of territory under military occupation. Serbia and Armenia initially claimed to have no involvement, until the fiction of their protestations became impossible to defend.

The United Nations, and most knowledgeable diplomats, know these conflicts are wars of territorial expansion, yet the world has done very little to stop the aggression. We get nice United Nations resolutions, telling the aggressors to stop, but nothing seems to happen. We have an excess of sympathy and a shortage of effective support.

However, there is an ironic difference between Bosnia's and Azerbaijan's relationship with the United States Government.

Bosnia receives very strong support in the U.S. Congress, but has had difficulty with the Executive Branch under Presidents Bush and Clinton.

Azerbaijan, on the other hand, has asked the American government to be impartial and play the role of an honest broker. Both the Bush and Clinton administrations have faithfully sought to play that role, but it is Congress that has tilted U.S. policy toward Armenia, in direct contradiction to the United Nations and U.S. administrations.

I have thought a lot about the similarities between Bosnia and Azerbaijan, and about the manner in which our countries have been dealt with by Congress and American administrations.

I can only conclude that many Americans do not understand the importance of and danger to the small, emerging secular Muslim countries of the world.

This inability of Congress and the Executive Branch to agree on policy reduces American effectiveness, confuses America's friends, and encourages the prolongation of conflicts.

The Washington Times
May 16, 1995
"Ethnic Politics Trump Humanitarian Concerns and U.S. National Interest"

Let me comment on the April 30 op-ed article by former Secretary of State James A. Baker III regarding Macedonia.

I found the article to be refreshingly candid and honest about the role of domestic politics in the formulation and execution of U.S. foreign policy. The resulting distortion of American foreign policy is quite disturbing, but it is often ignored because the media do not draw attention to these discomforting facts.

In the case of Azerbaijan, new democratic Republic, Armenian forces currently occupy 20 percent of our country, and they have looted, burned and destroyed hundreds of towns and villages. In the process, they have created more than one million refugees, about a seventh of the entire population. Yet, because of the domestic Armenian lobby, Congress has banned any direct assistance—even for humanitarian reasons—to Azerbaijan. So far as I know, Azerbaijani refugees are the only refugees in the world who cannot receive U.S. humanitarian assistance. Congress has done this despite the strong opposition of both the Bush and Clinton administrations.

Concerning Macedonia, Mr. Baker writes," The United States is in the grotesque position of defending the territorial integrity of a nation we refuse to have full diplomatic relations with." In the case of Azerbaijan, we have just signed a $9 billion oil contract with major oil companies—including Amoco, Unocal, Pennzoil, Exxon and McDermott from the United States. The expected daily production of 600,000 barrels will help secure energy independence for the West and America at this time of great uncertainty in the Middle East and Iran.

Yet because of congressional domestic ethnic politics, the United States does not have the kind of complete and equitable diplomatic relations with Azerbaijan that allies should enjoy. As Mr. Baker pointed out; allowing domestic politics to distort U.S. foreign policy is dangerous and shortsighted.

The Washington Times
August 22, 1995
"Up Against the Lobby" **by James Morrison**

The Ambassador from Azerbaijan spent much of the summer trying to persuade Congress to approve humanitarian aid to his country, but he ran smack into the powerful Armenian lobby.

Ambassador Hafiz Pashayev had the support of the State Department and several normally pro-Armenian lawmakers who believed in granting an exception to the prohibition of aid to Azerbaijan, imposed because of its economic blockade of Armenia.

The two countries went to war in 1991 over Nagorno-Karabakh, an Armenian enclave inside Azerbaijan. Both sides have observed a cease-fire in the area for more than a year.

The defeat of the amendment to the 1992 Freedom Support Act puzzled the Ambassador.

"It is hard for me to imagine how any member of Congress could be against such a provision," Mr. Pashayev wrote in a recent letter to Embassy Row, "After all, humanitarian assistance and democracy-building are, one would have thought, what the United States is all about." He defended the blockade, saying Azerbaijan "was not about to give [Armenia] fuel for use of their tanks against us."

In the debate in the House in late June, Representative Peter J. Visclosky led the fight to maintain the total ban on aid to Azerbaijan. "Any attempt [to lift the ban] must be viewed as support for Azerbaijan's blockade of Armenia, as a weapon of war, and as an obstructionist position in the ongoing peace negotiations" the Indiana Democrat said. "If the Azerbaijani government wants to drink from the cup of the United States' generosity, they should wash their hands of this blockade," he said.

Representative Robert L. Livingston argued in support of the humanitarian aid and said the United States should not be seen as taking a position on either side of the conflict. "The point is that the United States does not have a dog in this hunt," the Louisiana Republican said. "We should be in the position of helping people."

Representative Frank R. Wolf, Virginia Republican, said he is "pro-Armenian" but supported humanitarian aid to Azerbaijan.

Another supporter of the amendment was Representative Christopher H. Smith, chairman of the House Helsinki Commission, who said no one can challenge his commitment to human rights.

But the New Jersey Republican sounded as if he expected defeat. "I know [...] it is against the Armenian lobby, of which I am very often in support and they in support of me," he said. "But when somebody is suffering and we can provide tangible assistance, we ought to try to do it."

The Washington Times
December 9, 1995

"Dueling Diplomats" by James Morrison

The ambassadors from Azerbaijan and Armenia have traded diplomatic barbs over a recent conference on the conflict between the two countries.

Azeri Ambassador Hafiz Pashayev has condemned Armenia for blocking a resolution at the recently concluded Lisbon summit of the fifty-four-member Organization for Security and Cooperation in Europe.

He said Armenia's refusal to support the resolution endorsed by the fifty-three other members is "further evidence that Armenia is orchestrating" the conflict in Nagorno-Karabakh, an Armenian enclave in Azerbaijan. Armenian forces currently occupy 20 percent of Azerbaijan, including Nagorno-Karabakh, Mr. Pashayev said.

The resolution, which required unanimous consent, would have recognized the enclave as an autonomous part of Azerbaijan. "The Republic of Armenia refuses to acknowledge the sovereignty of Azerbaijan because it still wants to acquire Nagorno-Karabakh through military means," Mr. Pashayev said in a statement. "This also removes any doubt that it is Armenia itself, not ethnic Armenians in Nagorno-Karabakh that is behind this war."

Armenian Ambassador Rouben Shugarian dismissed Mr. Pashayev's complaints. Armenia has always "been very constructive in negotiations on Nagorno-Karabakh, and this fact is acknowledged by the international community," Mr. Shugarian said. "It has been and is our goal not to make noise and propaganda but... reach a resolution for the Nagorno-Karabakh conflict," he said.

Mr. Shugarian said the solution should be based on the "right to self-determination and territorial integrity and should be an outcome of peaceful negotiations."

The Washington Post
May 7, 1996
"Needed: A Redoubled Search for Peace"

Lally Weymouth ["Making Hay of Karabakh," op-ed, April 24] well summarizes the conflict between Armenia and Azerbaijan: Armenia occupies 20 percent of Azerbaijan, recent diplomatic efforts by the United States and Russia have failed because Armenia refuses to withdraw from the occupied territory and the Armenian American lobby exercises an inordinate (some would say decisive) influence on U.S. foreign policy in this matter.

President Clinton, Deputy Secretary of State Strobe Talbott, and deputy national security adviser Sandy Berger exerted much time and effort recently to resolve the issues. So did Russia. Lack of mission success should cause all concerned to redouble their efforts, not to give up. Solving the Karabakh problem requires the same kind of diplomatic effort the United States employed in Bosnia.

Mrs. Weymouth also correctly states that Russia is active diplomatically in the Caucasus. Russia now appears to be seeking an evenhanded policy. But return of the former Azerbaijani defense minister to face trial in Baku is pursuant to existing treaties between Russia and Azerbaijan, not some scheme to undermine U.S. influence in the area.

After enacting legislation in 1992 to prevent any aid to Azerbaijan, some members of Congress are now lobbying

President Clinton to ignore legislation offered by Representative Charles Wilson (D-Tex.) to allow direct U.S. humanitarian assistance to the one million refugees in Azerbaijan. If that effort is successful, Azerbaijan will remain the only country in the world denied direct American humanitarian assistance.

The Washington Post
October 7, 1996
"Tragedy in Azerbaijan"

The article "Karabakh Smooths Its Lifeline" [news story, Sept. 19] is a relatively accurate description of the situation in Nagorno-Karabakh, with one exception: the writer implies that the military conquest and occupation of western Azerbaijan was carried out solely by Karabakh Armenians. In fact, the aggression was conducted under the auspices and in many cases with the soldiers of the Republic of Armenia itself. Ethnic Armenians in Karabakh alone could not have overrun, ethnically cleansed and militarily occupied 20 percent of Azerbaijan.

The article accurately reports that negotiations to resolve this conflict are at a standstill. Much like the situation in Bosnia for several years, the world community has yet to muster the political will to help end the war, much less than the military occupation of one-fifth of Azerbaijan. In too much of the Western world, policy regarding our region is determined more by ethnic diaspora lobby groups than either the merits or the national interest of the country itself.

I commend The Post for bringing attention to the issue, and I encourage it to send a reporter to Azerbaijan to report on the tragic consequences for my country. Maybe that will inspire the international diplomatic community to make a stronger effort to resolve the conflict.

Hafiz Pashayev

The Washington Times
January 6, 1997
"What about the Crisis in Azerbaijan?"

The Washington Times carried an article on December 30 by Reuters News Agency that summarized the various regional wars and conflicts and the attendant refugee crisis throughout the world ("For refugees, '96 was a devastating year"). The article cites the situation in Bosnia, the Middle East, Northern Ireland, Central Africa and Afghanistan.

I would like to remind your readers that one of the longest-lasting conflicts, which began in 1988, involves my country, Azerbaijan, and the Republic of Armenia. Armenian forces currently occupy 20 percent of Azerbaijan and have created, by UN estimates, about one million refugees. In other words, one of every seven citizens in the Republic of Azerbaijan is a refugee. Adding insult to injury, the Armenian-American lobby, through its friends in Congress, maintains a ban on direct assistance—even for humanitarian purposes—to Azerbaijan.

The Reuters article reflects the larger problem of solving this conflict. The world at large, and especially the American public, has very little knowledge or understanding about this war. If it did, I am convinced that most Americans would be outraged by the Armenian aggression accompanied by efforts to deny humanitarian assistance to the victims of that aggression.

Historically, Americans have stood against forceful, territorial expansion in World Wars I and II, in Korea, in Kuwait, in Eastern Europe, the Baltics and in Bosnia. It should do the same in Azerbaijan, a new, independent and democratic republic.

The Washington Post
March 12, 1997
"Aid to Armenia"

The *Post's* March 1 editorial "Aid to Armenia" was full of irony, because:

(1) Armenia receives the second largest per capita aid from the United States, while at the same time, Armenia's ethnic lobby groups in Washington are responsible for a ban on any direct U.S. assistance to about one million refugees in Azerbaijan.

(2) Armenian forces now occupy 20 percent of Azerbaijan, which has no territorial claims against Armenia or any other country. But because the U.S. Congress favors the Armenian aggressor, that created a million refugees and punishes the victims of aggression.

(3) Despite Armenia's flawed election and drift toward autocratic rule, the administration and Congress, at Armenia's behest, prevented U.S. officials from assisting in Azerbaijan's initial presidential and parliamentary elections and from promoting democratic institutions.

(4) America responded in World Wars I and II, Korea and Iraq to prevent territorial expansion through force. At a recent Lisbon summit of the Organization for Security and Cooperation in Europe, Armenia was the only country out of fifty-four that opposed a statement affirming Azerbaijan's territorial sovereignty. America's response: more aid for Armenia.

Foreign policy experts say countries always act in their own best interest. In this case, I wonder.

The Washington Times
April 15, 1997

"Russian Arms Shipments to Armenia are a Major Threat to arms to Azerbaijan"

Your April 10 article, "Armenia Armed by Russia for Battles with Azerbaijan" both highlights a grave security concern for the Caucasus region and answers many questions regarding events of the recent past.

In 1993, Armenian forces launched a series of offensives against Azerbaijan that resulted in the deaths of thousands of innocent civilians, the military occupation (still in effect) of 20 percent of Azerbaijan and the creation of about one million refugees.

At that time and since, the Republic of Armenia claimed that only the ethnic Armenians in Nagorno-Karabakh—a region of Azerbaijan—had been involved in the fighting. The world was told that all military equipment used by Armenian forces had been captured from Azerbaijan. Armenian success was attributed to courage and the strong desire for independence.

Now we know that more than $1 billion in military equipment—including tanks, rockets, surface-to-air missiles and ammunition—was secretly and illegally shipped from Russia to Armenia during that period. Azerbaijan had only a fraction of this type of equipment. These shipments occurred both during the offensives and during the current cease-fire, which has lasted almost three years.

As for the future, the tremendous imbalance created by these shipments is an extremely destabilizing development that threatens not only Azerbaijan, but Armenia's other neighbors as well. It certainly indicates a desire to settle the conflict militarily rather than through negotiations. Indeed, at the recent Lisbon summit of the Organization for Security and Cooperation in Europe (OSCE), only Armenia among fifty-four countries refused to affirm the territorial integrity of Azerbaijan.

When you combine these facts with the appointment of Robert Kocharyan as Prime Minister of Armenia, it is cause for great concern. Formerly, he was the pro-war "President" of the rump government created in Nagorno-Karabakh by Armenian separatists.

But truth has a way of spoiling the plans of dictatorships, authoritarian regimes and governments seeking territorial expansion by force. The truth about the territorial ambitions of ultra-nationalist Armenians is in the open, and those ambitions will not survive scrutiny by the world community.

The Boston Globe
April 24, 1997
"'Great Game' Continues to Threaten Azerbaijan"

The American foreign policy establishment and media are almost totally focused on China, NATO enlargement and the Middle East crisis. While each of these topics is worthy of consideration, foreign policy elites are underestimating an important and dangerous issue: what will happen to the independent republics of the former Soviet Union?

Consider recent developments in my country of Azerbaijan. At a December summit of the Organization for Security and Cooperation in Europe, the chairman proposed a statement endorsing the territorial integrity of Armenia and Azerbaijan, which have been in conflict since 1988. The proposal also endorsed a high level of autonomy for the region of Nagorno-Karabakh and a guarantee of individual rights for all its citizens. Of 54 nations participating in the summit, only Armenia refused to support the statement.

Moreover, the Russian Defense Ministry revealed in March that between 1993 and 1996 huge amounts of military equipment were illegally shipped to Armenia. This included eighty-four advanced tanks, more than fifty armored personnel carriers and an unknown quantity of rockets. The chairman of the Russian Duma's Defense Committee said this equipment was worth almost $1 billion.

Not only do these shipments pose a grave risk to Azerbaijan, but they also represent a serious violation of the Conventional Forces in Europe Treaty and show both the fallacy of Armenia's claims about being under trade "embargo" by its neighbors and its claim of financial desperation.

In addition, last month Armenian President Levon Ter-Petrossian announced the appointment of Robert Kocharyan as prime minister. Kocharyan was not even a resident of the Republic of Armenia, but rather was the so-called "President" of "independent" Nagorno-Karabakh.

As a result of a series of Armenian offensives, 20 percent of Azerbaijan (including Nagorno-Karabakh) is currently occupied by Armenian forces. Kocharyan's sole qualification for the job is that he has been a leader of this war of aggression for territorial expansion. His appointment is consistent with the fact that Armenia and the "independent" Nagorno-Karabakh share the same Defense Minister.

In early April, a political furor broke out in Russia over an anonymous article in a leading Moscow newspaper urging the Russian government to take all necessary steps, including destabilizing foreign governments, to prevent what it called "anti-Russian" actions by states on the territories of the former Soviet Union. After being denounced by members of the Commonwealth of Independent States as a threat to their independence, the Russian Foreign Ministry also denounced the article. But then it was revealed that the authors of the article were policy analysts with close ties to the Russian leadership.

Overlaying these developments, of course, are the developments of Azerbaijan's energy resources. To date, Azerbaijan President Heydar Aliyev has signed more than $15 billion in oil contracts with Western oil companies, as well as the state oil companies of Russia, Iran, and Turkey. Some analysts believe Azerbaijan has as much oil as Kuwait, and there is naturally no shortage of people who wish to control either the oil or the money derived from it.

One would have to be blind not to see a pattern in these developments, but they are not new. It is just the latest version of the "great game" that big powers in the region have played throughout the centuries.

We in Azerbaijan find these developments troubling because we have good formal relations with all our neighbors, and wish the same with Armenia. But there is no doubt that unofficial elements within the region are actively working with Armenia to destabilize and possibly dismember Azerbaijan.

Until the foreign policy establishment and the media pay more attention, U.S. policy toward Azerbaijan and the region will continue to be mainly influenced by ethnic Armenian-American lobby groups, who are motivated not by American interests but by the desire for a Greater Armenia. These lobby groups control U.S. policy within Congress and the American administration seems unable to overcome their influence. Such matters may not be as prominent as other foreign policy issues, but they have far-reaching consequences that the United States can ill afford to ignore.

The fate of the new independent states is far from certain, but one thing is sure: what happens to these republics will greatly influence what happens in Russia, Turkey, and Iran, and, consequently, Central Europe and Central Asia; and this raises vital issues relevant to the whole notion of European security.

The Washington Post
July 12, 1997
"Azerbaijan's Oil"

I read with interest your article "Former Top U.S. Aides Seek Caspian Gusher" [front page, July 6] about U.S. interests in oil in Azerbaijan.

When seeking to explain why the U.S.-Azerbaijan relationship has grown, one certainly cannot overlook the impact of oil and energy development. But one also must consider that Azerbaijan has adopted democratic rule and friendly policies toward the West, especially the United States. [Azerbaijan] developed the most stable government in the Caucasus, instituted market reforms, and resisted all efforts to impose fundamentalist rule. Azerbaijan also remains the only former Soviet republic (besides the Baltics) with no foreign troops on its soil.

In contrast, Armenia has suffered in U.S. public esteem for good reason. Armenia occupies 20 percent of Azerbaijan, has received more than $1 billion in illegal arms shipments from Russia (including Scud missiles), and destroyed hundreds of Azerbaijani villages, creating some 1 million refugees who are denied direct U.S. aid because of a congressional ban that Armenians lobbied for. In addition, Armenia is the only country among the 54-nation Organization for Security and Cooperation in Europe (OSCE) that refuses to support Azerbaijan's territorial integrity.

The Washington Times
August 11, 1997

"President Aliyev Has Come a Long Way since his Days in the Politburo"

I generally found your July 30 editorial, "The Caspian Sea's Black Gold" to be accurate and analytically correct. Your comments about lifting the sanctions on Azerbaijan and on settlement of the conflict over the Azerbaijan region of Nagorno-Karabakh were helpful, especially your admonition that "For too long, negotiations have languished for lack of international pressure and commitment." The fact that the United States now Co-Chairs the negotiating team with Russia and France, coupled with public pressure such as that from The Washington Times, will hopefully lend urgency to the task.

However, I must take issue with your comments about President Heydar Aliyev of Azerbaijan, whose first official visit to Washington was the focus of the editorial. Mr. Aliyev was indeed a member of the former Soviet Union's Politburo, but he resigned in protest in 1989 after Moscow invaded Baku. He has worked tirelessly since that time not only to stamp out the vestiges of communism but to establish a free-market democracy in Azerbaijan.

Perhaps the best antidote to your stated concerns can be found in the excellent commentaries by Frank Gaffney ("Awakening to our Caspian Concerns," July 30), Ariel Cohen ("The New Silk Road to Central Asian Oil," Op-Ed, Aug. 4), and Georgie Anne Geyer ("Voyages through Shifting Ideologies," Aug. 6). Ms. Geyer recounts Mr. Aliyev's "personal ideological voyage" from the Soviet Politburo to become the anti-communist, nationalistic President of Azerbaijan.

Anyone who listened to his speeches throughout Washington, Houston, New York and Chicago could have little doubt about where Mr. Aliyev sees our country's future in democracy, free markets, independence and friendly relations with the United States and the West. His excellent reception by President Clinton and five members of the Cabinet, as well as leading Republican foreign policy experts, would not have occurred otherwise. The Communist Party is dead, not only in Russia but also Azerbaijan, and Mr. Aliyev helped bury it.

The Journal of Commerce
August 13, 1997

"Insightful Coverage of the Caspian Region"

Since arriving in Washington in early 1993 as Azerbaijan's Ambassador to the United States, it has been a struggle to educate Americans about Azerbaijan, its past and future, and especially the role it will play in energy and geo-strategic issues over the next several decades.

Your newspaper has consistently been among the most insightful and knowledgeable in covering these issues. It recognized the importance of the Caspian Sea energy and strategic issues long before most members of the American media. The coverage of President Heydar Aliyev's first official visit to Washington is further evidence of its insight ("Foreign policy, oil, Azerbaijan." July 29).

While I obviously do not always agree with what your newspaper says, it has helped focus American attention on the strategic and economic stakes in the region. The purpose of Mr. Aliyev's visit was to solidify relations with Washington and highlight the issues your newspaper has been reporting on for several years.

Azerbaijan seeks friendly relations with all its neighbors and with the West, based on mutual respect, because that is the way to ensure the independence we achieved in 1992 after seven decades of domination by the Soviet Union.

I commend The Journal of Commerce for its excellent coverage of issues affecting Azerbaijan, the Caucasus and Caspian Sea energy matters.

The Washington Post
August 20, 1997
"Azerbaijan: Cooperative and Sovereign"

I agree with the basic premise of Fred Hiatt's Aug. 4 op-ed column, "Don't Cold Shoulder Russia," that Russia should not be left out in the development of Caspian Sea energy resources. That is why Azerbaijan President Heydar Aliyev has made a point of including the Russian state oil company, Lukoil, in several of the projects, including proposed pipeline projects. Azerbaijan has no desire to exclude Russia; indeed, Russia is our main trading partner and our historic neighbor. Azerbaijan also has included Turkey, Georgia, Iran, France, Britain as well as U.S. oil companies in the development of pipeline projects or proposals.

While we are happy to have all of these countries participate in our good fortune, we have and will continue to insist on our sovereign rights over resources legally within our sector of the Caspian. We also will insist that the people of Azerbaijan receive their fair share of the proceeds from these developments.

After hundreds of years of domination by various regional empires, Azerbaijan finally achieved real independence in 1992. As a nation, we want to use our energy resources to benefit our people and help guarantee our independence. To achieve this, President Aliyev has skillfully sought to include all our neighbors and ally with the United States. That was the purpose of Mr. Aliyev's first official visit to Washington. This

is the best way to ensure regional and international cooperation and a free and independent Azerbaijan.

Embassy Flash (The Washington Diplomat)
October 1997

Interview with Azerbaijani Ambassador Hafiz Pashayev
Following a Clear Objective
by John Shaw

When Hafiz Pashayev arrived in Washington, D.C., in
February 1993 as Azerbaijan's first ambassador to the United
States, he did not bring with him elaborate theories of diplo-
macy, a bulging Rolodex or a lengthy brief from home.

Instead, the physics professor from Baku State University
brought to his first diplomatic post a sharp mind, a record of
accomplishments, and a clear objective: to persuade the
United States to help Azerbaijan remove the shackles of its
troubled past as part of the Soviet Union and become a prosperous, independent nation.

Pashayev has pursued this objective relentlessly for four
years and is now reaping the rewards of his hard work and
the fortuity of Azerbaijan's abundant natural riches, especially
its massive reserves of petroleum. Azerbaijan is now a hot
item and the ambassador's small nation on the shores of the
Caspian Sea is getting the full attention of the United States
and the other countries of the world.

In his office on McPherson Square, Pashayev says he was
selected for his job because the leaders of Azerbaijan were
looking for a representative to Washington who was untainted by the Soviet past and was familiar with the United
States.

As a professor and director of the metal physics laboratory at the Academy of Sciences in Azerbaijan, Pashayev

hadn't been involved in politics during the Soviet era and had lived in the United States for a year in the mid-1970s while doing research at the University of California at Irvine. "I was very happy in science," says Pashayev. "I was not looking for a new career." Pashayev has written more than one hundred scientific articles and books. But events changed his mind, including the deployment of Soviet troops to Baku in 1990, the continuing struggles with Armenia over Nagorno-Karabakh, and the unique opportunity to represent his new nation in the United States.

So he accepted the post, moved to Washington in early 1993 and quickly discovered the differences between the rigid discipline of science and the hurly-burly of international politics. "In physics, there are certain facts, or truths, that are universally accepted by those dealing with the matter," he says. "But I have found that in politics and diplomacy, facts and truths are all relative."

The ambassador admits he is sometimes frustrated by the relativity of political truth and the strictures of diplomacy. "As a scientist in the Soviet Union, I was free in an un-free society. As a diplomat, I'm working in a free country, but I'm not free because I'm a government official," he says.

But for an un-free person Pashayev speaks with remarkable frankness. In speeches and interviews, he is unfailingly polite but also very direct. He has scolded the U.S. Congress, chided the White House and blasted Armenia, a nation Azerbaijan now has a war truce with after nearly a decade of war. "In my view, the best diplomacy is to be straightforward," he says. "When you're open and sincere, you're credible, you are taken seriously, you are understood. Life is easier when you're simple and direct."

Pashayev recalls his first two years in Washington as a frustrating, often discouraging time. Few in Congress were familiar with Azerbaijan, and those who were familiar with it were only because of its bitter dispute with Armenia.

Festering tensions between the two countries broke out in the open in 1988 when Nagorno-Karabakh, a mostly Armenian enclave in Azerbaijan, asserted its independence with the support of Armenia. Azerbaijan then imposed an embargo on Armenia.

Armenia still controls about 20 percent of Azerbaijan. A cease-fire has been in place since 1994, and international efforts led by the United States, Russia and France to broker a peace agreement continue. But no settlement is in sight.

The U.S. Congress passed the Freedom Support Act in 1992 to aid the new nations of the former Soviet Union and has authorized about $2.2 billion for this effort. However, Section 907 of the law prohibits direct U.S. assistance to Azerbaijan until the embargo by Armenia is lifted. It also prevents the United States from helping Azerbaijan in elections, economic reform and energy development efforts.

Pashayev has made it his personal crusade to get Section 907 repealed, an effort that has thrust him into the center of fierce American and international politics. "Section 907 is such a political issue, it has nothing to do with reality," Pashayev says. "And for the people of Azerbaijan, it seems very unfair. It seems like the United States is punishing us for a war we didn't start."

A spokesman for the Armenian embassy disputed the genesis of the war between the two countries and said his government believes the provision should remain. "Nothing has changed since the day Section 907 was imposed," he says. "We believe it should remain until the embargo is lifted."

Both the Bush and Clinton administrations have supported Azerbaijan's efforts to repeal Section 907, but Congress has resisted. Pashayev has met with about 150 lawmakers to press his case. He has won some converts but not enough to change the law.

Pashayev's message to Congress is blunt: Section 907 is an "affront" to Azerbaijan's sovereignty. It's a "discriminatory piece of legislation that is a constant source of disharmony" between the United States and his country. Azerbaijan wants to resolve the dispute with Armenia, but Armenia is dragging its feet, and U.S. support is crucial as his country tries to build democratic institutions and a market economy.

While Pashayev spends most of his time in Washington working with Congress, he has traveled to thirty-two states to promote Azerbaijan and encourage greater U.S. involvement and investment in his country. He cites three reasons for closer U.S. ties to Azerbaijan: oil, geopolitics and support for a fledgling democracy.

Azerbaijan sits on the western shore of the Caspian Sea, at the southeastern corner of the Caucasus. It is bounded by Russia to the north, Iran to the south, and by Georgia and Armenia to the west. Azerbaijan also has about a ten-mile border with Turkey.

It has a population of 7.5 million and is about the size of the state of Maine. Azerbaijan is a relatively poor nation, with a per capita income of about $1,790. But that is about to change.

The Caspian Sea basin is believed to have the largest reserves of oil outside the Persian Gulf, with much of it in Azerbaijan's sector. Energy analysts say there are up to 200 billion barrels of oil in the region worth about $4 trillion at current prices. And it has comparable reserves of natural gas.

The existence of petroleum in the Caspian region has been known for centuries. During the Czarist era, Baku was the center of Russian oil production. And it was with a covetous eye on the petroleum resources of Azerbaijan that Hitler decided to invade the Soviet Union in 1941.

Western oil companies have explored the Caspian basin aggressively in the past five years and have invested large sums to extract oil and natural gas from the region and ship these fuels to world markets. Much of this investment has flowed into Baku. Azerbaijan has signed more than $25 billion in contracts with oil companies from the United States, Western Europe, Russia, Turkey and Iran.

Two pipelines are being built to ship oil from Baku to the Black Sea: a northern route through Russia and a western route through Georgia. And a third major pipeline will be built soon, probably one that runs through Turkey to the oil terminal at Ceyhan in the Mediterranean Sea. "Oil is not new to Azerbaijan," Pashayev says. "We have a 150-year history of oil exploration. Our first oil boom came at the end of the last century, and we have had other booms. So I'm not worried that Azerbaijan will be spoiled by new wealth, new opportunities."

Pashayev says his country is determined to take advantage of the oil and natural gas wealth to fund economic development. Azerbaijan will build on its strong oil equipment, petrochemical, and agricultural sectors, and also expand its tourism and small business industries, he says.

Azerbaijan plans to upgrade its physical infrastructure, including crumbling roads and inadequate water treatment facilities, and Pashayev repeatedly refers to the need to create a "broad middle class" in his country.

The new oil boom has sweeping domestic and international consequences for Azerbaijan. In addition to helping the nation rebuild its economy, oil has made Azerbaijan a very popular country in the world. Azerbaijan is attracting much notice in the United States. In recent months, many U.S. foreign policy luminaries have spoken out in support of Azerbaijan, including James Baker, Henry Kissinger, Brent Scowcroft, Richard Cheney, John Sununu, Zbigniew Brzezinski and Lloyd Bentsen.

Pashayev argues their support is prompted by more than just oil. "People who understand geo-strategic issues realize the importance of Azerbaijan. We are in a crucial region of the world, in the Caucasus, at the gateway to Central Asia. Because of geography, natural resources and geopolitical circumstances, Azerbaijan will be at the center of international diplomacy for the next several decades," the ambassador predicts.

Pashayev is concerned outside powers may push for pre-eminence in the region, launching a twenty-first century version of the nineteenth century's "Great Game." This refers to the historic fight for control of the Caucasus and Central Asia that primarily involved the British and Russian Empires, but also included the Persian, Ottoman and Chinese empires.

The United States should be focused on the strategic importance of this region, Pashayev says, adding that it's in America's interests to support his nation. If Azerbaijan succeeds and becomes "truly independent," other Central Asian and Caucasus nations will be fortified in their efforts to build democratic institutions and will be open to a partnership with the United States, he notes.

Azerbaijani President Heydar Aliyev traveled to the United States for his first official visit this summer, a trip that demonstrated his nation's new clout.

During his visit, Aliyev met with President Bill Clinton, Vice-President Al Gore and Secretary of State Madeleine Albright among others. While in New York, he was hosted by Kissinger.

Aliyev and Gore presided over a ceremony in which Azerbaijan signed $8 billion in oil contracts with U.S. petroleum companies.

"The president had a very successful visit," says Pashayev. "Even better than I expected. It was the culmination of four years of hard work. The American mass media is starting to understand the importance of Azerbaijan."

The ambassador says he spoke with President Aliyev about his returning home for good, but the president made it clear he wants Pashayev to stay in Washington and keep working to improve links with the United States and repeal the Section 907 provision.

"I'm not tired, but I really want to go back to my beautiful city of Baku. I am homesick," he says. But Pashayev vows to press ahead, with a clear goal in sight. "I think we're making progress on 907," he says. "Many members of Congress now understand the realities, and those that are politically free support us. We're not there yet, but I think we can repeal Section 907 next year. Then I can go home."

TIME Magazine
June 15, 1998
"Azerbaijan: Oil & Diplomacy"

The status of U.S.-Azerbaijan relations can best be described as vastly improved but still lacking in one major respect.

When I arrived in America in 1993 as Azerbaijan's first U.S. Ambassador, U.S.-Azerbaijan relations were nonexistent. Few American policymakers and even fewer American lawmakers had even heard of Azerbaijan. Little was known about Azerbaijan other than it is a former Soviet Republic.

Since early 1993 vast changes and improvements in U.S.-Azerbaijan relations have taken place. Azerbaijan has adopted democratic and free market reforms, as evidenced by holding three nationwide elections, after gaining its independence in 1991, as well as the fact that small businesses are already privatized and extensive land privatization is taking place, Azerbaijan has signed nine major oil contracts valued in excess of $30 billion, with American and Western oil companies participating in most of them.

Major conferences on U.S.-Azerbaijan relations and Caspian Sea oil development are organized regularly in Washington, with government principals from both countries actively participating [including] Energy Secretary Federico Pena, Commerce Secretary William Daley, Deputy Secretary of State Strobe Talbott. Under Secretaries of State Stuart Eizenstat and Thomas Pickering, former Defense Secretary Dick Cheney, former Treasury Secretary Lloyd Bentsen, former Secretary of State Lawrence Eagleburger, and former National Security Advisor Zbigniew Brzezinski have all more than once advocated close cooperation between U.S. and Azerbaijan.

Government-to-government exchanges have also increased dramatically, highlighted last August by meetings in Washington between Azerbaijan's President Heydar Aliyev and U.S. President Bill Clinton. During his historic official visit to the U.S. President Aliyev also met with Vice-President Al Gore, Secretary of State Madeleine Albright, Defense Secretary William Cohen and others in the American government leadership. He also conferred with leaders of Congress. As a result, the U.S. and Azerbaijan have established bilateral working relationships in the security and energy areas.

The American business community is also becoming more active in Baku, Azerbaijan's capital, led by all the major American oil companies. But it is not just oil that attracts U.S. businesses. We are also seeing interest in Azerbaijan from American telecommunications, construction and mineral development firms. In fact, the American presence in Baku has become so prominent that American restaurants and the English language are now commonplace.

What has led to this enhanced relationship between the U.S. and Azerbaijan? It can be related to three things: (1) Azerbaijan's key role in geo-strategic issues affecting Caucasus; (2) Azerbaijan's future as a major oil producing state; and (3) shared American and Azerbaijani values about independence, democracy and free markets.

Let us take a look at each of these.

Azerbaijan's geography dictates that it is a key in geo-strategic consideration of the Caucasus. At the crossroads both commercially and diplomatically for all major issues facing the region, Azerbaijan has resisted efforts by those who wish to dominate Azerbaijan from outside its borders. In fact, it is the only former Soviet republic other than the Baltics with no foreign troops on its soil. Azerbaijan has resisted efforts by zealots who wish to impose an Islamic republic in Azerbaijan. And, Azerbaijan has strongly resisted efforts by Armenian extremists to create a Greater Armenia through conquest of Azerbaijani territory. Azerbaijan also is a key to the future of the Central Asian republics, whether they will be independent or dominated by regional powers, democratic or totalitarian, free market or centrally planned economies.

Most world energy experts believe there is as much oil in the Caspian Sea Region as there was in the North Sea, and some have estimated that Azerbaijan has as much oil as Kuwait. Due by the end of this year, the Main Export Pipeline will be located to deliver Azerbaijan's, and possibly other Caspian states' oil to the Mediterranean and Western oil markets. This prospect of huge oil supplies means a great deal to the United States and the Western industrialized world in terms of reliable energy supplies at reasonable prices.

Early oil is already being produced and shipped through an existing pipeline through Russia to the Black Sea. Still another early oil pipeline will probably transit Georgia to the Black Sea. Azerbaijan, the United States, and Turkey are supporting a pipeline through Georgia and Turkey to the Turkish Mediterranean port city of Ceyhan for the main export pipeline. Once that is accomplished, Azerbaijan will once again become a major player in world energy production.

The third reason for increased U.S.-Azerbaijan relations has to do with shared values about political independence, democracy and free markets. During our 70 years of subjugation by the former Soviet Union, Azerbaijanis always admired the U.S. for its role as a former colony turned independent country.

We also admired the U.S. for its position as the world's foremost supporter and promoter of democracy and free markets. An additional election for President is scheduled for later this year. Most real estate and small businesses have been privatized, as are major business enterprises. We have introduced a new currency, the manta, and have brought our inflation down to less than 4 percent over the past year. The growth of the Gross Domestic Product is 5.8 percent over the same period, and the share of the private economy will increase from 30 percent in 1997 to 70 percent by the end of 1999.

As I said before, U.S.-Azerbaijan relations can be characterized as one of vast improvement with one major obstacle, that being Congressional action in terms of the conflict between Azerbaijan and Armenia. In 1992, before Azerbaijan had an ambassador or embassy in Washington, pro-Armenian forces within Congress .succeeded in enacting Section 907 of the Freedom Support Act, which bans any direct U.S. assistance to Azerbaijan. One year after that ban was enacted Armenia launched a series of military offensives that resulted in the occupation of 20 percent of Azerbaijan, including the region of Nagorno-Karabakh. These offensives killed thousands of Azerbaijanis, resulted in hundreds of towns and villages being looted and destroyed, and created (by UN estimates) almost one million refugees. Despite these offensive actions, Congress has still been unwilling to repeal Section 907, which tilts American foreign policy towards Armenia.

We have now completed four years of a ceasefire in the war between Armenia and Azerbaijan. During this four-year period, the Organization for Security and Cooperation in Europe has made valiant attempts to settle the conflict Now, however, the hard-line former Prime Minister has assumed the office of Armenian President, making settlement of the conflict much more difficult and putting Armenia into confrontation with the international community.

The United States Government has been firm in its response to these developments. It stated on January 26, "The actions taken by the government of Armenia in the context of the conflict over Nagorno-Karabakh are inconsistent with the Helsinki Final Act: Armenia supports Nagorno-Karabakh separatists in Azerbaijan both militarily and financially. Nagorno-Karabakh forces, assisted by units of the Armenian armed forces, currently occupy the Nagorno-Karabakh region and surrounding areas of Azerbaijan."

In order for America to play the role of honest broker in trying to settle this conflict, the U.S. Congress should repeal Section 907 of the Freedom Support Act. I believe that this ill-conceived piece of legislation will soon be repealed or waived by the Administration because it is so discriminatory that it makes a mockery of the values America stands for more and more Members of Congress are speaking out against Section 907, and in favor of an even-handed American policy in the area.

In summary, U.S.-Azerbaijan relations have progressed tremendously in the past five years, to the point that we can now talk confidently of the U.S.-Azerbaijan partnership. Five years from now, I predict a very strong and enduring U.S.-

Azerbaijan relationship built on mutual trust and understanding, complemented by shared values.

The Washington Post
July 2, 1998
"Azerbaijan's Pledge of Reform"

I wish to respond to the June 11 editorial, "White House Pledge." President Heydar Aliyev is conducting democratic and free-market reforms in Azerbaijan for the benefit of the Azerbaijani people, not because of a pledge to the White House during his visit here last August.

Because of his background in the former Soviet Politburo, some people cannot accept that President Aliyev is today a dedicated nationalist devoted to securing the independence and sovereignty of Azerbaijan. People of my country highly appreciate his historic role in 1993, when the very existence of Azerbaijan was threatened. He believes in democracy and has committed himself to its realization in Azerbaijan, which has already held three nationwide democratic elections since independence in 1991.

One should take into account the environment in which President Aliyev is conducting democratic reforms. We are still in a precarious economic situation, especially as a result of the aggression of Armenia. We have almost 1 million refugees (one out of seven Azerbaijanis), 20 percent of our land mass is under Armenian military occupation, and reforms are occurring while Azerbaijan is under immense pressure from regional powers.

Regarding [to] the Election Law passed by the Parliament, its draft was subjected to the independent review of the Organization for Security and Cooperation in Europe, and, as a result, 32 of 59 articles were changed to comply with the international standards. The electoral commission likewise is designed to correspond to these standards.

The editorial also said free-market reforms have not kept pace with the development of oil in Azerbaijan. In the past two years, almost all small businesses have been privatized, land privatization is proceeding at a fast pace, and major industries are being converted. Azerbaijan has brought the rate of inflation down from 1,600 percent in 1995 to less than 4 percent today. Both the International Monetary Fund and the World Bank have expressed satisfaction with the degree and pace of free-market reforms.

Finally, concerning White House pledges: the White House has also pledged to move quickly to secure congressional removal of Section 907 of the Freedom Support Act, a ban on direct U.S. assistance to Azerbaijan. Now, almost a year later, Section 907 remains in place, undermining our efforts during this transitional period.

The Washington Times
July 15, 1998

"Oil in the Caspian Basin is Crucial to U.S. National Security"

Your July 9 article, "Senator Warns of Focus on Caspian Oil" does not present a complete reflection of the views voiced at the recent hearing of the Senate Foreign Relations subcommittee on export and trade promotion of "U.S. Policy on the Caspian." Senator Paul S. Sarbanes' opinion that oil in the region is overemphasized was countered by Assistant Secretary of State, Marc Grossman, Special Adviser to the Secretary of State, Stephen Sestanovich, and former National Security Adviser Zbigniew Brzezinski. All three pointed out that the oil being developed in the Caspian basin is very important to American national security interests as well as to the future economic and democratic development of all the independent states of the region.

Mr. Sarbanes also raised the issue of human rights. However, as Mr. Brzezinski rightfully pointed out, it is unrealistic to expect countries that have lived under Soviet rule for seven decades to establish democracies within a short period of time. A good example is presented by Armenia, another post-Soviet republic, with already two flawed presidential elections.

In Azerbaijan, the situation is aggravated by continuing Armenian military aggression that has created almost one million refugees and displaced persons. Nevertheless, Azerbaijan has a presidential election scheduled for October, and the government is inviting observers from throughout the world to witness the freedom and fairness of this election, including 140 from the Organization for Security and Cooperation in Europe and hundreds of other observers as well. President Heydar Aliyev of Azerbaijan is committed to holding free and fair elections for the benefit of his people.

Your report is accurate in describing the Clinton administration's opposition to Section 907 of the Freedom Support Act. This discriminatory provision, mainly a result of ethnic politics, treats Azerbaijan differently from all other former Soviet republics by denying it direct U.S. assistance. I believe that its repeal will be mutually beneficial for our two countries.

The Washington Times
August 14, 1998

"Azerbaijan Has Paid Enough"

Azerbaijan is one of many nations around the world currently subject to unilateral U.S. sanctions. The recently-appointed Senate Economic Sanctions Task Force is currently reviewing the impact of all U.S. sanctions and will soon make recommendations to Congress. Section 907 represents an excellent example of a U.S. sanctions policy that has no justification in current political or diplomatic reality, and which serves only to interfere with the building of construc- tive relations between the United States and a key partner na- tion in a strategically and economically important region of the world.

This month marks the first anniversary of Azerbaijani President Heydar Aliyev's first official visit to the United States, an event that culminated in strengthening political and commercial relations between our two countries. President Aliyev recently completed an equally successful official visit to the United Kingdom, which reaffirmed Azerbaijan's grow- ing diplomatic and business ties to the West.

The anniversary of the U.S. visit and the recent UK visit offer an appropriate opportunity to take stock of bilateral and regional relations and interests. Why are Azerbaijan's efforts to build strong ties to the U.S. and Europe significant? The reason is that the U.S. has vital interests in Azerbaijan and the Caucuses.

First, Azerbaijan and many of its neighbors are former republics of the Soviet Union—young, independent nations seeking to develop democratic institutions and free market economies and to address long-standing ethnic and social conflicts. Americans are uniquely able to understand the chal- lenges we face and to lend support. The U.S. will benefit from a Caucuses region characterized by stability, economic cooperation and secure internationally recognized borders. Azerbaijan is a small nation surrounded by several large ones: Russia, Iran and Turkey. Stability and security issues have ramifications beyond our own borders.

Second, Azerbaijan and the U.S. are currently cooperating on critical decisions regarding oil pipelines from the Caspian region to the Mediterranean. These decisions will determine who will manage (or possibly prevent) the flow of the Cas- pian Sea's abundant oil and gas reserves in the 21 century. Both Mr. Aliyev and the Clinton administration are promoting the Baku-Ceyhan route that would permit future oil flows to go through Azerbaijan, Georgia and Turkey.

Third, Azerbaijan has instituted a broad program of economic reforms that is yielding impressive results. GDP rose by 9 percent in the first half of 1998. Azerbaijan is openly welcoming U.S. and other Western businesses as partners in its development, not just in the critical energy sector, but also in construction, mineral exploration, business services and telecommunications.

Fourth, Azerbaijan is demonstrating real progress in developing democratic institutions, with multiparty presidential elections scheduled in October. The government has implemented many steps to bring this election into compliance with international standards. Numerous NGOs, including the National Democratic Institute for International Affairs and the International Foundation for Election Systems, as well as the Organization for Security and Cooperation in Europe (OSCE) structures, have helped Azerbaijan draft a new election law and will be monitoring the upcoming elections.

Yet problems in the U.S.-Azerbaijan relationship remain unresolved. The most important issue is the lifting of sanctions imposed by Congress under Section 907 of the Freedom Support Act of 1992. These sanctions, resulting from a ten-year-old conflict between Azerbaijan and neighboring Armenia over Nagorno-Karabakh, bar direct U.S. assistance to Azerbaijan "until it ceases economic blockades and other offensive uses of force against Armenia and Nagorno-Karabakh." But in reality, no blockade against Armenia exists. Trade regularly flows through its borders with neighboring Georgia and Iran, and an internationally-recognized cease-fire in Nagorno-Karabakh has now been in place for four years. There are no offensive actions on either side.

In fact, about 20 percent of Azerbaijani territory today remains under the control of Armenia. Almost one million

Azerbaijani citizens—about 15 percent of the nation's total population—are refugees and displaced persons in their own country, having been dislocated from the Nagorno-Karabakh region and other surrounding regions of Azerbaijan.

The task of bringing a peaceful, internationally recognized solution to this conflict has been made more difficult by the recent change in government in Armenia. Former Armenian President Levon Ter-Petrossian, who favored a compromise plan supported by the U.S. and the OSCE through the Minsk Process, was forced from office by Armenian hard-liners earlier this year.

The new Armenian president and Armenian-American lobbying groups are against OSCE's proposed solution to the conflict based on two stages. First, Armenian withdrawal from seven of the eight occupied regions of Azerbaijan, and second, final talks on the status of Nagorno-Karabakh within Azerbaijan. In effect, Armenia is proposing to kill or at least to subvert years of negotiations through the Minsk Process, which is co-chaired by the U.S., France and Russia and includes the active involvement of several European nations.

Despite Azerbaijan's commitment to the Minsk peace process and the fact that the Clinton administration supports a congressional repeal of Section 907, U.S. sanctions continue because Congress is under strong pressure from Armenian lobbying groups. Azerbaijan has taken sufficient "demonstrable steps" in recent months to permit the Clinton administration to make a presidential determination, in effect waiving Section 907.

The Washington Post
November 3, 1998
"Democracy in Azerbaijan"

The *Post's* Oct. 17 editorial, "Missed Chance in Baku," concerning the Azerbaijan presidential election, reminds me of the proverbial question about whether a glass is half full or half empty. The *Post* obviously has chosen to declare the Azerbaijani election half-empty. A more sober judgment, in my opinion, would have declared the election half full.

We did not expect perfect elections, but almost all observers agree that this election represented significant improvements over previous elections. Election laws were improved, censorship was abolished, each candidate received free time on national television, open campaigning was encouraged, opposition candidates flourished, and hundreds of election monitors and observers were invited to witness the election. And while irregularities were reported, no one really questions the outcome.

With reference to the often cited criticism of the International Republican Institute, it is worth mentioning that long-term monitors usually sound much more constructive and understanding. While we appreciate IRI's comments, we would have welcomed the institute's full-scale participation in the educational pre-election process.

The Boston Globe
February 23, 1999
"U.S.-Azerbaijan Ties and National Security"

John Ellis correctly understands the correlation between the national security interests of the United States and Azerbaijan ("U.S. Should Build a Military Base in Azerbaijan," op-ed, Feb. 6). Azerbaijan wants closer security ties with the United States to help maintain its independence, resist regional pressures, and protect its vital natural resource development. As the saying goes, Azerbaijan lives in a tough neighborhood.

The United States, on the other hand, should seek closer ties with Azerbaijan to help promote the growth of secular, democratic Muslim states in the region, prevent the reestablishment of regional empires, and encourage development of Caspian oil and gas reserves for Western industrialized countries.

The need for greater security ties is apparent for both nations. Azerbaijan is willing. The question is whether the United States shares that willingness.

The Washington Post
March 8, 1999
"Azerbaijan Responds"

The *Post's* Feb. 9 Federal Page article, "Jewish-Armenian Split Spreads on the Hill" is accurate in most respects; however, it states that "in imposing sanctions seven years ago, Congress cited Azerbaijan's blockade of Armenia, which has continued despite a 1994 ceasefire between the two waning nations."

While this statement reflects the thinking of some members of Congress, it is untrue. Just take a look at the map. Azerbaijan is in no position to blockade Armenia, which has borders with Iran and Georgia, as well as easy trading access to Russia. Through Georgia, Armenia has access to ocean trading. Besides, most communication links between Azerbaijan and Armenia have been either destroyed or occupied by Armenian troops (as is the case with 20 percent of western Azerbaijan). What has occurred is a normal cessation of commerce between two countries in a declared state of war, not a "blockade."

In fact, there is no sound reason why Azerbaijan should be the only former Soviet republic that is denied direct U.S.

Government assistance. By continuing this policy, Congress is rewarding the aggressor in this conflict and punishing the victim.

The Washington Times
April 21, 1999
"East Looks West for Security"

The most interesting topics for discussion at the upcoming fiftieth anniversary celebration of NATO will be revision of NATO's strategic concept and the next phase of NATO enlargement. How these matters are resolved will affect the future peace and security of all of Europe, from Norway to Spain in the West and from Russia to the Caucasus in the East.

Optimists see NATO enlargement as eventually guaranteeing an end to large European wars of the kind that we have witnessed twice during this century. But pessimists are warning about the danger of a new Yalta, without regard to the interests of other European nations.

Let me cite my own nation of Azerbaijan as an example. After centuries of domination by various regional powers, Azerbaijan finally achieved true independence in 1991. Because Azerbaijan sees NATO as a stabilizing factor, we support the concept of NATO expansion, and we are actively involved in the Partnership for Peace program. At the same time, we are concerned about the reaction of Russia to NATO expansion, and, in turn, the United States' reaction to Russian concerns. The current Russian opposition to NATO expansion can lead it to one of two modes of behavior. It can either try to oppose further NATO expansion, or it can try to create regional security treaties to counterbalance NATO.

Where does this leave Azerbaijan in the critical year of 1999? We are the only ex-Soviet country, other than the Baltics, that has no Russian military bases on its soil. Azerbaijan is among the most pro-Western of the former republics. But we are only one of three Caucasian countries, which are united geographically but separated politically. Armenia has already thrown in its lot with Russia, and is the recipient of the most modern Russian arms. Georgia is pro-Western but is limited in action by the existence of Russian military bases in the country.

Beyond expansion, it is important that NATO's strategic concept also envision and deal with the security needs of nations like Azerbaijan. That is why we are so sensitive about the possibility of the United States and Russia reaching expansion-related accommodations that overlook the independence and security needs of other countries. To understand our security concerns, consider the following: Armenia, with more than $1 billion in illegal arms shipments from Russia, has conducted aggression against Azerbaijan and occupied 20 percent of my country, causing one million refugees, whose sufferings remain greatly unnoticed in the West due to lack of media attention. Armenia has consistently frustrated efforts of the Organization for Security and Cooperation in Europe to settle the conflict. And this year Russia announced plans to ship modern Mig 29 fighters and long-range S-300 missiles to Armenia.

This is why Azerbaijan objects when the United States so casually accepts Russian ideas such as the "common state" proposal for settlement of the conflict with Armenia. That is why it is beyond reason to the average Azerbaijani that the U.S. cannot find the political will to repeal Section 907 of the Freedom Support Act, an Armenian Diaspora—inspired piece of legislation that bans direct U.S. Government aid to Azerbaijan, including military assistance.

We have made our choice to join the West and the European Community. We think the best hope for our continued independence and sovereignty, as well as for successful development of Caspian energy resources, is to become part of the European and Euro-Atlantic security structures.

Russia is a regional power that has historically sought to dominate its neighbors. We do not wish to be dominated any longer. The region as well as its individual countries faces a choice of collective security arrangements. The options are either to follow the "proposal" for a collective security treaty (CST) under the auspices of the CIS, or work out some form of guarantees with participation by the West. The first option will inevitably lead to a standoff between an enlarged NATO and a strengthened, Russian-sponsored CST, which would lead to the same bipolarity we witnessed during the post-World War II decades. In the second case the U.S. participation would be essential.

I'd even like to see some form of charter on cooperation between the states of the region and NATO established (not unlike the arrangements NATO has with Russia or Ukraine). This is very likely to remove walls of distrust between feuding parties in the South Caucasus, and at the same time it would address the region's security concerns.

There is also the question of balance of forces in the region. It is over the means of striking that balance that the parties may differ. It can be achieved either by building up forces, or by reducing them to the lowest possible level. Azerbaijan believes the latter course is preferable, not only from a security standpoint, but also in the interest of development of a market economy and democratic societies.

The Washington Times
December 28, 2001

"History Sheds Different Light on U.S. Sanctions Against Azerbaijan"

Allow me to make several points regarding your Dec. 23 editorial, "The Importance of Armenia and Azerbaijan." As you state, Americans are not very knowledgeable about realities in the region. This is especially true with regard to the conflict between Armenia and Azerbaijan as well as to the consequences of Armenian aggression against my country. It is an internationally established fact that Armenia has occupied 20 percent of Azerbaijan, turning almost a million of my compatriots into refugees and internally displaced persons. Yet even experts writing on these issues sometimes present a distorted picture of the situation, be it intentionally or involuntarily.

Lack of knowledge is the main reason why the powerful Armenian lobby has succeeded in misrepresenting the cessation of normal trade relations, quite natural between two warring parties, as a blockade. Thus, it misled the U.S. Congress into adding insult to injury and passing Section 907 of the 1992 Freedom Support Act, containing sanctions against Azerbaijan. Despite the opposition of successive U.S. administrations to 907, it was only after September 11 that U.S. policy on this matter was reconsidered.

As far as Armenia's "admirable restraint" and "gracious response to the relaxation of U.S. sanctions against Azerbaijan" are concerned, I would like to set the record straight. After September 11, the President of Armenia himself went on record viciously opposing any modification of Section 907. At the same time, a high-ranking Armenian delegation was dispatched to Washington to enforce this position.

We do welcome the Bush administration's engagement in the process of peaceful settlement of the Armenian-

Azerbaijani conflict, and the congressional decision to provide the president with authority to waive 907 is an important step toward making this engagement truly unbiased. That is precisely the sort of U.S. involvement in world affairs that is needed to counter the aggressive separatism that, merged with international terrorism, threatens to destroy our values and way of life.

Finally, with respect to both Armenian-Azerbaijani and Turkish-Armenian relations, I believe the only way to settle these kinds of disputes is to look to the future, not appeal to what took place or is claimed to have taken place in the past.

The Washington Post
October 30, 2003
"Critiquing the Election in Azerbaijan"

The Oct. 22 editorial on Azerbaijan, "A 'Strong' Performance?" cited the "fraudulent presidential election" and "massive irregularities, including bribery, beatings and arrests of opposition supporters" while conveniently omitting the "unprecedented transparency" of the election cited by the Organization for Security and Cooperation in Europe's International Elections Observers Mission and the "progress over previous elections in Azerbaijan" and "significant efforts towards international standards" noted by the European Union presidency. Where the European approach encourages Azerbaijan to build upon this foundation, the U.S. media effectively discourage my country from further progress toward democracy.

Does the *Post* believe that Europe adheres to different standards of democracy?

As for "scores of opposition supporters" being rounded up, an opposition leader predicted before the October 15 election that the streets of Baku would "bathe in blood," and another urged his supporters to protest the outcome before the outcome was known. That's why they were detained. Many of the participants in the riot have been released, and the cases against the rest are being' reviewed carefully.

Let's not forget that my country's support for the United States in Afghanistan and Iraq has not been limited to the "easy grant of over flight rights." Our soldiers and officers stand shoulder to shoulder with the men and women of the U.S. Military. It is typical of the *Post* to find a conflict between oil and democracy and between geo-strategy and human rights. Why can't those factors be combined, with energy and geo-political considerations supporting and strengthening a policy of democratic development? My country strives to be a good example of that.

The Washington Times
November 5, 2005
"Country 'Under the Microscope' Envoy Says" **by David R. Sands**

Hafiz Pashayev, a physicist by training, has been Azerbaijan's Ambassador to Washington since 1993, the only ambassador to the United States since his country achieved independence with the collapse of the Soviet Union. He talked with staff writer David R. Sands this week about the significance of tomorrow's parliamentary elections.

Q: Do you feel there is increased international scrutiny over how the government conducts this vote? Do you feel that is fair?

A: I think there is no question that Azerbaijan is under the microscope. We feel we have proven we are an important friend and ally of the United States, and with President

Bush's clear doctrine in support of democracy around the world, we know a lot of people will be watching what happens. Is it fair? I think it's both fair and unfair. In my view, Azerbaijan from the first day of our independence has intentionally chosen to be considered among the democratic states of the world. We had our problems and perhaps that is understandable, taking into account the political culture we inherited from the Soviet times. But from that first day, all of our elections—four presidential and two parliamentary votes—have been held in a timely fashion, and each election has been an improvement, technically, on the one before.

Q: The Rose Revolution in Georgia and the Orange Revolution in Ukraine have sparked talk of a democratic transformation across your region. How has that affected the political debate in Azerbaijan?

A: Some of our opposition groups are trying to use those very different situations in Azerbaijan also, but we strongly believe that the peaceful, evolutionary path to reform would also be a very important example for others in our region.

   All the opinion polls show that the party of President Ilham Aliyev can win a clear majority in any free and fair vote. The reason why Azerbaijanis want to conduct a good, clean election is not because we are trying to escape the experience of Ukraine and Georgia, but because our own citizens deserve it. The government understands that while we are well advanced in economic and social terms, we have to maintain a stable and progressive political situation to move forward.

Q: There was violence in the days after President Aliyev won [the] election in 2003. Are there similar concerns about this vote?

A: I think in some ways our government is more concerned about the day after the vote than the day of the election. Yes, there was violence in 2003, even though the most hard-line opposition groups had to concede that the president was the clear winner.

The anti-government forces used violence to try to undermine the credibility of our vote internationally, and, I have to say, there were instances where our own security forces overreacted. We have been working very hard to ensure not just the fairness of this vote, but also that it can take place peacefully.

Q: Private groups such as Human Rights Watch have been particularly critical of the run-up to the vote. How do you respond?

A: The president and the government have taken a number of documented steps since May until just last week to ensure the vote is fair. We do not fear a clean election, because the government is genuinely popular.

I hear this talk that the press is not free or that the government is suppressing the opposition. But when I travel back to Baku and read the newspapers and watch the television, I don't know how anyone can say that. It seems to me, sometimes, as if every achievement or improvement we make just means that the level demanded of us goes that much higher.

The Washington Times
March 1, 2005

"Azerbaijan Vote, If Imperfect, Still Important Step Forward"

I read the February 10 article, "Democracy Rising in Ex-Soviet States" with utmost interest, mostly because democracy is indeed, as the article stated, on the rise in the nations that used to be called the Soviet Union. We in Azerbaijan welcome this development, since democratization is undoubtedly one of the pillars of our country's policy in building civil society.

Yet, I would most vehemently disagree with the article's portrayal of the 2003 election in Azerbaijan.

Unlike the cases of Georgia and Ukraine, where the initial elections were obviously stolen from the majority of the electorate, in Azerbaijan independent polls taken both weeks before and just prior to the election by domestic and foreign NGOs, showed Ilham Aliyev with a commanding lead over his closest opponent.

With no doubt as to the outcome, the Azerbaijani opposition began to disrupt public order and discredit the winner through public confrontation and violence. Unfortunately, some NGOs and media outlets took the bait, accepting the distorted vision of the election proper and the post-electoral process.

While I acknowledge that the 2003 elections did not meet all international standards, it was a step forward compared to previous elections.

It is important that your readers gain a clear and accurate perception of the democratic process in Azerbaijan.

The Washington Times
September 11, 2005

"Azerbaijan's Democratic Transition"

In a recent visit to Azerbaijan as National Democratic Institute chairman, former Secretary of State Madeleine Albright said, "Election day is important, but the months leading up to the elections are also crucial."

She referred to the parliamentary elections to be held [on] November 6, when the citizens of Azerbaijan go to the polls to elect their representatives to Parliament, or Milli Mejlis.

The Bush administration views these elections as a litmus test of the Azerbaijan government's commitment to democracy. The U.S. Congress has weighed in by passing a resolution calling on Azerbaijan "to hold orderly, peaceful, and free and fair elections in November 2005 in order to ensure the long-term growth and stability of the country."

We are the first to recognize that independence, stability and prosperity depend on successful democratic reform. President Ilham Aliyev wants an orderly transition, as our last few years of unprecedented economic growth would be jeopardized by political instability. Toward this end and to conduct elections according to international standards, the president issued an Executive Order outlining steps to be taken:

(1) Allowing all political parties to organize rallies free from violence and intimidation.

(2) Welcoming domestic and international election observers.

(3) Providing access to media, thus ensuring fair coverage.

(4) Ensuring central and regional authorities create the necessary conditions for exit polls.

Among many provisions of the Order already carried out are those that concern participation in the political arena by opposition parties. There has been dialogue between ruling and opposition parties, all opposition parties may freely conduct rallies and demonstrations and, thus far, all opposition activists—including those who called for overthrow of the government in October 2003—have been allowed to become candidates if they wish. During his visit to Azerbaijan at the end of August, Senator Richard Lugar (R-Indiana) said, "The opposition leaders underlined that the registration process of the MP candidates went well, which is a step forward compared to the previous elections." President Aliyev went further by warning all regional election officials not to interfere in the old Soviet fashion, when ballot-stuffing was common. President Aliyev's insistence on free and fair elections in November is based on the idea that Azerbaijan's secular government can co-exist with its Muslim traditions.

Our vision is premised on the belief democratic pluralism will ensure a peaceful outlet for dissent eliminating the need for violent alternatives. Citizens of all ethnicities and political persuasions are free to advocate their positions peacefully.

Today, Azerbaijan is a vibrant, independent state. We have faced many challenges in our young country's life; preserving our independence in a tough neighborhood; making the transition from a shattered to a market economy; building government institutions and an independent judiciary; finding a peaceful solution to our conflict with Armenia; and developing and delivering our natural resources to world markets.

Throughout these difficult years, the United States has been a friend and ally of Azerbaijan. Our strategic partnership has blossomed since the attacks on America on September 11, 2001. Immediately after, the late President Heydar Aliyev visited the U.S. Embassy in Baku not only to express his condolences but to offer his full support. "Today, we stand side-by-side in the global war on terrorism. Our troops proudly serve in Afghanistan and Iraq."

Azerbaijan's location between Russia, Iran and Turkey, coupled with our desire to integrate into the Euro-Atlantic community, requires that we conduct a balanced foreign policy fostering development of democratic institutions and a strong economy. Azerbaijan has come this far without tangible foreign aid and expects to continue democratic and economic development, primarily through its own resources. According to a recent survey by the International Republican Institute sponsored by U.S.AID, an overwhelming majority of Azerbaijanis want economic and social development to be their government's priority concerns.

This November, the people of Azerbaijan will elect a Parliament I believe will accelerate our transition toward democratic pluralism to match the country's unprecedented economic growth. Mr. Lugar told the press in Baku: "I sense in Azerbaijan a yearning for building strong democratic institutions."

Appendix I
Background on Azerbaijan

Geography and Population

Azerbaijan is located on the western shore of the Caspian Sea in the South Caucasus region. The country is bounded by Russia to the north, Iran to the south, Georgia to the northwest, Armenia and Turkey to the west and the Caspian Sea to the east. Azerbaijan is a secular state with predominantly Muslim population of eight million. While the majority of the country's population is ethnic Azerbaijanis, who are of a Western Turkic descent, over seventy different ethnic groups, including Russians, Armenians, Georgians, Kurds, Udins, Talishes and others live in the country. Several religions, including Islam, Judaism and Christianity are being freely practiced in Azerbaijan.

Independence, 1918-1920

Azerbaijan's first opportunity for independence was between 1918-1920 in the aftermath of World War I and the overthrow of the Russian czar. On May 28, 1918, the Azerbaijani National Council adopted a declaration of Independence, much as the American forefathers did. A new country was born—the Democratic Republic of Azerbaijan.

Azerbaijan Democratic Republic (ADR) is considered to be the first democratic republic in the Muslim world, and its democratic standards were higher than in many western democracies. ADR was officially recognized at the Versailles Peace Conference in February 1920, but its request to enter into the League of Nations was rejected due to the conflict with Armenia over the Nagorno-Karabakh region. Although ADR was a short lived (only twenty-three months) state, it rapidly developed and established diplomatic relations with several countries. Within this short period of time, the Republic managed to establish its own parliament, army and the currency.

Soviet Era, 1920-1991

Unfortunately, on April 27-28, 1920, the Russian Bolshe-vik Army invaded Azerbaijan and put an end to the newly established Democratic Republic. This cleared the way of incorporation of Azerbaijan into the new Soviet Empire. With the signing of the treaty on formation of the USSR on December 30, 1922, Azerbaijan became the Azerbaijan Soviet Socialist Republic. Once again, the country fell under the domination of its neighbors, and the possibility of developing as an independent state was eliminated.

While Azerbaijan was no longer independent, it was not without basic governmental institutions. It had a constitution, a parliament, a judicial system, and even a foreign ministry. These institutions were, of course, controlled by Communist Party elites—often from outside Azerbaijan—but they did exist. This was important, because it gave Azerbaijan the experience needed in operating governmental institutions, despite the artificial nature of those institutions under the communists. Yet, the people of Azerbaijan never gave up their aspirations for true independence and self-government. These desires grew much stronger during the perestroika period of the Gorbachev era.

The growing desire for freedom in Azerbaijan coincided with the outbreak of hostilities due to the conflict in Nagorno-Karabakh region, Azerbaijan's autonomous region with predominantly ethnic Armenian population. With support from some official groups in Moscow, the Republic of Armenia and separatists in Nagorno-Karabakh began their ethnic cleansing policy against Azerbaijanis in an attempt to annex this region and merge it with Armenia. This policy merely served to enhance the nationalistic feelings of Azerbaijanis, who were already trying to escape the domination of the Soviets.

Independence Arrives in 1991

In January 1990, thousands of Azerbaijanis took to the streets of Baku to demonstrate for freedom and independence from the Soviet Union. In order to quell the uprising, the Soviet troops entered the capital on the night of January 19-20, and began indiscriminately shooting at unarmed civilians. Hundreds were killed, and Azerbaijani people became more determined to gain independence. This tragedy accelerated the process.

On August 30, 1991, the Supreme Soviet of Azerbaijan (same as the parliament) adopted the Declaration on Restoration of the State Independence of Azerbaijan. This declaration was a descendant of the Declaration of Independence adopted in 1918, and led to the adoption of the Constitutional Act on October 18, 1991. This act was a milestone in the development of Azerbaijan as an independent and democratic state. It established the basis for political and economic systems of a free and independent state. Azerbaijan did not have time to create a new constitution, so it kept the old Soviet constitution for the time being. This is important because in doing so, newly independent Azerbaijan accepted the concept of sovereignty based on constitutional law, not on the whims of whoever happened to be in power. The Republic of Azerbaijan adopted its new constitution on November 12, 1995.

The arrival of true independence has not brought an end to the troubles of Azerbaijan. The conflict between Armenia and Azerbaijan over the Nagorno-Karabakh region of Azerbaijan has not been resolved yet. The conflict erupted in 1988 and turned into a full scale war in 1991, which ended with a cease-fire singed in May, 1994. This war led to the occupation of about one fifth of Azerbaijan's territory by the Armenian forces, including seven districts surrounding the Nagorno-Karabakh region. The country was also inundated with almost one million refugees and internally displaced persons (IDP) from Armenia and all the occupied territories. In a country of eight million people, Azerbaijan has the highest per capita number of IDPs and refugees in the world.

Political System

The government of the Republic of Azerbaijan is organized on the principles of separation of power. In line with the traditional concept of separation of power, the Constitution of the Republic of Azerbaijan determines that the executive power is held by the President of the Republic of Azerbaijan, the legislative power is carried out by the Parliament (Milli Majlis), and the judicial power is held by independent courts, the Constitutional Court being the highest court of Azerbaijan.

The executive power of the Republic of Azerbaijan is held by the President of the Republic of Azerbaijan. The Executive Branch is made up of the president, his apparatus, a prime minister, and the cabinet of ministers.

The President of the Republic of Azerbaijan is elected for five-year terms by general and direct elections. The President is the Supreme Commander-in-Chief of the armed forces of the Republic of Azerbaijan. No person can be elected President of the Azerbaijan Republic more than twice.

The President forms a Cabinet of Ministers for the realization of the executive authorities. A Cabinet of Ministers is the superior body of the Executive power of the President; it submits to the President and is accountable before him.

The legislative power of the Republic of Azerbaijan, the Milli Majlis consists of 125 members. The members are elected for five-year terms on the basis of a majority system by direct elections. Every citizen of Azerbaijan who has reached the age of twenty-five can be elected to the Milli Majlis and there are no election term limits.

The Constitutional Court of Azerbaijan is the highest juridical body on matters under the authority allocated to it by the Constitution of the Republic of Azerbaijan. The Constitutional Court is not dependent on legislative and executive organs. The purpose of the Constitutional Court is to provide the supremacy of the Constitution of the Republic of Azerbaijan and to protect the rights and the freedoms of everyone. The Constitutional Court of the Republic is composed of nine judges appointed by the Milli Majlis on the nomination of the President. The Constitutional Court is considered authorized with the participation of seven judges. The judges are appointed for fifteen-year terms. There is no second term appointment.

Political Parties

The political life of Azerbaijan is characterized by a multiparty system. The political parties have the opportunity to participate in the political life of the country through representation in the legislative and local municipal bodies. There are forty-two registered political parties in Azerbaijan as of today.

Article 58 of the Constitution states: every one has a right to unite with others; everyone has a right to join any association including any political party, trade unions and other social unions as well as existing units; the free activity of such associations is ensured; no one can make any other person to join or to remain the member of any association; the activity of the associations aiming at the forceful overthrow of the legal state power on the whole territory of the Republic of Azerbaijan—or its part—is prohibited; and the activity of the associations violating the Constitution and the Law can be ceased only through the court.

Foreign Relations

Turkey was the first country to recognize Azerbaijan's independence in November 1991, followed by the United States on Christmas Day of 1991. Diplomatic relations with the United States were formally established in March 1992 and now the two countries enjoy a high level of cooperation within political, economic, military and security fields. Since independence Azerbaijan has opened embassies, permanent missions and general consulates in thirty-six countries and is planning to open more missions in the near future. There are also a growing number of foreign embassies in Baku.

Azerbaijan is a member of the United Nations (UN), Organization of Security and Cooperation in Europe (OSCE), Council of Europe (CE), Commonwealth of Independent States (CIS), GUAM, Organization of the Islamic Conference (OIC), Black Sea Economic Collaboration (BSEC), and Organization of Economic Cooperation (OEC). Azerbaijan also actively cooperates with the European Union, NATO, International Monetary Fond, European Bank for Reconstruction and Development, Islamic Development Bank and other organizations.

Economic Overview

During the past decade, Azerbaijan has been implementing ambitious structural reforms and adopted numerous laws and legislative changes, paving the way toward further integration with the global economy. The country is aggressively moving to diversify its economy to achieve sustainable growth and meet the social and development needs for its population.

Azerbaijan's macroeconomic performance in recent years, as reported by the IMF "has been impressive with strong growth, low inflation and a stable exchange rate." Real GDP grew by an annual average of over 10 percent between 1997-2004, driven by investments in energy sector and related spillover effects in the construction and transportation sectors, as well as, substantial gains in agriculture following land reform in mid-1990s. In 2005, GDP growth was 26.4 percent and IMF forecast for 2006 is 38 percent.

Azerbaijan has the highest ratio of Foreign Direct Investment per capita among countries of Eastern and Central Asia. During 1993-2005, about $25 billion was invested in the economy.

Azerbaijan was a pioneer in opening the Caspian Sea to international cooperation and oil and gas exploration. After gaining independence in 1991, Azerbaijan has attracted significant international interest to its substantial oil and natural gas reserves and is currently involved into the implementation of huge energy projects.

Since the "Contract of the Century" was signed in 1994, with American and other Western companies, Azerbaijan has developed its energy resources to diversify Western energy supplies. The Baku-Tbilisi-Ceyhan oil and the Baku-Tbilisi-Erzurum gas pipelines will bolster the political and commercial independence of the countries in the region. The oil and gas revenues will contribute to a doubling of the size of Azerbaijan's economy by 2008. Completion and expansion of new pipelines will allow Azerbaijan to become a significant regional energy exporter over the next decade.

Azerbaijan and the Geo-Politics in the Region

The Republic of Azerbaijan's foreign policy aims to preserve the country's pro-Western orientation and accommodate its national interests in a tough neighborhood.

Azerbaijan was the first country in the former Soviet Union to remove Russian troops from its territory and was successful in persuading Russia to tune down its opposition to the Western sponsored Baku-Tbilisi-Ceyhan Pipeline. Russia is one of the Co-Chairs of the OSCE Minsk group mediating the Nagorno-Karabakh conflict between Armenia and Azerbaijan, and home to about two million ethnic Azerbaijanis.

Turkey and Azerbaijan have a strategic alliance strengthened by mutual interests and kinship. Located at the strategic crossroads between Russia and Iran, Azerbaijan plays an important role for Turkish and American security interests, and is a vital link to Central Asia as well as an alternative source of oil and gas.

Iran and Azerbaijan have had uneasy relationship over the past fifteen years. Iran has viewed Azerbaijan with suspicion due in part to the presence of large Azerbaijani population in northern Iran (roughly twenty-five million). Iran has also complained about Azerbaijan's close ties with the West and especially with the United States and opposed American energy companies' involvement in the development of the Caspian hydrocarbons. In addition, Iran and Turkmenistan are the only countries that have yet to agree to a sectored division of the Caspian Sea bed endorsed by Azerbaijan, Kazakhstan, and Russia.

Georgia and Azerbaijan have cooperated on many issues including the construction of two oil and gas pipelines that link Azerbaijan, Georgia and Turkey to the West. Both states share similar views regarding integration with the Euro-Atlantic Community and have a common position against separatist movements within their borders.

Armenia's foreign policy priorities are different from those of Azerbaijan and Georgia. While Azerbaijan and Georgia have been closely cooperating with the United States in security and energy issues, Armenia has chosen Russia and

Iran as its security guarantors. Today, Russia dominates Armenia's economic, political, and security sectors, and Armenia hosts a significant number of Russian military bases on its soil. Armenia and Iran have become strategic partners. Armenia has been used as a transfer point for narcotics from Iran and, in some cases, sensitive nuclear technology to Iran. Armenia still occupies roughly 20 percent of Azerbaijan.

The United States has supported ongoing Caspian energy projects that will bring additional oil and gas supplies to the global energy market. Since 9/11, the U.S. has increased its presence in the region helping Georgia and Azerbaijan to improve their security capabilities to make the borders secure and non-proliferation efforts more effective.

Azerbaijan is a staunch ally in the Global War on Terrorism (GWOT). While cooperation in anti-terrorism and counter-terrorism activities between two countries existed for many years, the 9/11 attacks elevated collaboration to a profoundly higher level.

Azerbaijan was amongst the first countries to offer the United States unconditional support in the war against terrorism, providing its airspace and the use of its airports for Operation Enduring Freedom in Afghanistan. Azerbaijani troops are serving under the International Security Assistance Force (ISAF) in Kabul and were praised for their performance by NATO officials. Since 1999, a peacekeeping platoon of Azerbaijan's Armed Forces has been participating in peacekeeping operations in Kosovo within Kosovo Force (KFOR).

Azerbaijan was the first Muslim nation to send its troops to serve shoulder-to-shoulder with U.S. forces in Iraq. "I have been working with the Azerbaijani soldiers for six months and they have been a fantastic asset for us [...] we haven't had a single negative incident at the Haditha Dam on their watch," said Lt. Glenn Page of the 3 Armored Cavalry Regiment serving in Iraq.

As a chair of the GUAM Working Group (Georgia, Ukraine, Azerbaijan, and Moldova) on the fight against terrorism, organized crime and drug trafficking, Azerbaijan represented GUAM at the special meeting of the UN Counter Terrorism Committee with international, regional and sub regional organizations on March 6, 2003. At the 2006 GUAM summit, the Heads of GUAM member-states signed the Kiev Declaration to found GUAM Organization for Democracy and Economic Development, thus transforming it into an international organization.

Human Rights and Democratic Reforms

Since regaining its independence in 1991, the Government of the Republic of Azerbaijan has been developing a democratic society based on such fundamental principles as the respect for political and civil rights and liberties; the protection of interest of every citizen irrespective of his or her ethnic, religious or any other affiliation; the division of power; and the rule of law.

Achievements in the field of democratic state-building include political pluralism, more than eight hundred functioning mass media outlets, abolition of censorship in 1993, development of civil society with approximately fourteen hundred non-governmental organizations, and the establishment of a modern judiciary system.

Three Parliamentary and two Presidential elections were held in the country after the adoption of Azerbaijan's Constitution in 1995.

Azerbaijan is a party to a number of international legal instruments in the promotion and protection of human rights and civil liberties, rule of law and democratization, including the International Covenant on Civil and Political Rights and International Covenant on Economic, Social and Cultural

Rights which are the cornerstone documents in the protection and promotion of human rights.

Azerbaijan has also joined more than forty Conventions of the Council of Europe, which ensure human rights and democracy. Ratification of the European Convention on Human Rights and its relevant protocols allows Azerbaijani citizens to appeal directly to the European Court of Human Rights.

Appendix II
Steps Taken to Repeal or Modify Section 907

In 1994 Timothy Penny (D-MN) and in 1997 Peter King (R-NY) unsuccessfully attempted to repeal 907, acting in spite of mounting pressure from the Armenian Diaspora.

Congress has made several other attempts to modify Section 907, which were successful. These include allowing assistance for direct humanitarian aid, democracy-building programs and efforts to establish a market economy. Armenian lobbying groups have opposed most of these efforts. However, in FY 1997, Congress approved language exemption the Nunn-Lugar program to prevent the spread of weapons of mass destruction, as well as allowing for the use of state facilities and doctors to provide humanitarian assistance.

In FY 1998, Congress approved language as part of the Foreign Operations Appropriations Bill to provide additional exceptions to Section 907. These exceptions, proposed by Senators Byrd and Leahy, included "democracy-building" programs, as well as activities of the Export-Import Bank, the Overseas Private Investment Corporation (OPIC), the Trade and Development Agency (TDA) and the Foreign Commercial Service. The Byrd-Leahy Amendment was intended to stimulate US business activity in Azerbaijan.

Congress during consideration of the FY 1999 Foreign Operations Appropriations bill retained all these exceptions and added a blanket exception for all humanitarian assistance. This action by Congress came after the full House Appropriations Committee voted 30-19 to repeal Section 907 on what became known as "Livingston Amendment". This repeal was later overturned by a full House vote of 231-182.

With the convening of the 106th Congress, Senator Sam Brownback introduced his Silk Road legislation, which was originally approved in 1998 by the Senate Foreign Relations Committee. The Brownback Silk Road legislation, which provided for a Presidential "national interest" waiver for Section 907, was again approved that year by the Senate Foreign Relations Committee and offered as an amendment to the FY 2000 Foreign Operations Appropriations Bill. However, during debate on the Senate floor, the "national interest" waiver authority for Section 907 was stricken from the amendment on a 53-47 vote.

During other consideration of the FY 2000 Foreign Operations Appropriation Bill, all of the previous exceptions to Section 907 were again approved. The House of Representatives approved some harmful report language, but this language was not adopted by the House-Senate Conference committee.

Legislative process for FY 2001 brought no changes on 907.

The discussions on foreign ops appropriations for FY 2002 have brought new hope for additional carve-outs. Specifically, the area of exempting law-enforcement has been mentioned by the executive branch on several occasions. Nevertheless, those efforts bore no fruit. It also became obvious that the U.S. side started placing its expectations for the success of peace talks above any immediate action to eliminate or modify the sanctions.

Waiver Provision

Deliberations on the foreign ops appropriations for the Fiscal Year 2003 were undoubtedly influenced by the tragedy of 9/11, after which Azerbaijan has shown immediate and unconditional solidarity with the United States. It was rather ironic that the terrorist attacks of September 11, 2001 triggered Washington's abandoning its short-sighted policy of punishing Azerbaijan for imaginary wrong-doings.

Fall 2001 became turning point in that regard. As a result of heated behind-the-scenes debates the foreign ops bill was amended in Senate by introducing the waiver language on 907. Despite initial efforts of the proponents of "unconditional waiver" in the US Senate, who pushed forward with the idea of a "national security" waiver, as proposed by the US Secretary of State in his October 2001 letter to the leadership of the Foreign Relations Committee and supported by a dozen of leading US businesses, the Senate majority agreed to a language which granted the US President to waive the sanctions provided that this waiver "is necessary to support United States efforts to counter terrorism; or is necessary to support the operational readiness of United States Armed Forces or coalition partners to counter terrorism; or is important to Azerbaijan's border security; and will not undermine or hamper ongoing efforts to negotiate a peaceful settlement between Armenia and Azerbaijan or be used for offensive purposes against Armenia." This legislation was passed in December 2001 and signed by President Bush into law on January 10, 2002. Almost immediately after that, on January 25, the US President exercised his newly granted authority waiving the Section 907.

Appendix III
Quotes on Section 907

Many Americans in the government and private sectors have recognized that Section 907 is counter-productive to the American interests, and called for its repeal. The following are some quotes:

Madeleine Albright, Secretary of State, January 8, 1997: "We have very substantial economic, political and humanitarian interests in this region, and are prepared to play a more visible role in helping to arrange a settlement. One step that Congress could take to increase our influence would be to lift restrictions on non-military assistance to Azerbaijan."

Dick Cheney, former Secretary of Defense, February 12, 1997: "Azerbaijan is of great significance not only to the futures, of the region, but to the future of a diversified and balanced global oil market... I also believe that our current posture—prohibiting US assistance to Azerbaijan—is misguided. In my experience, this kind of unilateral sanctions based primarily an US domestic political consideration is unwise. Such a policy limits US influence in any given situation. And, in this ease it reduces rather than enhances prospects for ultimately resolving a very complex and important set of regional issues... Azerbaijan has its own priorities: nation building, solidifying its independence, developing its economy, fostering political stability, and ensuring its defense and security...Most Americans even here in Washington, do not know that much about Azerbaijan, but they should. It is of great importance to the region, to world oil markets, and to global economic and political stability."

Senator Robert C. Byrd, February 18, 1997: "The time for American policy toward the [Caucasus] region to be dominated by ethnic and campaign politics in the United States should be brought to an abrupt close. America's strategic interests in the region are far too important to be subjected to such politics."

Congressman Lee Hamilton, July 23, 1997: "A problem for our democracy is the continuing ban on U.S. assistance to the government of Azerbaijan. It limits our ability to be an effective intermediary [to the conflict]."

Congressman Peter King, July 25, 1997: "While there are as many as one million refugees suffering in Azerbaijan, it remains the, only non-terrorist State in the world that is barred from receiving direct U.S. humanitarian aid."

Stuart Eizenstat, Under Secretary of State, July 22, 1997: "Section 907 [of the Freedom Support Act] hinders our ability to act as an unbiased honest broker in our role as co-chair of the Minsk Group [OSCE] and prohibits technical assistance to Azerbaijan in support of market reform and democratization."

Senator Sam Brownback, Monday July 21, 1997: "The countries of the South Caucasus... are all looking to the United States for support. In Azerbaijan, Russia used pressure tactics...for refusing to accept Russian troops on its soil. Russia bas intervened mostly on the side of Armenia, supplying weapons and covert intelligence assistance. In return Russia gained a 25 year military base right on Armenian soil. The time to focus and take action in the region is now. We have the opportunity to help these countries rebuild themselves from the ground up and to encourage them to continue their strong independent stances, especially in relation to Iran and the spread of extremist, anti-western fundamentalism, which is one of the most clear and prevent dangers facing the United States today."

Strobe Talbott, Deputy Secretary of State, July 21, 1997: Section 907 of the Freedom Support Act... has the negative effect of limiting our leverage with Baku and complicating our ability to be an honest broker [to the peace process]. It has also made it impossible to provide the Azerbaijanis with assistance on elections, economic reform, energy development, and its other areas of national interest... hence our opposition to Section 907."

Thomas Dine, USAID Assistant Administrator, May 6, 1997: "The [Clinton] administration is strongly opposed to Section 907 of the Freedom Support Act because its restrictions impede the United States' government's ability to implement more effectively our development assistance program in Azerbaijan and thereby slows the advancement of U.S. interests in a strategically significant region."

Richard Armitage, Ambassador At Large, May 21, 1997: "I understand fully the sensitive domestic political implications of an activist American policy toward resolving the Nagorno-Karabakh controversy... it is time for Armenians, for American friends of Armenia and for Members of the U.S. Congress to recognize that it is the policy of the most reactionary elements of Russia to fight to the last Armenian in order to re-establish Russian political control over Armenia and Azerbaijan alike. If, in the name of responding positively to a domestic lobby, Members of Congress wish to advance such an agenda, let them at least understand the implications of what they are doing.

Senator Dennis DeConcini, November 1993: "[In] view of the humanitarian needs of the large numbers of Azerbaijani refugees, we should consider whether that course (the sanctions), which I initially supported—is the wisest and fairest course of action. The Nagorno-Karabakh conflict has seated hundreds of thousands refugees on both sides, and refugees are deserving of humanitarian assistance, whether they are Armenian or Azerbaijani."

Washington Post Editorial, May 2, 1996: "One country—friendly, needy and working to build a democracy—is denied direct American humanitarian assistance by law. The target of this rare legislated violation of American ethical tradition is Azerbaijan."

Index